Praise for *The Global Sexual Revolution*

"I am delighted to know that readers in Britain, the U.S., and other English-speaking nations will have the opportunity to read Gabriele Kuby's important book *The Global Sexual Revolution: Destruction of Freedom in the Name of Freedom*. As the carnage of untrammeled sexual license piles up in cultures that have embraced sexual revolutionary ideology, we need the kind of sober and thoughtful analysis Gabriele Kuby provides. Her work will help readers understand that false visions of freedom are highways to slavery, and that true freedom is to be found in self-mastery and virtue."
—ROBERT P. GEORGE, Princeton University; author of *Conscience and Its Enemies: Confronting the Dogmas of Liberal Secularism*

"Cardinal Robert Sarah's statement that 'What Nazi fascism and communism were in the 20th century, Western homosexual and abortion ideologies . . . are today' could serve as the principal theme of Gabriele Kuby's devastating critique, which gives detailed expositions of those ideologies, their origins, and ill effects. Kuby maps the topography of horror that sex unleashed from the moral order visits upon any society that allows it. She also offers a strong, much-needed dose of moral realism that offers a way out of an otherwise totalitarian result."
—ROBERT R. REILLY, American Foreign Policy Council; author of *Making Gay Okay: How Rationalizing Homosexual Behavior Is Changing Everything*

"I have eagerly awaited the English-language publication of this important book from a vital voice in the European debate on human sexuality. Gabriele Kuby is a global treasure and a remarkably brave soul, speaking as she does from the very heart of European secularism. In this book, Kuby gets to the heart of the matter: the grotesque distortion of the human person at the hands of the sexual left, through what Pope Francis and the African bishops properly call 'ideological colonialism.'"
—AUSTIN RUSE, President, Center for Family & Human Rights

"Gabriele Kuby is a contemporary Joan of Arc in Europe. Through her books, translated into several languages, and unceasing public talks and media exposure in various nations, she is awakening the conscience of a generation. Writing with utter lucidity, in *The Global Sexual Revolution* she gives us a comprehensive understanding of the war for the future of mankind that has spread with astonishing speed throughout the world. Not only the nature of man, woman, and family are under relentless assault by the top-down imposed revolution, but the nature of reality itself—and of freedom. Kuby presents her fastidiously researched analysis of the gravity of our civilizational crisis without any defect in charity. There is not only knowledge here, but a wisdom sorely needed in our modern age."

—MICHAEL D. O'BRIEN, author of *Elijah in Jerusalem* and *The Island of the World*

"The sexual revolution has never been about true freedom, but rather, about destroying it. Gabriele Kuby makes an eloquent and factual case for why *all those concerned with liberty and rights of conscience* must stand up—before it is too late—to those agendas that seek, even demand, to take away our freedom."

—ALAN E. SEARS, President, Alliance Defending Freedom; co-author of *The Homosexual Agenda: Exposing the Principal Threat to Religious Freedom Today*

"All who read this book will join Pope Benedict in saying 'Thank God that you speak and write.' It is the most comprehensive primer ever on the culture wars. Without it, one fights half-blind; read it and be changed. Kuby shows how the radical 'deep pan-sexual state' is history's ultimate means for those who would dominate the world through the internationally-shared linguistic, intellectual, academic, media, legal and policy tools of control that we experience daily. But her ending is upbeat: the growing effective resistance in Europe, a resistance that we in the land of freedom must quickly emulate. Buy a dozen copies and form your own battalion of counter-revolutionaries."

—PATRICK F. FAGAN, Director, Marriage and Religion Research Institute (MARRI) at the Family Research Council

"Do you think the family simply 'declined' all on its own? Was it some inexorable Law of History or Force of Nature that caused the family to 'fall apart'? Gabriele Kuby shows convincingly how, against the wishes of ordinary decent people, global elites committed to a destructive ideology have commandeered the State to undermine the family. If you care about the early sexualization of children, the increasing unwillingness to form and sustain families, the relentless drive of political correctness, and above all the ever-increasing intrusiveness of the government, you must read this book."

—JENNIFER ROBACK MORSE, Founder and President of the Ruth Institute; author of *101 Tips for a Happier Marriage*

Praise for the German Edition

"Mrs. Kuby is a brave warrior against ideologies that ultimately result in the destruction of man."—POPE BENEDICT XVI

"I express my appreciation and gratitude for your courage to clearly speak the truth, without being impressed by the intolerant opinions that dominate most of the powerful media outlets."

—CARDINAL GIOVANNI LAJOLO, Cardinal Deacon, S. Maria Liberatrice a Monte Testiccio, Rome

"The term 'gender mainstreaming' may be unfamiliar to most citizens of our country. Therefore many are unaware of the fact that for years they have been subjected to a re-education program put forth by governments, European authorities, and elements of the media. The concept of political freedom was coined in ancient Greece and initially meant: allowing people to live in their customary ways. The tyrant was the one who hindered people from doing that, the one who wanted to 're-educate them.' This book is about just such a tyranny. . . . Gabriele Kuby courageously shows how our freedom is threatened by an anti-human ideology. She deserves our thanks for enlightening us through her work. As many people as possible should read this book in order that they may be aware of what to expect next if they do not fight back."

—ROBERT SPAEMANN (from the Foreword)

"The author shows in her book that the massive attack we are dealing with today is no accident and no passing fashion, but rather part of a global plan, a world strategy to effect fundamental changes in humankind and society by fundamentally altering our understanding and experience of human sexuality. She exposes the truth about gender-ideology, much as Kolakowski and Solzhenitsyn unmasked the truth about Communism."
—FR. DARIUSZ OKO, Assistant Professor of Philosophy at John Paul II Pontifical University (Poland)

"I read the book in breathless suspense and emotional shock."
—EDITH DUSING, Professor of Philosophy and Intellectual History, Freie Theologische Hochschule Gießen

"Gabriele Kuby testifies to the power of human dignity in the light of natural law and the divine image with a rare, bright, and fresh conviction."
—HARALD SEUBERT, Professor of Philosophy and Religious Studies, State Independent Theological College, Basel

"With the publication of this book, none can any longer say they did not know of a revolution that speaks of freedom, but aims at dictatorship."
—KATRIN KRIPS-SCHMIDT, *Die Tagespost*

The Global Sexual Revolution

Destruction of Freedom
in the
Name of Freedom

GABRIELE KUBY

THE GLOBAL
SEXUAL REVOLUTION

Destruction of Freedom
in the
Name of Freedom

Translated by
James Patrick Kirchner

Foreword by
Robert Spaemann

First published in German as
Die globale sexuelle Revolution:
Zerstörung der Freiheit im Namen der Freiheit
© Fe-Medienverlags Gmbh, 2012
First published in English by LifeSite, 2015
an imprint of Angelico Press
English translation © James Patrick Kirchner, 2015
Foreword © Robert Spaemann, 2012

For information, address:
Angelico Press
4709 Briar Knoll Dr.
Kettering, OH 45429
www.angelicopress.com

Pbk: 978-1-62138-154-9
Cloth: 978-1-62138-155-6
eBook: 978-1-62138-156-3

Cover design: Michael Schrauzer

CONTENTS

Foreword

MOST PEOPLE don't know the term "gender mainstreaming." As a result, they also don't know that for years governments, the European authorities, and part of the media have been subjecting them to a reeducation program that insiders know by that name. What this reeducation is supposed to remove from our heads is a millennia-old habit of humankind: the habit of distinguishing men from women. This includes extinguishing the fundamental truth that mutual sexual attraction between man and woman forms the basis of humankind's current and future existence. Therefore it is distinguished from all other ways of satisfying people's drives, subjected to certain humanizing rules, and given privilege through institutionalization. In the end, the reeducation intends to eliminate the beautiful custom we call humanity and human nature, which has been established since time immemorial. We are to emancipate ourselves from our nature.

The word "emancipation" once meant something like liberation. Emancipation from our nature can only mean liberation from ourselves. The term "political freedom" was coined in ancient Greece and initially meant being allowed to live in the customary manner. A tyrant was someone who prevented people from doing this—someone who wanted to re-indoctrinate them. This book is about that sort of tyranny. It is a book of enlightenment. It enlightens us about what is happening to us right now, the methods the "re-educators" use, and what reprisals await those who oppose this project. And this includes not only those who take sides in the discussion, but, as this book shows, all those who have ever advocated the freedom to express their opinion on these matters in an open discussion.

For years, all over Europe, discussion has been increasingly suppressed in the name of "political correctness." Someone deviating from the mainstream is not shown with reason why he is wrong, but is merely told, "You shouldn't say that." What lurks behind this is a relativism regarding truth. To assert the truth is considered intolerance, although the opposite is true. Making an assertion of truth means subjecting one's opinion to discursive tests. If there is no truth, then no such test

1

can exist. Consequently, discussions are just veiled power struggles in which an opinion is not true or false, but dominant or deviant, and the latter of the two brings ostracism. Naturally, the truth does not arise from discourse; it is only tested by it. Even before this test, it is true and intuitively convincing.

We have heard that in London kindergartens—and in Swedish ones, which are considered especially progressive—use of the words "father" and "mother" is forbidden; they must be replaced by gender-neutral words. Similar news is coming from Austria's government offices. This causes reactions from head-shaking to outrage, mainly because the people have not authorized their representatives to reeducate them.

What is the motive for these absurdities? It's stated loud and clear: children on whom adoption by a same-sex couple has been imposed should not have the feeling that others have something they are missing. Because there's no longer any such thing as abnormal, the concept of normal is taboo and placed under ideological suspicion. Nonetheless, normalcy is what constitutes every living thing. In inanimate nature— that is, in physics—there is no normalcy, but just strict laws. On the other hand, wherever there is life, species aim at fulfilling their nature in their own specific ways. And this very nature that drives them to fulfillment can miss its aim. As Aristotle wrote, there can be "errors of nature." The instinct to teach lion cubs to hunt is part of the mother lion's nature. Without it, her young would not be capable of living, and consequently, there would be no lions at all. The absence of this instinct is therefore an anomaly.

The concept of normality is indispensable when it comes to dealing with life processes. Mistakes in this regard threaten the life of humanity. Gabriele Kuby has the courage to show how our freedom is threatened by an anti-human ideology. She deserves our thanks for enlightening us through her work. As many people as possible should read this book to be aware of what to expect if they do not fight back.

PROF. DR. ROBERT SPAEMANN

Preface

THE BOOK you are holding cannot be read without an emotional reaction. The global sexual revolution affects everyone—man and woman, young and old, our personal existence and the future of society.

Because people are not the same as animals, programmed with barely any instincts at all, they have freedom and must decide which way to go. For this we need a standard of right and wrong. The standard of sexuality that has been binding for centuries is now being shattered, or will be shattered where it hasn't happened already.

This is claimed to be desirable progress toward freedom, as if an individual's subjective freedom to do anything he finds fun and pleasurable is the fast track to happiness. But is that true?

Let's take a hard look at the state of society—at broken families, mothers or fathers raising their children alone, and at the young people with deep emotional and spiritual wounds. Let's also look at the pornography addicts, at the millions of sexual abusers of children, at the millions of aborted babies, and at our own path through life. If we ask teachers, doctors, psychiatrists, therapists, social workers and youth service workers, it appears we should avoid this kind of happiness like the plague. We claim that youth is the happiest time of life, but we are creating a society in which there are fewer and fewer laughing children and more and more depressed elderly men and women.

All of this is as plain as day. The causes are researched and discussed, but one cause—perhaps the most important—is shrouded behind taboo: the deregulation of sexual norms now shaping society. Because these norms are part of society's "operating system," every society protects sexual norms with social and legal penalties. While monogamy once was the standard, now it's the permissiveness of hedonism and sexual promiscuity that the law is forcing through under the banner of equality and non-discrimination.

The fairy tale "The Emperor's New Clothes" is an ingenious metaphor for the taboo against perceiving reality as it truly is. The taboo exists because speaking the truth would threaten the power structure, which sooner or later must collapse due to its denial of reality.

Some swindlers convince the emperor that they can weave "the most beautiful fabric" with the amazing quality that clothing made from it is invisible to anyone who is "not fit for his office or is unforgivably stupid." To state the obvious—that something that's not there really isn't there—can get touchy. The emperor doesn't want to lose his position or reveal his stupidity, and that's how the swindlers take him in.

Everyone gets entangled in a web of lies, and all claim to see something that doesn't exist. The emperor gets into a predicament where everyone knows he's clothed in lies, and not in truth. But only a child dares to call out, "The emperor is naked!" The child has no job or reputation to lose.

In this book, I take on the eyes of a child when I speak of the demoralization of political power. This is demoralization with a double meaning: Good is called evil and evil is called good, taking away people's direction and courage to follow the vocation of love.

I describe the global sexual revolution, prepared by the intellectual trailblazers from the French Revolution to the post-modern gender ideology of one Judith Butler, which involves:

- Destruction of the inherited value systems of all cultures and religions.
- Support for the revolutionary agenda by the international political elites.
- Totalitarian endeavors, as seen in the program set forth in the Yogyakarta Principles.
- Concrete imposition of gender ideology on society to the point of politically motivated changes to the language.
- The pornography epidemic, from which children and youth can no longer be protected.
- The homosexual movement as the activist engine that drives this revolution.

Even though important aspects of this movement can no longer be discussed without incurring severe personal attack, this comprehensive chapter presents scientific research on the reality of homosexual life and the internal contradictions of the homosexual agenda.

A special chapter looks into the Christian position on homosexuality and how the church deals with the movement's demands.

The chapter entitled "Sex Education from K through 12" details how mandatory school sex education actively initiates children and teenagers into a hedonistic sexuality, so that the values that make marriage and parenthood possible are not taught.

In "Intolerance and Discrimination," I give examples of how the sexual revolution culminates in an attack on basic democratic freedoms and is especially directed against Christians.

But there is hope. In the second-to-last chapter I describe the growing resistance against the cultural revolution.

All this leads to the final chapter and the real concern of the book: a warning against a new totalitarianism that is destroying freedom in the name of freedom.

We are contemporaries of a cultural revolution that reaches into every home and heart. There is no neutral territory to which we can escape. This revolution increases its speed and the fierceness of its attack on democratic freedoms from one day to the next. Its current culmination is the US Supreme Court decision *Obergefell v. Hodges,* which forces homosexual "marriage" on the United States of America and beyond. This book, originally published in September 2012, has required updating with every new edition and translation. For the American edition I have eliminated some of the material that is only relevant to German-speaking or European readers and included material relevant to the US, especially cases that demonstrate intolerance and discrimination against Christians.

You, the reader, have a right to know where the author stands. As a sociologist, I observe society's developmental trends. As a mother of three children, I devote myself to the future of the next generation. And as a Catholic (since 1997), I strive to live what I believe. This includes goodwill toward people, even if I don't share their convictions and they don't share mine.

I thank everyone who helped bring this book to fruition. That it can now appear in English in the United States I owe to several people who appeared out of the blue to open the doors to a book they thought important: my friend, the late Dr. Justinus Hüppe, who, at over 90 years of age, did everything he could to make people aware of the hidden threats to our culture; Alvino-Mario Fantini and Brian Gill, who found the translator and the publisher; translator James Patrick Kirchner, who did a wonderful job of producing a book that seems to have been originally written in English; and editors Kendra Shriver and Michael Martin, who spared no pains to bring my notes and references up to the required standard. Finally, I thank my publisher, John Riess of Angelico Press, for standing with me against the tide.

GABRIELE KUBY, Rimsting, July 2015

1

The Destruction of
Freedom in the Name of Freedom

*The excess of liberty, whether in States or individuals, seems only to pass
into excess of slavery. And so tyranny naturally arises out of democracy,
and the most aggravated form of tyranny and slavery out of the most
extreme form of liberty.*

Plato, *The Republic,* Book VIII[1]

The Dismantling of Sexuality

WE ARE in the middle of an astonishing process. Fundamental standards of human behavior that were generally considered valid just a few
decades ago have now been put to pasture. What was good back then is
now considered bad. These standards affect the propagation of humankind and the universal institution for its fulfillment: the family. In 1948,
the countries shattered by the Second World War drew up the Universal
Declaration of Human Rights. It states: "The family is the natural and
fundamental group unit of society and is entitled to protection by society and the State" (Art. 16). Family comes about through the marriage
of a man and a woman, who vow to share their lives with one another
and are willing to have and raise children. Family requires monogamy—sexual fidelity between spouses. If monogamy is abandoned as a
moral orientation, the family breaks down. Guiding ideals, customs and
laws anchor this high moral standard in the way people live their lives.

But in the past 40 years, these ideals, customs and laws have been dis-
mantled. In affluent Western cultures, this started with student rebellions. Now it is the revolutionary cultural agenda of the world's power
elites. Since the 1960s, with help from the United Nations (UN), the

---

1. Plato, *The Republic,* trans. Benjamin Jowett (Gutenberg Project, 2008), Book VIII,
https://www.gutenberg.org/files/1497/1497-h/1497-h.htm (accessed January 8, 2015).

European Union (EU), and the media, a powerful lobby has been fighting to change the value system. The goal is absolute freedom, unfettered by any natural or moral limitations. It sees the human being as merely a "naked" individual. For such absolute freedom that wishes to free itself from the "tyranny of nature," any natural precept is an obstacle that must be removed. When freedom is understood in this way, there is no "good," no "evil," and no system of standards. The concrete weapons in this war include deconstruction of male-female sexuality, alteration of the population's social norms and attitudes (especially among youth), complete legal equivalency of homosexual partnership with marriage, and even social ostracism and legal criminalization of any opposition to these new "norms."

The process is astonishing, because this attempt to create a new human being, and the consequent dissolution of any system of norms, get priority treatment in the activities of the UN, the EU, and many individual countries, even though this strategy of cultural revolution makes no contribution to solving the great problems of our time. On the contrary! The epochal demographic shift will do more than just derail the social structure. Over the past 40 years, most European countries' birth rates have sunk far below replacement levels. As they try to make up the shortfall through immigration, it comes at the expense of their own cultural backbone. Politics oriented toward the public good must make strong families a priority of social policy. Instead, sexual norms have been deregulated in the service of small minorities, thus robbing the family of the values that make it possible.

This process is also astonishing because it destroys the conditions that brought forth European high culture—a model of success for the entire world. Until a few centuries ago, this culture had a Christian foundation. Christianity provided the basic morality that was passed from generation to generation. The essence of this culture is our forbears' decisions in favor of what is good and true—decisions that have always demanded renunciation and sacrifice by the individual. Violent, power-hungry rulers, wars, corrupt church leaders, and even the horrific atheistic systems of terror of the twentieth century could not eradicate Christian culture. Not only was it families who made survival possible in the midst of hunger, but they also passed on this culture under the most adverse circumstances. After every catastrophe, the green growth of Christianity sprouted back, eventually in the unification of Europe on the bedrock of its Christian founders' higher values.

What is happening now goes deeper. This is not about the dictatorship of the proletariat or the dominance of a master race. The terror regimes were recognizable as oppressors and could be eliminated after twelve years—or sixty years, as the case may be. Now the attack is aimed at the person's innermost moral structure—the one that empowers him to be free. The axe is now being taken to the root.

This book's basic premise is that the beautiful gift of sexuality requires cultivation if it is to allow people to have successful relationships and a successful life. The opposite—the coarse acting-out of all desires—distorts the person and the culture. A person sexualized from childhood is taught: "It is *right* to live out all of your instincts without reflection. It is *wrong* for you to set boundaries for them." He uses his own body, and the bodies of other people, for satisfying his sex drive, instead of for expressing personal love. This drive is powerful, because it has the task of ensuring the survival of humankind. The person who does not learn to cultivate it for the expression of love and the creation of new life is ruled by it. A person driven in this way loses his freedom. He no longer hears the voice of his conscience. He loses the ability to love and the ability to bond. He loses the desire to give children the gift of life. He becomes incapable of cultural achievement. He becomes mentally and physically sick. He loses the desire and ability to maintain his own culture, thereby setting it up for domination by a more energetic one.

The Christian idea that humans are made in the image and likeness of God was the basis for the inviolable dignity of every person and led to the formation of state and society on the principle of freedom. High culture, shaped by Christianity, with its commitment to reason and truth, allowed open-minded inquiry into reality, giving rise to unique scientific and technological development. But the acknowledgment of God the creator, the sanctity of human dignity, the validity of universal moral values, and the non-ideological search for truth have come under pressure.

The results are dramatic. Many people no longer want to pass on the life they have received. Families are disintegrating. The next generation's performance is declining—20 percent of 15-year-olds are functionally illiterate.[2] More and more children and teenagers suffer from psychological disorders.[3] The right of the unborn, handicapped and elderly to live is no longer protected. Freedom of religion, expression, science, and parental discretion in childrearing have been undermined.

This is all happening in the name of an ideology that denies that individuals exist as man or woman, that this polarity molds their identity, and that it is required for the propagation of humanity. (Psychological

---

2. Bildung in Deutschland 2012. Autorengruppe Bildungsberichterstattung (Bielefeld: Bertelsmann Verlag, 2012).

3. Cf. Kiggs study of the Robert Koch Institute: www.rki.de/kiggs.

and physical anomalies do not alter this fact.) Never before has there been an ideology that aims to destroy the gender identity of man and woman and *every* ethical standard of sexual behavior. This ideology is called *gender mainstreaming*.

There are many other factors dramatically changing in our time—ecological, economic, technological, and scientific—but none of these factors are strategically aimed at the human being's very core—his or her identity as man or woman—as the individual is increasingly delivered to a sex drive stripped of all moral standards.

It was previously reserved for men to develop ideological systems that left outrageous destruction in their wake and cost countless millions of people their lives. Gender ideology was made up by radical feminist women, and its implementation has been secured—with unimaginable consequences. Many cultures have perished from moral degeneration. For moral degeneration to be forced on people by the rulers of this world is something new.

High Culture and High Morality

Every culture penalizes violation of its sexual standards. While people previously thought it a feature of primitive societies to have taboos that were enforced by everything from social ostracism to the death penalty, today we are finding that new taboos apply. They gain their validity through social exclusion and gradual criminalization, specifically in the domain that all cultures protect with strict standards—the domain of sexuality. A reversal has taken place. Today the dissolution of moral standards is being enforced, and opposition is being punished with exclusion and legal sanctions.

In a comprehensive scientific investigation, the anthropologist J.D. Unwin researched the relationship between sexuality and culture.[4] In the early 1930s, he wanted to test Sigmund Freud's thesis that culture is based on the "sublimation of the sex drive."

The results in a nutshell: the greater the sexual restrictions, the higher the cultural level; the fewer the sexual restrictions, the lower the cultural level.[5] If one looks at the development of our society, it appears this principle is being confirmed once more.

A New Soft Totalitarianism?

It would seem that our current conditions are light years away from the terror systems of Nazism and Communism. However, we can see that

4. J.D. Unwin, *Sex and Culture* (London: Oxford University Press, 1934).
5. Ibid., Foreword, 7.

our freedom is becoming ever more constricted. The people who notice this first are those whose values get in the way of the strategies of the powerful—namely, Christians.

There is no identifiable system of state rule that visibly strives toward world domination, but there are global networks that follow a unified agenda.

It appears there is no ideology enforced by the state, but this is a delusion: The new gender ideology is firmly established in politics and in universities, but it works behind the scenes. Although ordinary people don't know the term yet, the whole society is being "gendered." Like every utopian ideology, this one intends to create a new human being that it designs in accord with its own wishes.

Disfavored ethnic groups have not been (completely) eradicated in Europe so far, but every year, around the world, more than 40 million children are killed in the womb before they can be born.

There is basic democratic order, but there are uncontrollable powers that exert their will over voters and their elected representatives: the media and the financial oligarchy.

There is no one-party system, but a growing portion of the public feels it is no longer represented by the parties in power. This is shown in political detachment and a continuous decrease in voting.

There is no ministry of propaganda, but there is growing uniformity in the media, which is pushing for the dismantling of sexual norms.

There is no state censorship board, but there are government and academic speech policies—rules of Newspeak that must be followed lest one become conspicuous and suffer the consequences.

There is no terror-wielding police or secret-service system, but thanks to digital data storage, we all live in glass houses, where there is no private nook or cranny left. This is a prerequisite for completely new forms of totalitarian monitoring and control.

There are no mass movements dazzled and manipulated by a Führer, but there are atomized, rootless masses, who are kept calm by government entitlements—their potential for radicalization in an economic emergency is incalculable.

There is no prohibition against religious worship, but in the name of anti-discrimination, religious freedom is being insidiously curtailed, and the social conditions for handing on the faith to the next generation are being undermined.[6]

6. Martin Schulz, reelected president of the European Parliament, demanded the abolition of crosses from the public square a few days before the elections for the European Parliament in May 2014.

Totalitarianism has made a costume change and now appears in the mantle of freedom, tolerance, justice, equality, anti-discrimination and diversity—ideological backdrops that prove to be amputated, distorted terms.

These processes are global, and are driven forward by influential lobbies in international institutions. The core of this global Cultural Revolution is the dismantling of sexual norms. The lifting of moral limitations on sexuality would appear to increase people's freedom, but it creates rootless individuals, leads to the dissolution of the supporting social structure, and creates social chaos.

Today, anyone in the political, academic, media, or even ecclesiastical realms who brings forth reasons why the sexual act belongs exclusively within the marital relationship between a man and a woman, and should be open to conceiving children, puts himself at risk. Anyone who scientifically discusses the risks and consequences of non-heterosexual behavior, or flat-out opposes sexual deregulation, opens himself up to becoming a social pariah. He may be excluded from public discourse, stigmatized with obscenities, lose his professional position, be harassed in many ways by interest groups, or otherwise discriminated against. In Germany, demonstrations on behalf of family values need heavy police protection. Criminalization through anti-discrimination laws and new punishable offenses such as "homophobia" and "hate speech" is already a reality in some countries and is being promoted globally.

Do those who consider themselves firmly on the side of good—who today so courageously battle the state terror of a bygone century—have the will to oppose the increasing curtailment of freedom in our own time? The dividing line between standing for freedom and relinquishing freedom is a willingness to pay the price today for not swimming with the sharks.

Brave New World

Sometimes authors can see beyond the borders of the present. In his 1930 novel *Brave New World,* Aldous Huxley described what arises when fun becomes the meaning of life and sex becomes the everyday pleasure of young and old. In his foreword to the 1946 edition, he wrote, "The really revolutionary revolution is to be achieved, not in the external world, but in the souls and flesh of human beings."

Thus, in the *Brave New World,* people want to do what they're supposed to do, and they take their enslavement for freedom.

In his foreword Huxley continues:

As political and economic freedom diminishes, sexual freedom tends compensatingly to increase. And the dictator . . . will do well to

encourage that freedom. In conjunction with the freedom to day-
dream under the influence of dope and movies and the radio, it will
help to reconcile his subjects to the servitude which is their fate. . . .
All things considered, it looks as if Utopia were far closer to us than
anyone, only fifteen years ago, could have imagined. Then, I pro-
jected it six hundred years into the future. Today, it seems quite possible that the horror may be upon us within a single century.[7]

Aldous Huxley wrote this when there was still no artificial insemination, prenatal selection, sperm and egg banks, surrogate motherhood,
"Parent 1" and "Parent 2," daycare, sex-game instruction in kindergarten, obligatory sex-education in school, rampant drug consumption, or
pornography as mass entertainment; and when there was no TV in
every living room, no Internet, and no smartphones.

People had just survived World War II, and put their hope in the new
organization called the United Nations, which passed the Universal
Declaration of Human Rights in 1948. It was to be a bulwark against the
unspeakable horror that sent millions upon millions of people to their
death. They had been degraded, deprived of their rights, dispossessed,
agonized, tortured and murdered by people who had been blinded by
ideology and dehumanized by the corruption of power. Half a century
later, this same United Nations is where the battle is being fought to
raise the murder of children in the womb to a human right, and for the
nations of the world to give same-sex relationships the legal status of
marriage.

As Huxley foresaw, the core of this attack on fundamental values is
human sexuality. The battle to abolish sexual norms has begun an
epochal victory march. At the same time, we witness an epochal cultural
decline in the Western world. What was praised by Plato and Aristotle as
truth, beauty and good has now fallen into disrepute. No big money can
be made from truth, beauty, and good, but lies, ugliness, and malice will
bring in plenty—billions through horror and pornography alone.

We are born with the potential for freedom, but the ability to use our
freedom for good needs formation and work within the individual. Virtue is the precondition for culture. We must learn the cardinal virtues
that allow our humanity to flourish: wisdom, justice, bravery, and
restraint. When a culture stops valuing virtue, and stops passing to the
next generation what is appropriate, tried and true, and precious—by
example, upbringing, and education—it is digging its own grave. There

---

7. Aldous Huxley, *Brave New World* (1932; reprt., New York: Everyman's Library,
2013), http://www.everymanslibrary.co.uk/ (accessed January 8, 2015).

is still freedom, and it is not too late to defend it. But one must know who is curtailing it in their own selfish interest. That's what this book is about.

2

Trailblazers of the Sexual Revolution from the French Revolution to Today

On today's thoughts depends what is being lived in the squares and streets of tomorrow.

José Ortega y Gasset

The Trailblazers

THE FRENCH REVOLUTION elevated autonomous reason to the level of a goddess, a women's libber who had freed herself from God and his imperatives. The people were enticed by beautiful words that spoke to the longings everyone harbors: *Liberté, Egalité, Fraternité* (Liberty, Equality, Fraternity). But people didn't notice that freedom can only be increased at the expense of equality, that equality only gains at the expense of freedom, and that brotherhood falls by the wayside where there is no justice.

From a well-furnished cell in the Bastille prison, the Marquis de Sade wrote what freedom meant in the sexual realm. Incarcerated there at the end of the *Ancien Régime*, he had plenty of time to commit every imaginable perversity to paper. His name is forever bound to them in its dreadful variant *sadomasochism*. His 1791 novel *Justine* contributed like no other to the politicization of sex and the sexualization of politics. Sade showed the way to revolution: from sexual freedom to sadism to death. It took only four years for the French Revolution's initial promises to give way to terror, with heads rolling off the guillotine by the minute. Voltaire's battle cry, "Crush the infamy!" (Crush the vile thing, the Church!), led to the death of thousands of priests and other religious.

With the abdication of Napoleon in April 1814, the return of King Louis XVIII, and the rehabilitation of the Jesuits by Pope Pius VII (the order had been banned by Pope Clement XIV in 1773), the first sexual revolution spent some time buried under the ashes of the political restoration. However, it merely smoldered there for 200 years to become a

15

global conflagration ignited by the strategist of today's global sexual revolution.

Many great, highly learned, devoutly revered minds have contributed philosophical and psychological ideas, cultural revolutionary expertise, and culture-altering works to the effort. Jean-Jacques Rousseau, August Comte, Henri de Saint-Simon, Charles Fourier, Friedrich Nietzsche, Sigmund Freud, C.G. Jung, John Watson, Wilhelm Reich, Alfred Kinsey, and Jack Kerouac are just a few of the most notable. They all had one thing in common: rejection, if not outright hatred, of the Catholic Church, because this church never stops preaching the message of Christ: "*If you love me, you will keep my commandments*" (John 14:15).

They did not keep these commandments, did not want to keep them, and dedicated their lives and considerable creative energy to justifying this and to recreating humankind in their own image. Both then and now, the Church has stood in their way, preaching the unchanging message of God in an ever-changing world.

Friedrich Nietzsche expressed it in this way: "Christianity has thus far always been attacked in the wrong way. As long as one does not perceive Christian morality as a capital crime against life, its defenders will always have an easy game. The question of the *truth* of Christianity . . . is something entirely secondary as long as the question of the value of Christian morality is not addressed."[1] Nietzsche said that Christianity promulgated a "slave morality" for the weak, which can only be despised by the neo-pagan master race.

In his work *Libido Dominandi: Sexual Liberation and Political Control*,[2] the American author E. Michael Jones describes those taking the intellectual match to the gasoline. Jones shows that they live in sexual chaos and shattered relationships; they neglect their children, are dependent on drugs and alcohol, and end in despair, insanity, the occult, and suicide. Their life-stories echo a Bavarian proverb: The devil helps his people, and then he snatches them.

Those who have themselves become enslaved to their urges, and have the power to forge them into ideological and political tools for creating an autonomous, sexualized people, blaze the trail to personal and social chaos for their contemporaries. On the other hand, people achieve inner freedom when they learn to cultivate their desires through the

---

1. Quoted by Joseph Ratzinger in Marcello Pera, Joseph Ratzinger, *Ohne Wurzeln* (Augsburg: Sankt Ulrich Verlag, 2005), 134.

2. E. Michael Jones, *Libido Dominandi: Sexual Liberation and Political Control* (South Bend: St. Augustine's Press, 2000), 200.

willing bond of love. But when people fall for the lie that unrestrained satisfaction of their urges is freedom, or leads to freedom, they become subservient to those urges. Another word for that is *addiction*. As Jones writes:

> This was the genius of Enlightenment politics, which is in reality nothing more than a physics of vice: Incite the passion; control the man. This is the esoteric doctrine of the Enlightenment, one that has been refined for over 200 years through a trajectory that involves everything from psychoanalysis to advertising to pornography and the role it plays in *Kulturkampf*.[3]

He further observes how "that discovery was so ingenious because vice as a form of social control is virtually invisible. Those who are in the thrall of their passions see only what they desire and not the bondage those desires inflict on them."[4]

The 200-year culture war to create autonomous, manipulable, controllable people had various drivers that developed into powerful coalitions of interests:

- Malthusianism, which aimed to reduce the world population, because the population was allegedly growing faster than food production.
- The eugenics movement, which aims to increase the quality of people and reduce their quantity.
- The ruling interests of the rich and powerful of the United States, generally white Anglo-Saxon Protestants (WASPs), who perceived the danger of "differential fertility." They feared that the low birth rate of the upper class and the high birth rate of the underclass, especially blacks in the US and poor Third World countries, would cause them to lose political and economic power.
- Eloquent individuals who delivered philosophical, political, and psychological ideas and methods for transforming social reality.
- Communist revolutionaries who destroyed family and religion and wished to transform the State into a Utopian classless society.
- The feminist movement, which aimed to free women from the "slavery of marriage and motherhood" (Simone de Beauvoir).
- The homosexual movement, which wishes to abolish "compulsory heterosexuality."

3. Ibid., 59.
4. Ibid., 61.

All of these interest groups overlap; their protagonists' affiliations can be varied and span more than one group.

Malthusianism

While occupying a professorial chair for "political economy," in 1798 Thomas Robert Malthus (1766–1834) wrote *An Essay on the Principle of Population,* in which he formulated his "Iron Law of Population." He claimed that catastrophic famines were inevitable, because the population would increase geometrically (2–4–8–16, and so on), while food production increased only arithmetically (1–2–3–4, and so on). To prevent this, birth rates had to be reduced.

To this day, the theory has influenced the fate of people and nations throughout the world. Malthus wanted to eliminate excess mouths at "nature's mighty feast." He expressed it this way:

> A man who is born into a world already possessed, if he cannot get subsistence from his parents on whom he has a just demand, and if the society do not want his labor, has no claim of right to the smallest portion of food, and, in fact, has no business to be where he is. At nature's mighty feast there is no vacant cover for him. She tells him to be gone, and will quickly execute her own orders . . . [through] sickness, misery and death.[5]

And, we might add, this reduction in population could also be effected by the worldwide efforts of the population controllers, for whom natural decimation is not enough. Malthus saw people whose numbers may threaten the affluence and power of the ruling classes as unnecessary eaters to be eliminated, rather than as people whose creative spirit and labor create prosperity.

If food shortages really arise, as is the case in many of the world's countries, there are two options: increase food production and distribute it fairly, or reduce the population. According to the United Nations Food and Agriculture Organization (FAO), per capita food production—the amount of food available to each person in the world if divided equally—grew 30 percent from 1951 to 1992.[6]

The UN expects the world population to top out at 8.9 billion by 2050 and then to *decrease.* For the first time, the UN assumes, fertility in most developing countries will drop to below 2.1 children per woman in the twenty-first century. It is expected to fall below replacement level in three out of four developing countries by 2050. This is the estimate of

---

5. http://de.wikipedia.org/wiki/Thomas_Robert_Malthus.

6. Roland Rösler, *Der Dämon des Thomas Robert: Oder Was heisst hier Überbevölkerung* (Abtsteinach: Derscheider, 1997), 42ff.

the Population Division of the United Nations in its 2002 revision of official UN population projections (UN, 2002).[7]

Fear of a population explosion was first stirred up in the mid-twentieth century. Paul Ehrlich began his famous book *The Population Bomb* with the words: "The battle to feed all of humanity is over. In the 1970s and 1980s, hundreds of millions of people will starve to death in spite of any crash programs embarked upon now."[8] In a tone of infallible scientific authority, in 1972 the Club of Rome published *The Limits of Growth*, predicting that by the year 2000 the world's mineral resources and oil deposits would largely be exhausted. The main reason was allegedly the population explosion. The Club of Rome's goal was to "build a global society in the twenty-first century."

Can that be achieved? The Rockefeller Foundation has billions to use for guiding the development of society according to its own interests, and they have bet on birth control. The twentieth century brought improved and completely new technical options—the birth-control pill in 1960, and gradual legalization of abortion.

To this day, reducing the world population is a priority of the United States and international organizations (see chapter 4, 54). This could explain why the power elites promote the feminist and homosexualist movements and support abortion organizations operating worldwide.

Margaret Sanger and the Eugenics Movement

Margaret Sanger (1879/1883–1966) played a decisive role in population control. She made it her life's mission to eliminate supposedly undesirable elements of the population through contraception, sterilization, and abortion. In the United States, the climate was right for the ideology of eugenics. "Racial hygiene" wasn't invented by the Germans. As Jeremy Rifkin relates, Theodore Roosevelt, the twenty-sixth president of the United States (from 1901 to 1909), waved the flag for it:

> Some day we will realize that the prime duty, the inescapable duty of the good citizens of the right type is to leave his or her blood behind him in the world; and that we have no business to permit the perpetuation of citizens of the wrong type. The great problem of civilization is to secure a relative increase of the valuable as compared with the less valuable or noxious elements in the population. . . . The problem cannot be met unless we give full consideration to the immense influence of heredity. . . . I wish very much that the wrong people could be

---

7. http://www.un.org/esa/population/publications/wpp2002/WPP2002-HIGH-LIGHTSre v1.PDF.

8. Paul Ehrlich, *The Population Bomb* (New York: Ballantine Books, 1988), xi.

prevented entirely from breeding; and when the evil nature of these people is sufficiently flagrant, this should be done. Criminals should be sterilized and feebleminded persons forbidden to leave offspring behind them. . . . The emphasis should be laid on getting desirable people to breed.[9]

The original Communist-oriented feminist, Margaret Sanger could be exploited for these purposes by the powerful; they opened all doors to her. She practiced the free sexuality she preached and had numerous affairs with influential contemporaries. She left her first husband and three children to marry oil magnate James Noah H. Slee, who financed her eugenics activities. The early death of her disabled daughter haunted her throughout her life. In séances, she tried again and again to contact her.

Sanger did not shy away from breaking the law in pursuit of her eugenics mission, or from being locked up for it. She crisscrossed America, and later Europe and Asia, to fight for the legalization of birth control and to convince women to reduce their fertility.

In 1921, Sanger founded the American Birth Control League, which openly advocated eugenics for racist purposes. At the same time, Marie Stopes opened a birth-control clinic in London in 1921. Today Marie Stopes International is one of the world's largest abortion organizations.

In the 1930s, the Rockefellers began to back Margaret Sanger's push for birth control as a solution to mass poverty at the time of the Great Depression. At a congressional hearing, Sanger called for "more children from the fit, fewer from the unfit." But she had a powerful opponent in Catholic moral theologian Msgr. John Ryan. What he said about the American Birth Control League would apply no less to the policies of the United Nations today:

To advocate contraception, as a method of bettering the condition of the poor and unemployed, is to divert the attention of the influential classes from the pursuit of social justice and to relieve them of all responsibility for our bad distribution and other social maladjustments. We simply cannot—those who believe as I do—subscribe to the idea that the poor are to be made responsible for their plight, and instead of getting justice from the government and a more rational social order, they are to be required to reduce their numbers.[10]

Ryan vanquished Sanger at the congressional hearing, with the result

9. Jeremy Rifkin, "Was macht euch so ängstlich? Eine Anfrage an die Deutschen," *Frankfurter Allgemeine Zeitung*, no. 269 (November 18, 2000), 41.
10. Jones, *Libido Dominandi*, 284.

that John D. Rockefeller III personally committed himself to the contraception crusade for the rest of his life. To many Americans, contraception, abortion and sterilization were and still are the answer to an estimated billion people on this earth suffering from hunger and some 9 million dying from it per year.

In 1942, the Birth Control League changed its name to International Planned Parenthood, because Nazi attempts at ethnic cleansing had given forthright eugenics a bad smell. Ten years later, the German branch was founded under the name *Pro Familia*. This name takes the guise of family-friendliness even farther. The organization "supports" the family by performing 77% of all abortions in Germany.[11]

Before she died at the age of 86, Margaret Sanger had left a long trail of accomplishments. She had initiated the 1927 World Congress for Population Control in Geneva and ignited a mass movement for "free sexuality." She financed research for the birth control pill, and fought with incredible doggedness for changes to the law until finally, in 1965, the United States Supreme Court declared laws against birth control unconstitutional, in the ruling on *Griswold v. Connecticut*. She had achieved her life's goals.

Karl Marx and Friedrich Engels

In the early nineteenth century, Karl Marx and Friedrich Engels developed the philosophy of dialectical materialism and their utopia of a classless society. At its core, this was a battle against God, belief, and the Church. Marx and Engels had been Christians in their youth—just as Soviet strongman Joseph Stalin was even a seminarian for several semesters. They fell away from the faith and elevated themselves and their teaching to the status of an ultimate principle that drove a superhuman potential for violence, bringing bloody terror and destruction to a large portion of the earth. When Marx and Engels were devising this ideology in the mid-nineteenth century, who could have imagined that they were writing the history of humanity?

In a poem written in his youth, Karl Marx revealed his gloomy objectives:

In a prayer of despair I will build myself a throne.
Cold and huge will be its summit,
Its bulwark will be superhuman horror,
And its marshal will be gloomy agony![12]

---

11. www.profamilia.de/fileadmin/dateien/fachpersonal/spin 0202.pdf.
12. *Marx-Engels-Gesamtausgabe* (MEG), vol. 1, 182–83.

In the *Manifesto of the Communist Party* of 1848, it is still there for everyone to read:

> But Communism abolishes eternal truths, it abolishes all religion and all morality, instead of constituting them on a new basis; it therefore acts in contradiction to all past historical experience. . . . [Communists] openly declare that their ends can be attained only by the forcible overthrow of all existing social conditions.

Marx's private life was a wreck. His two daughters and his son-in-law committed suicide. He lived on financial assistance from Friedrich Engels and from seeking inheritances. For example, of his uncle he said: "If the dog dies now, I'll be out of this jam."[13] Not only was his own family ruined, but the family as an institution was to be shattered; and for Marx, deep down, it was always a battle against God: "The secret to the Holy Family is the earthly family. To make the former disappear, the latter must be destroyed, in theory and in practice."[14] Marx and Engels reinterpreted the matter of women as a class issue. In his 1884 work *The Origin of the Family, Private Property and the State,* Engels wrote: "The first class antagonism appearing in history coincides with the development of the antagonism of man and wife in monogamy, and the first class oppression with that of the female by the male sex."[15] He saw integration of women into the production process as a necessary condition for their liberation. To Communist revolutionaries, "bourgeois morals" impeded achievement of the classless society, because it was in marriage that the first class antagonism arose.

All sexual revolutionaries in the twentieth century have their spiritual roots in Marxism. It didn't bother leftist intellectuals a bit that those executing this ideology subjugated entire peoples through State terror and slaughtered countless millions who stood in the way of their "Utopia." Apparently not every ideology is discredited by the mass murder it brings.

Alexandra Kollontai

During the Russian Revolution, Alexandra Kollontai was the first woman on the St. Petersburg Revolutionary Council and commissar for

---

13. Richard Wurmbrand, *Das andere Gesicht des Karl Marx* (Uhlinden: Stephanus Edition, 1987), 33.

14. Marx-Engels-Gesamtausgabe, vol. 3, 6.

15. Friedrich Engels, *The Origin of the Family, Private Property and the State* (Project Gutenberg, 1902), http://www.gutenberg.org/files/33111/33111-h/33111-h.htm (accessed January 8, 2015).

public welfare under Lenin. She was also the one who legalized divorce and abortion, established communal houses, and promoted free love to liberate women from the "choice between marriage and prostitution." The Bolsheviks wanted to control the rearing of children in order to make them obedient Communists. Women were to work in production and no longer for their husbands and children at home.

Kollontai did what she could to make her dream a reality: "[T]he home fire is going out in all classes and strata of the population, and of course no artificial measures will fan its fading flame."[16] However, the moral excesses of the Revolution threw Russian society into such chaos that there was a backlash. This roiled Wilhelm Reich—Germany's own sexual revolutionary—because Russia could no longer serve as a model of true Utopia.[17] Reich's lament over the "sexual reaction" in the Soviet Union in the early 1930s is interesting, because all of the Bolsheviks' revolutionary measures—which they actually reinstated after a short experimental phase—are on the agenda of the ruling political classes *today*. With sorrow Reich complained that:

- Homosexuality restrictions had been reinstated.
- "Pregnancy termination" had been made more difficult.
- The sexual freedom of Soviet youth and the "rational sexual enlightenment" of children and teenagers were being undermined by an "ideology of asceticism."
- The "compulsory family" was being supported again, and the 1918 dissolution of marriage law had been repealed.
- Collectivization of childrearing was stopped and responsibility placed back with the parents.
- The "destruction of authoritarian schooling" through children's autonomy had been reversed. Reich knew this was threatening the revolution, because he had recognized that "The sexual process of society has always been the core of its cultural process."[18]

Wilhelm Reich

At the time of the Weimar Republic, Wilhelm Reich was one of the most effective sexual revolutionaries. Reich was severely affected by his mother's suicide when he was 14 and the death of his depressive father a few years later. As a medical student, he was already making a name in the Vienna Psychoanalytic Society, founded by Sigmund Freud in 1908.

16. Jones, *Libido Dominandi*, 159.
17. Wilhelm Reich, *The Sexual Revolution: Toward a Self-Regulating Character Structure* (New York: Farrar, Straus and Giroux, 1974). Cf. *Sexual Revolution in Russia*.
18. Ibid., 159.

Without ever completing a training analysis, he was already working as a psychoanalyst at the age of 23.

Reich's orgasm theory grew from Freud's libido theory and—to put it simply—said that people need three orgasms a week to be healthy and to build the classless society as citizens of the Revolution. How a person induced them was beside the point. It could be by one's own hand, with alternating partners, or with either sex. For this, "compulsory marriage" and the "compulsory family" as a tool of childrearing had to be destroyed. The means for doing this was sexualization of the masses, particularly of children. In his work *The Sexual Revolution*, Reich states that "The patriarchal family is the structural and ideological breeding ground of all social orders based on the authoritarian principle." He goes on to say: "We do not discuss the existence or non-existence of God—we merely eliminate the sexual repressions and dissolve the infantile ties to the parents." [19] The rest of the subversive goals then take care of themselves, through the dynamic set in motion.

What is based on the authoritarian principle? One's relationship to God, to the church, to tradition, to one's parents—especially to one's father—and to teachers. Reich made it crystal-clear that sexualization was the vehicle for destroying all these relationships, and thereby the structural order of the whole society.

For this agenda he built a massive theoretical superstructure with scientific pretensions. Marxism had entered the scene as infallible, objective science, and Reich added to it with the newly invented "science" of psychoanalysis. As with any ideology, Reich used a massive intellectual edifice to sell his destructive agenda as objective and good. According to his theory, war, exploitation of the proletariat, "religious mysticism," and fascism[20] all have the same cause: the 6,000-year "sexual suppression" that had made humanity sick throughout the world.[21] All the scourges of human life would disappear forever if people were to satisfy their sexual desires without any limitations.

This is what Reich fought for, and it is why he joined the Communist Party, from which he was expelled in 1933. He founded the Sex-Pol movement, which organized proletarian mass rallies in prewar Berlin. The agenda: "Sexual affirmation as the core of a life-affirming cultural policy based on the socialist planned economy."[22] In a nutshell: Satisfy

19. Jones, *Libido Dominandi*, 261.

20. Wilhelm Reich, *The Mass Psychology of Fascism* (New York: Farrar, Straus & Giroux, 1970).

21. Wilhelm Reich, *The Sexual Revolution*.

22. Ibid., 268.

your sexual urges, and you'll create paradise on earth. It was an early forerunner of the more graceful hippie slogan "Make love, not war."

Children and youth were crucial in Reich's strategy. Sexually active children are natural revolutionaries who rebel against any authority. Reich wanted to abolish the "sex-negating atmosphere and structure of the family" by using sexualization to release children and youth from their family ties: "revolutionary youth is hostile and destructive to the family."[23] Reich promoted masturbation as a "way out of the harm of abstinence" and sexual intercourse starting at puberty, because "suppression [of youth sexuality] is essential for maintaining compulsory marriage and family as well as for producing submissive citizens."[24]

Wilhelm Reich recognized that total sexualization of the culture would mean extermination of the churches and the traditional state, and this was his goal. E. Michael Jones pinpoints what a society in transition from a Christian to a hedonistic model refuses to discern: "The state must come down with both feet in favor of one or the other form of government—either the rule of reason and self-control or the rule of sexual revolution. . . . The classical state must foster virtue; the revolutionary state must foster vice . . . but vice leads sooner or later to the demise of the revolutionary state as well."[25]

Strangely enough, Reich subjected himself to the constraint of marriage three times. He also divorced his third wife, whom he had wed in exile in New York and with whom he fathered a third child.

Reich developed an "orgone accumulator," a machine for production of "life energy." He and his colleague Dr. Silvert were convicted of fraud and sent to prison for selling this device. Reich died in 1957 in the federal penitentiary at Lewisburg, Pennsylvania. His cohort was released a year later and soon committed suicide.

Wilhelm Reich was extraordinarily influential. Fritz Perls, the founder of Gestalt Therapy, completed his training in analysis with Reich in Vienna, and Alexander Lowen's successful bioenergetics was influenced by Reich's theory of "character armor through sexual suppression." He achieved his great cultural revolutionary breakthrough postmortem, however, through the upheavals of the late 1960s. His messages were clothed in the theories of the "Frankfurt School" and planted into the hearts and minds of students by the works of the émigrés Adorno, Horkheimer, and Marcuse, who had returned to Germany. How seductive the message was: Free yourself of repressive Christian

---

23. Ibid., 89 et seq.
24. Ibid., 115.
25. Jones, *Libido Dominandi*, 260.

sexual morality, live out your urges, and thus create the paradise of a "society free of domination."

Magnus Hirschfeld

One of the first activists for legitimization of homosexuality was Magnus Hirschfeld. As a "pioneer of sexology," he developed the theory that the binary gender system must be abolished in favor of radical individualization. Each man and each woman, he claimed, was a unique mixture of male and female traits. In an age of scientific gullibility, he sold his political agenda for changing the value system as "science." In Nice, where he died in 1935, his gravestone reads, "*Per scientiam ad justitiam*" (Through science to justice).

As a homosexual, Hirschfeld was an enigmatic figure. On the one hand, he fought for acceptance of homosexuality, while at the same time he called homosexuality a "congenital deformity" that should be classified among "sexual anomalies and perversions."[26] In his book *Berlins Drittes Geschlecht* ("Berlin's Third Sex"), he calls homosexual men and women "unfortunate, disenfranchised people who drag a mysterious riddle of nature through their lonely lives. We must be thankful to any doctor who has new treatment options, because many homosexuals feel the certainly justified desire to feel inherently heterosexual."[27]

In 1908, Hirschfeld founded the Zeitschrift für Sexualwissenschaft ("Journal of Sexology"), and in 1919 the Institut für Sexualwissenschaft ("Institute for Sexology"), which organized congresses for "scientifically based sexual reform," where he promoted the "scientific" idea that homosexuality was part of nature's variety. Hirschfeld understood the potential of the media to change culture and launched production of the first homosexual film, *Different from the Others,* in which he himself performed. In 1923 he founded the Institut für Freikörperkultur ("Institute for Nudism") and in Copenhagen the World League for Sexual Reform in 1928. With this, he laid the cornerstone of the international homosexual network. Hirschfeld also advocated eugenics, such as "grafting" and "improving" beings of greater and lesser value through selection, and was a member of the German Society for Racial Hygiene.[28]

In the Weimar Republic, Hirschfeld was the epitome of "cultural bolshevism," which was perceived as Jewish. He was opposed by the Nazis,

---

26. Magnus Hirschfeld, *Sappho und Sokrates*, 15. Quoted here: http://sex-needs-culture.blogspot.de/2011/12/magnus-hirschfeld-das-falsche-idol_16.html (accessed October 6, 2015).

27. Ibid.

28. Ibid.

his lectures were disrupted by squads of thugs, and he was once severely beaten. In 1933, his Institute for Sexology was closed, and its files destroyed by the Nazis, possibly also to do away with compromising material. The Nazis persecuted homosexuals and killed them in concentration camps, yet at the same time, their ranks were full of them.[29] Hitler used repudiation of homosexuality among the populace to get opponents out of the way.

Magnus Hirschfeld lives on. The German Society for Social-Scientific Sexuality Research, founded in 1990, awards its Magnus Hirschfeld medal for outstanding contributions to sexual science and sexual reform. Rosa von Praunheim has made a film of Hirschfeld's life, called *The Einstein of Sex*. The Hirschfeld Eddy Foundation works to achieve "human rights for sexual minorities." How that is to take place is laid out in the Yogyakarta Principles, which are gradually being implemented with the authority of the UN (see Ch. 5). For this, the German federal government has provided 10 million euros to the Magnus Hirschfeld foundation.

Magnus Hirschfeld tried to overcome the painful contradiction between his own homosexuality and condemnation of this tendency as a "deformity" and "perversion" by dissolving gender identity. As such, he is the forerunner of gender ideology.

Sigmund Freud and C. G. Jung

The sexualization of society was given a powerful boost by depth psychology, which in the twentieth century was regarded as one of the great new discoveries regarding human nature. Sigmund Freud's message was that human consciousness was just the visible tip of the iceberg. Hidden beneath it was the subconscious, which was what really controlled people.

This subconscious revolved around repressed sexual desires, such as the "Oedipus complex," "penis envy," and "castration anxiety," which Freud claimed to have discovered in his patients. A child's sexual desires were directed at the parent of the opposite sex, while the child perceived the parent of the same sex as a rival, triggering feelings of jealousy and hatred.

Religion, morality, and parental authority were said to be anchored in the "superego" and exert repressive power over a person, especially when it came to his sexual desires. It was believed that years of psycho-

29. Cf. Scott Lively and Kevin Abrams, *The Pink Swastika: Homosexuals and the Nazi Party* (Keizer, Oregon: Founders Publishing Company, 1995).

analysis could deprive the "superego" of its power and, with the help of an emancipated "ego," the needs of the "id" could be satisfied without guilt. Alienated from his Jewish religion, Sigmund Freud considered religion to be infantile wishful thinking, and—strictly according to Feuerbach—as a projection that fulfilled important functions in the human psyche: the fantasy of security and protection, a higher purpose to life, and moral control. He thought religious practices were the neurotic compulsions of a person who did not want to grow up.

Freud falsified his case descriptions, was addicted to cocaine, had a relationship with his wife's sister, smoked 20 cigars a day, contracted palate cancer, for which he had 30 operations, and died of a heroin overdose that he had administered by his family doctor when life became unbearable for him. His was the life of a major mind who had eloquently formulated psychological theories that played an important role in the twentieth century's dismantling of Christian values and the sexualization of the culture. Freud's crown prince, nineteen years younger, was C. G. Jung. However, Jung broke away from Freud and founded his own school of psychology. Jung is considered to have united psychoanalysis with "spirituality," and for that reason seems to many Christians to have built a bridge between faith and depth psychology. Jung preferred to speak of "numina" rather than of God. It is a term from Roman paganism indicating the presence of nonspecific divinities in a tree, stone, emperor, the cosmos, or even the Jungian "archetypes."

Behind his concept that displaced "shadows" of the personality must be "integrated" into the "persona" is the view that God is good and evil at the same time, and that people can contain a unity of good and evil, "a nuptial union of opposite halves." In this way he removes the core of the Christian image of God, which rests on the belief that God *is* love: that he is completely good, and gives people the grace to overcome evil in, with, and through Jesus Christ. Martin Buber describes Jungian psychology as a new "pseudo-religious Gnosticism."

In her book *Healing Presence*, Leanne Payne reports of Jung's initiation into the "realm of darkness," which he himself describes in his autobiographical work *Memories, Dreams, Reflections*. When he was between 3 and 4 years old, he had a terrifying dream that occupied and pursued him for the rest of his life. He saw an enthroned phallus god three or four yards tall and heard the voice of his mother shouting, "Look at him. That is the man-eater!"[30] It is to this dream that Jung attributes his dismissive

---

30. Leanne Payne, *The Healing Presence: Curing the Soul through Union with Christ* (Grand Rapids: Baker Books, 1989), 228.

attitude toward Jesus: "Lord Jesus never became quite real for me, never quite acceptable, never quite lovable, for again and again I would think of his underground counterpart [the phallus god], a frightful revelation which had been accorded me without my seeking it."[31]

Leanne Payne considers the "initiation into the darkness" in Jung's early years as the key to his "integration" of the evil with the good and his openness to the occult. C. G. Jung's deep, sophisticated construct is the elitist way of invading Catholic spirituality with esotericism.

John Watson, Edward Bernays, Bernard Berelson

Depth psychology, however, is not suited to *social engineering*, the manipulation of the masses to serve hidden objectives. Behaviorism provided the foundation for this. Its founder was John Watson, whose book *Behaviorism* appeared in 1914. He saw each human being as a malleable object that could be conditioned by positive and negative stimuli. This was regarded as a new, strictly scientific understanding of people and as a method for changing them. Darwinism's message that man is nothing more than a highly developed ape had prepared the way. Because people were less and less formed by and tied to religion, tradition, and morality, they could and needed to be reconditioned.

The younger the person, the more this would succeed. In 1928, Watson published his book *Psychological Care of Infant and Child*, which sought to replace parental love and traditional standards of childrearing with "scientific" behavioral control. Since then, there has been a continuous process of denying mothers' and fathers' competence at raising their children. Watson's book was one of Aldous Huxley's inspirations for his novel *Brave New World*, in which people are conditioned to love slavery. Behaviorism promised to solve the problems of society by turning psychologists into social engineers.

Edward Bernays, a nephew of Sigmund Freud, was one of the first and most effective social engineers, and for his success at it *Life* magazine listed him as one of the 100 most influential people of the twentieth century. He had a passion for manipulating the masses. "If we understand the mechanism and motives of the group mind," he wrote, "is it not possible to control and regiment the masses according to our will without their knowing about it?"[32]

---

31. Cf. Jeffrey Satinover, *The Empty Self: C. G. Jung and the Gnostic Transformation of Modern Identity* (Cambridge: Grove Books, 1996), quoted by Leanne Payne.

32. Edward L. Bernays, *Propaganda* (New York: H. Liveright, 1928), 71.

He described this technique of forming mass opinion as the *engineering of consent*. Bernays' most famous book, *Propaganda*, appeared in 1928. Its first chapter, "Organizing Chaos," begins with the words:

> The conscious and intelligent manipulation of the organized habits and opinions of the masses is an important element in democratic society. Those who manipulate this unseen mechanism of society constitute an invisible government, which is the true ruling power of our country. We are governed, our minds molded, our tastes formed, our ideas suggested, largely by men we have never heard of. This is a logical result of the way in which our democratic society is organized. Vast numbers of human beings must cooperate in this manner if they are to live together as a smoothly functioning society. [. . .] in almost every act of our daily lives, whether in the sphere of politics or business, in our social conduct or our ethical thinking, we are dominated by the relatively small number of persons . . . who understand the mental processes and social patterns of the masses. It is they who pull the wires, which control the public mind.[33]

These insights were not lost on Joseph Goebbels, who, as propaganda minister of the Third Reich, soon used them to crank up Germany's anti-Semitic propaganda machine. They are also the views and motives of every spin doctor of our era.

Bernays was a dedicated atheist. According to Marvin Olasky, who had extensively interviewed Bernays, "[he was acutely aware] that a world without God rapidly descended into social chaos. Therefore, he contended that social manipulation by public relations counselors was justified by the end of creating man-made gods who could assert subtle social control and prevent disaster. . . . Pulling strings behind the scenes was necessary not only for personal advantage, but for social salvation."[34]

Behaviorist Bernard Berelson, of Columbia and Stanford universities, developed the techniques of mass manipulation even further, using the new technical capabilities of radio and television and social-scientific refinements in opinion surveys. He was in the service of the Ford and Rockefeller foundations, and the introduction to his pioneering work, *Reader in Public Opinion and Communication*,[35] clearly states that manipulating the masses requires manipulating their opinions. As Jones

33. Ibid., 37.

34. Jones, *Libido Dominandi*, 187.

35. Bernard Berelson and Morris Janowitz, "Reader in Public Opinion and Communication," *Public Opinion Quarterly*, vol. 14, no. 3 (1950).

sums up: "The goal of secularization was the reduction of all of life's imperatives to 'opinions,' which is to say not the expression of moral absolutes or divine law. Once this 'secularization' occurred, the people who controlled 'opinions' controlled the country."[36]

He knew what he was talking about, and he put it into practice as president of the Population Council under John D. Rockefeller III. With big money and plenty of know-how, he was able to fulfill Rockefeller's life mission—changing American attitudes toward contraception so that population-reduction programs could take hold.

E. Michael Jones explains the steps on the path to manipulated democracy in this way:

> Religious belief meant ipso facto the opposite of opinion, and therefore ideas not subject to the manipulation of the people who controlled the communications media. What needed to be done then was move large areas of thought from the realm of religion to the realm of opinion if any significant breakthroughs in political control through manipulation of the media were to take place. Sexual morality was the most important area of religious thinking that needed to be moved into the realm of 'opinion,' where it would then be under the control of psychological warriors like Berelson and those who paid his salary, namely, the Rockefellers.[37]

Alfred Kinsey

Alfred Kinsey achieved a breakthrough in the sexualization of the Western world with the publication of *Sexual Behavior in the Human Male* in 1948, and *Sexual Behavior in the Human Female* in 1953.

Kinsey, whose scientific qualifications were in the field of entomology, is rightfully considered "the father of sexology." His significance in the dismantling of the fundamental values of Western culture cannot be overestimated. In the meantime, it has been proven that he was a sadomasochist who abused children and prison inmates to arrive at his desired results, and that he falsified his statistics. This was revealed by Dr. Judith Reisman in the early 1980s.

Yet, sexologists to this very day cite him as a serious scientist. He reached his goal of eliminating the "repressive" sexual heritage of Judeo-Christian culture in both behavior and legislation. He claimed that the laws that had previously protected families, women, and children were relics of a hypocritical morality that no one adhered to and that stood in

36. Jones, *Libido Dominandi*, 415.
37. Ibid., 416.

the way of the blessings of a "sexually enlightened and honest era." The result is sexual anarchy. As Judith Reisman states: "Like a cancer spreading throughout the body, sexual anarchy has spread throughout the fabric of society, affecting every aspect of American life and every man, woman and child."[38]

Kinsey's works give the impression of strictly scientific empirical social research. Within two months, the first book sold 200,000 copies and made an astonished American public believe that it was "normal" to engage in premarital sex, to get divorced, to indulge homosexual tendencies, and to consume pornography. Kinsey's claim seemed self-evident: "Unless we want to close our eyes to the truth or imprison 95 percent of our male population, we must completely revise our legal and moral codes." Children, according to Kinsey's "scientific" results, were sexually active from infancy on, could have orgasms, and should be encouraged by adults to satisfy their sexual needs. Kinsey further stated that "The whole of our laws and customs in sexual matters is based on the avowed desire to protect the family and at the base of the family is the father. His behavior is revealed by the Kinsey report to be quite different from anything the general public had supposed reasonable or possible."[39] The rise of no-fault divorce (1970), the legalization of abortion (1973), extramarital sex, cohabitation, and toleration of fornication, sodomy, homosexuality, divorce, and prostitution had the effect Kinsey was looking for: disintegration of families, absent fathers, the explosive spread of sexually transmitted diseases, and an emotionally traumatized youth.

Kinsey had powerful allies: the Rockefeller Foundation for financing, *Playboy* publisher Hugh Hefner for media support through distribution of pornography, the American Law Institute for changing laws on sexual offenses, the Sex Information & Education Council of the United States (SIECUS) for pushing through mandatory sex education in schools, and International Planned Parenthood for legalizing and providing abortions.

Kinsey's rise to worldwide fame and influence was financed by the Rockefellers. Kinsey invited the heads of the Rockefeller foundation to his institute for sexual research at the University of Indiana (today known as the Kinsey Institute for Research in Sex, Gender and Reproduction), where he introduced them to his pornography collection, the

38. LifeSiteNews, August 24, 2011: http://www.lifesitenews.com/news/sexual-anar-chy-the-kinsey-legacy. Publications of Judith Reismann and online information on Alfred Kinsey here: www.drjudithreisman.com.

39. Jones, *Libido Dominandi*, 341.

largest in the world. To build his collection further, the Rockefellers financed two photographers and the necessary technical equipment.

However, as early as 1951, doubt began to arise as to the reliability of his empirical data. In that year, the American Statistical Society issued a negative assessment regarding the validity of Kinsey's statistics. Once the Kinsey Report had come into the crossfire of a congressional investigation, the Rockefellers withdrew funding, which did nothing to stop distribution of the Kinsey Report and the erosion of moral values. The *New York Times* played a large role in this (its publisher, Hays Sulzberger, was also on the board of the Rockefeller Foundation).

It was another 32 years before Judith Reisman brought Kinsey's criminal activities and his extreme sexual perversions to light. Her essay "The Scientist as a Contributing Agent to Child Sexual Abuse: A Preliminary Study" put her in the crosshairs of the media, from the *New York Times* to the *Washington Post* to *Playboy,* and ultimately cost her her position at the American University. At the center of her critique was Chart 34, which reported multiple orgasms in infants and toddlers. It indicated 14 orgasms in 38 minutes for an 11-month-old child, 7 orgasms in 9 minutes for a 2-year-old child, and 26 orgasms in 24 hours for a 4-year-old child. Judith Reisman pointed out the obvious, which was that the data had been obtained through criminal sexual abuse of children.

Kinsey was a homosexual sadomasochist. He practiced self-mutilation and was addicted to medication. He died in August 1956.

None of this prevented Kinsey from being honored to this day as "the father of sexology," a subject area that has established itself at universities and government and private institutions, from which it drives the sexual revolution as Kinsey intended.

John Money

A capable successor to Kinsey was John Money, a psychiatrist at Johns Hopkins Hospital in Baltimore. He played a key role in gender ideology, which promoted free choice of one's gender. In the 1960s, Money opened the first clinic for sex change operations, the Gender Identity Clinic. His success was based on an experiment with a pair of twin brothers. The penis of one of the twins, Bruce Reimer, was so severely injured in a botched circumcision that his parents subjected him to sex reassignment surgery, renamed him Brenda, and proceeded to raise him as a girl for 10 years under Dr. Money's therapeutic guidance.

The boy rebelled right from the start and felt the treatments were a type of torture. Starting at age 11, he was tormented by suicidal thoughts. At 13, when he found out what had happened to him, he instantly decided to live as a boy, but he never lost the feeling of deep shame.

Bruce Reimer, who had changed his name to David and even married, took a shotgun to himself at the age of 38. Two years earlier, his twin brother, Brian, had ended his life with an overdose of pills. The fact that his experiment resulted in two suicides did not stop John Money from using it for decades as proof that sex reassignment surgery was safe. He thereby attracted throngs to his clinic.[40] Like Kinsey, Money advocated "group sex and bisexuality." He promoted so-called "fucking games" for children and classified even extreme sexual perversions (even sex murder) as "paraphilias," merely differing preferences.

Simone de Beauvoir

The eugenics efforts of America's rich and powerful had made the Rockefellers financers of Margaret Sanger, Planned Parenthood, Alfred Kinsey, and many others who pushed for legalization and propagation of contraception and abortion and worked for changes to the laws on sexual offenses. In feminism, they found a powerful strategic partner. Its moment came with the publication of Simone de Beauvoir's book *The Second Sex.* The French edition appeared in 1949, the German edition in 1951, the first English translation in 1953, and it sold hundreds of thousands of copies in the 1960s.

Beauvoir had grown up Catholic, but was then attracted to the bohemian life in Paris: "I remained convinced that sin was the absence of God and I would perch on my bar-stool with all the fervor which made me kneel, as a child, before the Holy Sacrament."[41] She made a "pact" with Jean-Paul Sartre and became a role model for free love. Her novels *She Came to Stay,* about a love triangle, and *The Broken Woman* reflect the high psychological price she paid for this role.

"One is not born, but rather becomes, woman," was the fanfare of *The Second Sex.*[42] There is a simple logic behind this: because women were oppressed by men, women must deny their feminine identity to enjoy the same privileges as men. According to the promise of *The Second Sex,* the time had come for women to break free of the shackles of patriarchal oppression, flee the slavery of motherhood, fulfill themselves in careers, and indulge themselves in "liberated sexuality." For that, contraception and abortion were indispensable. For Beauvoir,

40. Volker Zastrow made this scandal known in "Der kleine Unterschied," *Frankfurter Allgemeine Zeitung* (September 7, 2006). Quotes from this essay.

41. Alice Schwarzer, *Simone de Beauvoir: Ein Lesebuch mit Bildern* (Rowohlt Verlag, Reinbek: 2008), 38.

42. Simone de Beauvoir, *Das andere Geschlecht* (Reinbek bei Hamburg: Rowohlt Taschenbuch, 1968), 265. English: *The Second Sex* (New York: Vintage Books, 2011).

pregnancy was a "mutilation," the fetus a "parasite" and "nothing like flesh." Beauvoir extolled her two abortions and set up an abortion station in her Paris salon, when killing unborn children was still prohibited. The campaign to accuse prominent women of abortion in order to bring down the ban was imported to Germany by Alice Schwarzer, an eager student of Beauvoir, Kinsey, and Money. And she got what she wanted—killing of children in the womb completely free of prosecution. Since then, more than 8 million children have been aborted in Germany. In the United States, the total is 56 million deaths since 1973.

The radical feminist agenda had been established: Rejection of sexual morality, rejection of marriage, motherhood, and family, abortion as a woman's "human right," the career woman as the only role model, and a power struggle against men.

Feminism boomed in the 1970s and 1980s. After Simone de Beauvoir broke the dam, then came Shulamith Firestone with *The Dialectic of Sex: The Case for Feminist Revolution,* Betty Friedan with *The Feminine Mystique*, and Kate Millet with *Sexual Politics.* These titles sold in massive quantities. Feminism hadn't been about equal rights for a long time. The goal was renunciation of heterosexuality and the destruction of the family and the church—social structures that cannot exist without the union of man and woman in marriage. Judith Butler, an American philosopher and chief ideologue of what became known as *gender mainstreaming*, took it a step further. Butler denied the importance of biological gender difference between man and woman and worked for its destruction in society (see Chapter 3).

Let's step back and look. Leftist atheist intellectuals tilled the seedbed. The media sexualized the masses. Psychologists and social scientists, drunk with the power to mold people and society to their objectives, delivered the methods of social engineering. The Rockefeller and Ford foundations ponied up the capital. And the political institutions implemented the program. The obvious objective: reducing the world's population.

Rockefeller and Berelson joined forces to convince President Johnson to set the course toward population reduction. In his January 4, 1965 State of the Union address, he explained, "I will seek new ways to use our knowledge to help deal with the explosion in world population and the growing scarcity in world resources."

The Breakthrough: The 1960s Student Rebellions

So far, we have shed light on the major currents of the Sexual Revolution. With the student rebellions of the late 1960s, these streams merged to form a raging torrent. In the 1960s, the seeds broke through the soil. Students' heads had been filled with Marx and Engels, Freud, Reich, Beauvoir, the theories of the Frankfurt School, Che Guevara and Mao Zedong. The University of California at Berkeley exported new forms of student political protests: sit-ins and teach-ins. The atmosphere was rabid. University lobbies and lecture halls were occupied for days at a time for preaching the revolution in the gibberish of dialectical materialism. Every day, the cafeteria at the Free University of Berlin was strewn with new flyers. The student councils, financed from the university budget, were almost all in leftist hands and repurposed by radical groups as instruments of revolt.

The idea peddlers were professors of the Frankfurt School. Strangely enough, for an idea to be effective at changing society, it made no difference whether the writing was generally intelligible or not. Marx's *Das Kapital* is hard to understand; yet it became the ideological foundation without which Communist dictatorships, the theoretical derivatives of the Frankfurt School, and student revolts would have been unthinkable.

During the Weimar Republic, Frankfurt's Institute for Social Research was the academic basis for socio-political change. The Institute was founded in 1923 as a research station for scientific Marxism. In collaboration with Moscow's Marx-Engels Institute, it published the complete works of Marx and Engels. Its founding members, Friedrich Pollock, Max Horkheimer, and Carl Grünberg, were all members of or sympathizers with the German Communist party. The institute published the *Zeitschrift für Sozialforschung* ("Journal of Social Research"), which was the most important pre- and postwar platform for Marxists, including Max Horkheimer, Theodor W. Adorno, Erich Fromm, Leo Löwenthal, Walter Benjamin, Herbert Marcuse, Ernst Bloch, and others.

The Frankfurt School's trademark was merging Marxist theory with Freudian psychoanalysis for the purpose of transforming society on Communist principles: abolition of private property, destruction of religion, and destruction of the family. The new skin for the old Marxist wine was called "critical theory." Since Marx's time, revolutionary propaganda has wrapped itself in the cloak of "science" and at the same time betrayed the very essence of science—the unbiased search for the truth. This high ideal is the basis for the unrivaled fruitfulness of Western science. If it goes down, science goes down with it and is reduced to being a servant for special interest groups.

The Nazis closed the Institute for Social Research in 1933. After a stopover in Geneva, it received a generous welcome at Columbia University in New York. This is where Adorno and others began their research into the "authoritarian personality," which is brought about by the "authoritarian family" and is "potentially fascist"—a theory legitimizing the deconstruction of the family.

As early as 1946, the mayor of Frankfurt and the rector of the University of Frankfurt overtook the exiled Marxists in reestablishing the institute in that city. This coincided with American interests in "reeducating" the German people.[43] The first large project for researching the political attitudes of Germans was financed by the US High Commissioner for Germany. Because most of those questioned denied complicity and were ambivalent about democracy, the need for reeducation appeared even more urgent.

Max Horkheimer and Theodor W. Adorno received professorial positions, and Horkheimer became dean and later even rector of the University of Frankfurt. They led the institute until 1964. In 1955 Ludwig von Friedeburg became head of the empirical research department. From 1956 to 1959 Jürgen Habermas was an assistant at the Institute, and in 1964 he succeeded Horkheimer to the chair of philosophy and sociology.

The Frankfurt professors closely collaborated with the Socialist German Student League ("SDS" in Berlin—not to be confused with Students for a Democratic Society in the United States), whose most prominent leader was Rudi Dutschke. Since then, streets in Berlin have been named after him. One of the most prominent media activists of the 1968 movement, Klaus Rainer Röhl, chief editor of a publication called *konkret,* wrote a self-critical book in 1994 in which he revealed that leftist cadres got their orders and the money they needed from across the wall in East Berlin. However, their intellectual preparation came from Frankfurt.[44]

An impartial observer must wonder how the offspring of the German middle class could find Marxist ideology attractive in a city split by the Berlin wall, where a death strip full of land mines and overseen by snipers prevented residents of the Communist side from heading west. In photos of the time, one sees fresh, well-fed, well-clothed young people—children of the German economic miracle and the free democracy in West Germany. There was no proletariat, but unprecedented prosperity. No one wanted to go "over there." Yet they were inspired by slogans like these:

---

43. Cf. Caspar von Schrenck-Notzing, *Charakterwäsche, Die Re-education der Deutschen und ihre bleibenden Auswirkungen* (Graz: Ares Verlag, 2005).

44. Klaus Rainer Röhl, *Linke Lebenslügen. Eine überfällige Abrechnung* (Frankfurt a.M.: Ullstein, 1994).

Destroy what is destroying you!
Battle the bourgeois nuclear family!
If you sleep with the same one twice, you're a slave of bourgeois vice!
The cassock conceals the mold of a millennium!

The German people were burdened by the guilt of the Holocaust. Dealing with that guilt started slowly and laboriously. And there was a taboo in the air: Only the Nazi criminals could be called by name, and they were considered incomparably worse than anything, past or present, that was done in the name of Communism. To this day, leftism is still acceptable in polite company. For a leftist, even a violent past and collaboration with the secret police are no obstacle to the highest-level jobs. At the same time, being labeled "right wing" or, worse, "radical right wing"—whether accurately or not—can lose a person his reputation and his job.

The Frankfurt School's ideology had taken hold: the Germans' authoritarian character was blamed for having caused the Holocaust.[45] The logical conclusion was that the family had to be destroyed if Germany were to be reeducated.

But how do you destroy the family? For this, Herbert Marcuse's book *Eros and Civilization* provided the crucial impetus. He thought the deepest cause of repressive power relationships was the suppression of eros, which triggered a socio-pathological dynamic that led to man's domination of man and ultimately to war and mass murder. He called for abolition of the achievement principle and its replacement with the pleasure principle. While Freud saw "sublimation of the sex drive" as the condition for culture to emerge, Marcuse spoke of a "libidinous morality" inherent in eros. Marcuse criticized "repressive tolerance" and promoted intolerance toward anyone who would prevent the revolutionary overthrow of traditional values. Living in the here and now, in keeping with the pleasure principle, was glorified as a revolutionary act. Anyone not convinced of this path of salvation was branded a "reactionary," a "revanchist," a "counterrevolutionary," a "shit liberal," or even a "fascist."

How is *that* for liberation! People in all high cultures had struggled with their impulses in order to be capable of commitment and family, achievement and culture, and now affluent German revolutionaries were claiming it was all for nothing. Unbridled indulgence of sexual

---

45. Cf. Theodor W. Adorno, Else Frenkel-Brunswik, Daniel J. Levinson, and R. Nevitt Sanford, *The Authoritarian Personality* (New York: Harper and Brothers, 1950). Max Horkheimer, Erich Fromm, and Herbert Marcuse, *Studien über Autorität und Familie. Forschungsberichte aus dem Institut für Sozialforschung* (Paris, 1936; reprinted Lüneburg: Klampen Verlag, 2001).

urges was to lead to a virtuous society free of domination and was to end war and genocide for all time.

A "liberated sexuality" free of "compulsory marriage," the incest taboo, and prohibition of pedophilia was openly practiced in Berlin at "Commune I" and "Commune II" and eagerly exhibited by the media. Sex with anyone—in front of children, with children, among children— was promoted with no bourgeois possessiveness. If children "wanted" it, why should they be denied it? The Green Party was still arguing this position in the 1980s and 1990s, attempting to legalize pedophilia.

A new kind of daycare center ("Kinderladen") was founded as experimental sites for creating the new person through anti-authoritarian childrearing, which soon entered schools and families as "emancipative education."

With the downfall of the Motion Picture Production Code (also known as the Hays Code) in Hollywood and the end of the pornography ban in Germany (1973), sex in all its forms became the rage in media and advertising. In 1951, Beate Uhse opened her sex shops; in 1956 *Bravo*, a German teen magazine dedicated to sexualization of children and teenagers, appeared; and in 1959 came *Playboy*. Russ Meyer, the American director of "sexploitation" films, released his first movie in 1959. Ingmar Bergman broke the prohibition on the public display of sex with his 1962 film *The Silence*, and, starting in 1967, the German public learned a wide array of sexual positions in the films of Oswald Kolle. The powerful medium of rock music brought the hippie subculture to the mainstream of youth culture. Hashish and psychedelic drugs became socially acceptable. In 1969, the legendary Woodstock rock festival was expected to attract 60,000 attendees, but 400,000 came. Complete with music and drugs, it became legendary proof that one of the most ingenious slogans of seduction could come true: Make love, not war. Feminists convinced society that men represented patriarchal machismo, while women, as wives and mothers, were oppressed and inferior. They claimed women could find fulfillment only in careers and through "liberated sexuality."

At California's Esalen Institute, the methods of humanistic psychology and group dynamics promised expanded states of consciousness as the groundwork for an approaching "New Age." These ideas penetrated secular and parochial schools and educational institutions. They lured people with the promise that they could achieve divine consciousness and fulfill all earthly wishes without the "moral slavery" of Christianity.

The upshot was that thanks to the student rebellions of the late 1960s, 200 years of persistent work by many major minds was coming to fruition—the Judeo-Christian foundation of Western culture was starting to crack. The message of "sexual liberation" had made it into every living room and most bedrooms. Through the media's constant stimulation of the sex drive, with ever more shameless images of all types of sexual behavior, the views and behavior of the masses had shifted at their moral core—sexuality.

Sexual norms are of the greatest public significance, because they powerfully influence the weal and woe of all society. *As sex goes, so goes the family; as the family goes, so goes society.* For this reason, all societies subject sexual norms to strict social and legal sanctions. This is understandable with *restrictive* sexual norms, because these are hard to adhere to. Now we are witnessing *libertine* norms being enforced through criminal law.

A person rooted in religion and family is hard to manipulate. First the moral bond to belief in God and the social bond to the family must be broken if people are to be seduced by the lure of absolute freedom and free sexual gratification. For decades, increasing prosperity made it possible to sell fun as the meaning of life, with sex front and center. Once the views and behavior of the masses had been altered in this way, the global cultural revolution could proceed unhindered through public debate and blatant opposition. Sexualization—even if it's just the occasional fling and a bit of pornography—blinds people and makes them unwilling to resist attacks on the fundamental pillars of society's value system, such as legalization of abortion and homosexual "marriage." Thomas Aquinas said it 750 years ago: "Blindness of the mind is the first-born daughter of lust."[46]

The Legal Deregulation of Sexuality

What was still an opposition movement in the streets in 1968 escalated to a "march on the institutions." As academically educated cadres, the '60s generation moved into key positions in politics, the media, jurisprudence, the universities, and the church. They even took the levers of power at the UN and EU. They had the cultural and political tools as well as the resources to continuously undermine the sovereignty of the member states and to destroy their value systems. Through determined manipulation of opinion and the sexualization of the entire society, the pressure on the dam of sexual law became stronger and stronger until, piece by piece, it began to give way. In Germany, these were the milestones, and they were similar in other Western countries:

---

46. Thomas Aquinas, Secunda Secundae Partis of the *Summa Theologiae*, Quaestio 153 a. 5 ad 1.

1961	Authorization of the birth control pill.
1969	Repeal of blasphemy law.
1969	Legalization of divorce.
1969	Introduction of mandatory sex education in schools.
1969	Legalization of pornography.
1973	Authorization of no-fault divorce.
1976	Full legalization of homosexuality.
1977	Abortions remain "illegal" but are not subject to prosecution up to the 14th week. Abortion of disabled children possible all the way to the delivery date.
1994	By order of the cabinet of Chancellor Gerhard Schröder gender mainstreaming becomes the "guiding principle" of politics.
1995	Civil unions for homosexuals.
1999	Prostitution recognized as a service and a profession qualifying for social insurance.
2001	Decision of Supreme Court: Financial benefits for families of civil servants must be granted to same-sex partners in civil union.
2001	Decision of Supreme Court: Tax advantages for married couples must also be granted to same-sex partners in civil union ten years backwards.
2001	Stepchild adoption of same-sex partners in civil union expanded to "successive-adoption": Since 2001 adoption of a biological child through same-sex partner is possible. Now the *adopted child* of one partner can be adopted by same-sex partner.

3

From Feminism to Gender Ideology[1]

With the denial of nature in human beings, not only the telos of the external mastery of nature but also the telos of one's own life becomes confused and opaque.

At the moment when human beings cut themselves off from the consciousness of themselves as nature, all the purposes for which they keep themselves alive ... become void.

Max Horkheimer, Theodor W. Adorno [2]

Who are you going to believe, me or your own eyes?

Groucho Marx

The Fight for Equal Rights

FOR THE FIRST TIME in history, power elites are claiming authority to change men's and women's sexual identity through political strategies and legal measures. They had previously lacked expertise in social engineering. However, today this is happening before our eyes on a global scale. The strategy's name: *gender mainstreaming*. This battle is being fought under the banner of equality of men and women, but that has proven to be a tactical transitional stage.

Women's fight for equal rights has lasted more than 150 years. Women had good reason to shake up the ruling social structure, because as late as the early twentieth century, many of them were not allowed to:

---

1. Previous books by Gabriele Kuby on gender ideology: *Die Gender Revolution. Relativismus in Aktion* (2006). *Verstaatlichung der Erziehung, Auf dem Weg zum neuen Gender-Menschen* (2007, twelfth edition 2015). *Gender. Eine neue Ideologie zerstört die Familie* (2014). All three published at Kisslegg: fe-medienverlag.

2. Max Horkheimer, Theodor W. Adorno, and Gunzelin Schmid Noerr, *Dialectic of Enlightenment: Philosophical Fragments* (Stanford, CA: Stanford University Press, 2002).

- Receive higher education.
- Vote.
- Open a bank account.
- Practice most professions.
- Hold public office or management positions.
- Follow an artistic vocation without serious obstacles.

Male supremacy was even justified by theories that represented women as mentally incompetent. In the nineteenth century, women began to rebel against this situation, partly because social conditions had changed through industrialization and this was eliminating the woman's role as the informal ruler of the extended family. At the beginning there were educated middle-class women who called for equal rights, organized themselves into Christian women's associations, and advocated protection for mothers and families. They wanted a war between the sexes and separation of sexuality from motherhood. They wanted political rights, the right to education, and better social conditions. In the western world, these demands have largely been met.

With the Communist opposition to early capitalism, a socialist current arose in the nineteenth century. Women's issues were taken up by Marx and Engels and converted into a class issue. In his book *The Origin of the Family, Private Property and the State*, for instance, Engels demanded the abolition of the family, the identical integration of men and women into the workplace, and the collective rearing of children in institutions run by the state.

The great overthrow of the Christian foundation of Western society was brought about by the battle for women's "sexual self-determination" through legalization of contraception and abortion. Simone de Beauvoir set the radical feminist gears in motion with her famous statement: "One is not born, but rather becomes, woman."[3] This triggered a strange dynamic. In response to their degradation and devaluation by radical feminism, men responded by feeling guilty and surrendering without a fight: "*Hold on!*" they seemed to say; "*We're not so bad—we're just lovable softies!*"

But that was not enough for those radical feminist leaders who aimed to make the sexes the same. They pretended to fight for still more "equality" for women, but they were really battling against marriage, the family, and the child, against women as mothers, and for the complete deregulation of sexuality. They fought against everything lesbians

---

3. Simone de Beauvoir, *Das andere Geschlecht* (Reinbek bei Hamburg: Rowohlt Taschenbuch, 1968), 265.

couldn't have. They battled for a transformation of society that would finally free them from abnormality, by deconstructing the binary sexual identity of man and woman and what they called "compulsory hetero-sexuality."

Deconstruction of Binary Sexuality

Enforcing this social policy required a new word, because language doesn't just reflect reality; it creates it. *Gender* was the magic word. The word *sex* had to be replaced; for prior to that, if someone was asked, "What is your sex?," they could answer only one of two things: man or woman.

Without question, there are cultural and historical variations in the form a society gives to the binary sexual identity of men and women. This is something sociologists and ethnologists deal with. However, these variations do not eliminate the reality of two genders any more than changes in the weather negate the reality of day and night. The term *gender* was repurposed to do just that. A political battle had been waged to "confound," "destabilize" and "deconstruct" binary gender identity. This was to become *mainstream,* the unquestioned spirit of the times.

What an undertaking! How great must be the mental trauma and the yearning to be normal for someone to submit the irrevocable laws of nature to the capriciousness of people's free choice! Now there was a project that gave non-heterosexuals the option of using activism to drive out the problem of their identity. Not only did the activist "community" declare any sexual orientation or practice good, they were also able to access money and power. The UN and EU, furthermore, were pumping millions into LGBTI organizations pushing gender mainstreaming. (LGBTI is the customary abbreviation in international documents for "lesbian, gay, bisexual, transsexual, intersexual.") For the clever ones among the homosexuals, the academically trained, a career was opening in international organizations, universities, the media, and the courts.

The Subversive Gender Theory of Judith Butler

The pioneer of gender theory is Judith Butler, born in 1956. She grew up in the United States in a family of Jewish academics of Hungarian-Russian origin. In 1984, Yale University awarded her a doctorate for a disser-tation on the concept of desire in Hegel. She is a professor of rhetoric at the University of California at Berkeley. Since 2006, she has held the Hannah Arendt Chair for Philosophy at the European Graduate School in Switzerland. It is no small mind that would dare to attack binary gen-der identity and the entire cultural tradition of our planet and try to shatter them.

Judith Butler is a lesbian. Evidently, she feels the system of binary genders to be a prison, a limitation on freedom, discriminatory by nature. For her the experience as a lesbian of taking on the masculine role at one moment and the feminine at another seems to determine her nature more than the fact that each of her cells, the composition of her body, her organs, and her voice are feminine and are recognized by anyone as those of a woman.

Her 1990 book *Gender Trouble: Feminism and the Subversion of Identity* is the fundamental work on gender ideology. Butler feels uneasy with the gender order and, as her foreword explains, wants to make trouble. Her question is, "What best way to trouble the gender categories that support gender hierarchy and compulsory heterosexuality?"[4] She goes on to say that "The task of inquiry is to center on—and decenter—such defining institutions: phallogocentrism and compulsory heterosexuality."[5] We are to "ask, what political possibilities are the consequence of a radical critique of the categories of identity. What new shape of politics emerges when identity as a common ground no longer constrains the discourse on feminist politics?"[6] Butler's opinion is that the "fictive" categories of sexual identity are only "constructed" through language,[7] so that political change to the language plays a central role in deconstructing the gender order.

As a post-structuralist philosopher, she has developed a complicated theory that uses an invented philosophical language intended to shake the foundations of the human order through "subversive confusion and multiplication of gender identities." If her views were expressed in simple words, anyone would see that she has lost touch with reality, but because she clouds her destructive ideas with highly philosophical terminology that is hard to understand, readers and listeners reverently nod their heads. As Butler says, "In other words, 'sex' is an ideal construct which is forcibly materialized through time. It is not a simple fact or a static condition of the body, but a process whereby regulatory norms materialized 'sex' and achieve this materialization through a forcible reiteration of those norms."[8]

In plain language: there are no such things as "men" and "women." One's sex is a fantasy, something we only believe because it has been

---

4. Judith Butler, *Gender Trouble: Feminism and the Subversion of Identity* (New York: Routledge, 1999), 8. German translation: *Das Unbehagen der Geschlechter* (Frankfurt am Main: Suhrkamp, 1991).

5. Ibid., 9.

6. Ibid.

7. Ibid., 10.

8. Judith Butler, *Bodies That Matter* (New York: Routledge, 1993), 21.

repeated so often. Gender is not associated with biological sex, which plays absolutely no role and arises only because it is created by language, and because people believe what they constantly hear. In Butler's view, identity is free-flowing and flexible. There is no masculine or feminine being, but only a certain *performance*; that is, behavior that can change at any time.

For Butler the incest taboo is the cause of the "phantasm" of gender identity as man or woman and of the taboo against homosexuality. It must therefore be abolished. For Butler, "The incest taboo is the juridical law that is said to both prohibit incestuous desires and to construct certain gendered subjectivities through the mechanism of compulsory identification."[9] "Hence," she adds, "the incest taboo not only forbids sexual union between members of the same kinship line, but involves a taboo against homosexuality as well."[10]

If there is no such thing as sexual identity, then the feminists fighting for female supremacy have a problem. There is a choice of expanding women's power at the expense of men or of completely abolishing binary sexual identity and leaving it up to individual choice. Butler is aware of the problem and asks "whether feminist politics could do without a 'subject' in the category of women."[11]

Even though she is working on exactly that, she pacifies her fellow feminist activists by stating that "it still makes sense, strategically and transitionally, to refer to women in order to make representational claims on their behalf."[12] But dissolution of sexual identity is really the goal, because not until then will the individual be emancipated from the dictatorship of nature and realize complete freedom of choice, the ability to reinvent oneself at any time. Only if women exist can women be oppressed. Only if there is "compulsory heterosexual normativity" can "other forms of desire" be ostracized.

Butler criticizes "the foundationalist reasoning of identity politics," which tends to assume that an identity must first be present for political interests to be formulated and then political action to be taken. For Butler, it is different: "My argument is that there need not be a 'doer behind the deed,' but that the 'doer' is variably constructed in and through the deed."[13]

Lines of thought like this lead to the claim that there aren't just two

9. Butler, *Unbehagen*, 118.
10. Ibid., 115
11. Ibid., 209.
12. Ibid.
13. Ibid.

genders, but many, depending on a person's sexual orientation. For Judith Butler, there is such a thing as identity; yet it is not determined by being a man or a woman, but by sexual orientation, whether a person is queer, lesbian, bi-, trans-, inter- or any other kind of sexual. Butler reduces human identity—which is formed from countless influences besides sex, including family, culture, and religion—to freely chosen, mutable sexual orientation.

In Butler's opinion, families are formed not by the bonds between spouses and children, but by arbitrary acts of momentary belonging. In Butler's parallel universe, children are not conceived, but "designed" and produced with the aid of artificial technical modes of reproduction, such as sperm donation, egg donation, surrogate motherhood, artificial wombs and gene manipulation.

Butler is one of the most important practitioners of *queer theory*. Like *gender*, the word *queer* has undergone some semantic changes. LGBTI activists use the word *queer* to overcome being imprisoned in the concept of homosexuality because it always points to heterosexuality as its opposite. *Queer* is simply anything that is not heterosexual. The polarity of hetero- and homosexuality should be eliminated in favor of complete dissolution of sexual identity, because only then will the "hegemony of compulsory heterosexuality" be completely overcome and will people have complete freedom to invent themselves.

According to the Oxford Dictionary, *queer* was once used as a "deliberately offensive and aggressive term" for homosexuals but has since been adopted by homosexuals as a substitute for the words *homosexual* and *gay*. Older observers will have noticed that the term *gay*, promoted as a positive euphemism in the 1960s, had come to be used as a pejorative in place of *queer*, particularly by younger people. It is strange that this negative word has gained the status of a noble term, used in theoretical disciplines like "queer studies," as part of gender studies at universities.

Now let us sum up what gender theory claims. According to this theory, the biological sex of individuals as man or woman is irrelevant to their identity, but represents a "dictatorship of nature" against their own self-definition, a dictatorship from which they must be freed. A person's identity is instead determined by his sexual orientation, and is therefore flexible, changeable and diverse. This illusion, or "phantasm," of two sexes is created by the incest taboo and by linguistic designations like *man* and *woman*, *father* and *mother*, which must be eliminated in favor of free self-invention. Society's heterosexual "signatures" must be eliminated in all spheres. Man and woman, marriage and family, father and mother, sexuality and fertility are not deemed natural; rather, it is claimed, they establish the hegemony of men over women and of heterosexuality over all other forms of sexuality. This must be destroyed at its roots.

In 1999, Butler received a Guggenheim Fellowship and in 2001 a Rockefeller Fellowship. In 2004, she received Yale University's Brudner[14] Prize for special achievements in "lesbian and gay studies." The year 2008 brought her the Andrew W. Mellon Award, which is endowed with $1.5 million and is meant to enable its recipients to teach and do research under favorable conditions. On September 11, 2012, she received the 50,000-euro Theodor W. Adorno Prize. In November 2014 she received an honorary doctorate from the Swiss University of Fribourg for her political involvement, especially for the rights of homosexuals, and her position in the Israel-Palestine conflict. (Judith Butler, as a Jew, calls for the support of Hamas and a boycott of Israel.) Since 2012, Butler has been a visiting professor at Columbia University.

Most remarkable of all is that the "subversive" theory of Judith Butler, along with the theories of her masters and comrades-in-arms,[15] is welcomed by the world's academic elites—and implemented by them. Back in the nineteenth and twentieth centuries, subversive activities were aimed at the ruling classes, and these elites were not willing to give up without a fight. Today international organizations like the UN, the EU, and a number of foundations with billions of dollars at their disposal drive the subversion themselves and force it on the world. What motivates them?

It has taken only twenty years for gender theory to become an influential ideology. Government-financed "gender competence centers" see to its political implementation. At universities, the new field of "gender studies/queer studies" has been established and its faculties expanded. The young generation is taught gender ideology as an achievement of modern thinking. The staff of public authorities, corporations, and educational institutions are shaped by gender. This is all happening with little public discourse, whether in the legislatures or in the media. Hardly anybody knows what gender theory is, yet it has gone mainstream—an eerie process whose specific effects will be described in Chapter 7.

---

14. James Robert Brudner, urban planner, musician and photographer, was a homosexual activist who studied at Yale and died of AIDS in 1998.

15. Simone de Beauvoir, Jacques Lacan, Luce Irigaray, Monique Wittig, Jacques Derrida, and Michel Foucault, among others.

4

The United Nations
Globalizes the Sexual Revolution

*The power of Man to make himself what he pleases means, as we have
seen, the power of some men to make other men what they please.*
C. S. Lewis[1]

The Universal Declaration of Human Rights

IN EARLIER TIMES, people thought of revolutions as coming from the
bottom up. The masses are so disgruntled with their exploitation and
oppression that they want to change the system of power through violence. It is an open conflict with the power elite, supported by a mass
movement, motivated by generally visible, intolerable social evils; and
has the goal of violently forcing a change in the power structure. Historically, revolutions mounted in the name of greater freedom and a better,
utopian future have usually led to dictatorial systems controlled by the
revolutionary elites.

In contrast, the current sexual revolution that has seized and changed
all aspects of life is a *top-down* revolution originating with the globally
active power elites. The visible objective is reduction of the world population. However, a change in the value system can only lead to a change
in the world order. It would be unreasonable to assume that this is an
unintended consequence.

With the fall of the Berlin Wall in 1989, the Western world thought it
was done with totalitarian forms of government once and for all. Since
then, a change in values has crept in that is taking hold of all aspects of
society—from the state to the family to the rearing of children. It's as if
our society's operating system is being replaced in the background with
no one knowing who is doing it or for what purpose. Everyone is notic-

1. Lewis, C. S., *The Abolition of Man* (1944; reprt., New York: Harper Collins, 2001).

ing accelerated changes, which have something eerie about them, since the cause and the objective are hidden.

In 1948, when the United Nations adopted the *Universal Declaration of Human Rights*, there was still agreement that there actually were universally applicable rights that protect human beings and the fundamental natural institutions of society. Those institutions included marriage, family and private property. These were rights that the family of nations agreed upon and committed itself to. The horror of World War II and the inhuman, totalitarian systems of rule under the Nazis and Communists made this declaration possible. Once and for all, the sacrosanct dignity of human beings was to be set forth as the "foundation of freedom, justice and peace in the world."

On December 10, 1948, the United Nations General Assembly proclaimed:

> *Article 1*: All human beings are born free and equal in dignity and rights. They are endowed with reason and conscience and should act towards one another in a spirit of brotherhood.

> *Article 2*: Everyone is entitled to all the rights and freedoms set forth in this Declaration, without distinction of any kind, such as race, color, sex, language, religion, political or other opinion, national or social origin, property, birth or other status.

> *Article 16* (1): Men and women of full age, without any limitation due to race, nationality or religion, have the right to marry and to found a family.

> *Article 16* (3): The family is the natural and fundamental group unit of society and is entitled to protection by society and the State.

The *Universal Declaration of Human Rights* expresses universal moral values derived from the Judeo-Christian image of man, based on biblical revelation: "God created mankind in his image; in the image of God he created them; male and female he created them" (Genesis 1:27). There is no higher image of humankind than that. The fundamental Christian concept that all people are equal before God was acknowledged by the proclamation as a basic human principle: "All human beings are born free and equal in dignity and rights." They are not to be considered better or worse based on *immutable characteristics*: race, skin color, sex, language, origin, social status, and religion. Religious conversion and social mobility aside, none of these characteristics is subject to moral freedom of choice.

The United Nations protects the family as the "natural and fundamental group unit of society," because it creates the connective tissue without which a culture crumbles: the bond between man and woman, and the bond between generations. Marriage and family antedate the state; they do not owe their existence to the state, but rather the state is dependent on them because they provide the fundamentals crucial to human coexistence—creating children and raising them to be people who can make a positive contribution to society as a whole.

What was once believed without question, however, was soon hollowed out step by step. Within a few decades, the UN became an institution that would use its power and resources to change the image of humanity as declared by the Declaration of Human Rights and to replace universal morals with relativistic postmodern "values" as the foundation of the culture.

God was deposed and the "autonomous human being" placed on His throne. People have had this temptation since time immemorial, but in no historical epoch have they succumbed to such a spiral of delusional radicalism as through the contemporary denial of men's and women's binary sexual identity.

Today the UN and its powerful sub-organizations fight for dissolution of men's and women's sexual identity, elimination of marriage and the family, for dividing the generations through autonomous "children's rights," for doing away with sexual morality, and for abortion as a "human right." It seems as if the powerful of this world have been abandoned by the benevolent spirits of reason, conscience, and brotherhood.

The Paradigm Shift after 1989

The collapse of Communism in 1989 ignited the hope that the end of all ideology had come and that world peace was within reach. It was thought to be the dawn of a New Age, in which all differences would merge, especially religious ones. Religions that made claims to absolute truth came under ideological suspicion, Christianity above all.

As a guarantor of hope for world peace, the UN drew on the moral capital from its Declaration of Human Rights. But the UN of 1989 was not the UN of 1948.

Marguerite A. Peeters analyzes this global counter-cultural revolution and its new ethics in her book *The Globalization of the Western Cultural Revolution*:

> Postmodernity implies a destabilization of our rational or theological apprehension of reality, of the anthropological structure given by God to man and woman, of the order of the universe as established by God. The basic tenet of postmodernity is that every reality is a social construct, that truth and reality have no stable and objective

content—that in fact that they do not exist. . . . Postmodernity exalts the arbitrary sovereignty of the individual and of his or her right to choose. The global postmodern ethic celebrates differences, the diversity of choices, cultural diversity, cultural liberty, sexual diversity (different sexual orientations). This "celebration" is in fact that of the "liberation" of man and woman from the conditions of existence in which God has placed them. Such an alleged "liberation" becomes an imperative of the new ethic. It goes through the destabilization and the deconstruction . . . of all that is considered universal, and as a consequence of Judeo-Christian values and divine revelation.[2]

Postmodernism has introduced new expressions and filled old ones with new content. Here are a few from Peeters's long list:

Judeo-Christian paradigm	Postmodern paradigm
Truth	Right to error
Absolute values and binding standards	Free choice by autonomous individuals
Hierarchy	Equality
Parental authority	Children's rights
Sex	Gender
Binary sexual identity as man or woman	Choice of gender
Heterosexuality as the norm	Legal and social acceptance of any sexual behavior
Spouse	Partner
Nuclear family	Adoption rights
Abortion	Family planning and "reproductive health"

2. Marguerite A. Peeters, "Willkür als Moralgesetz," VATICAN Magazin, October 2007. In this article M. Peeters sums up her book *The Globalization of the Western Cultural Revolution: Key Concepts, Operational Mechanisms* (Brussels: Institute for Intercultural Dialogue Dynamics, 2007).

National sovereignty	Global governance
Representative democracy	Participative democracy
Confrontation of varying interests	Dialog
Majority decision-making	Consensus
Tradition	Cultural diversity
Cultural identity	Multi-culturalism
Ten Commandments	Moral relativism
God	The autonomous individual

While the terms of the "new global ethics" sound vaguely positive and seem to promise something better, the old terms that have long supported Christian-influenced Western culture have taken on a bad ring. Using them with approval can ruin one's reputation. Such terms include truth, morality, authority, hierarchy, conscience, husband, wife, chastity, purity, evil, and many more. This deliberate change in the language is a political strategy (see Ch. 8).

Who even asks what the new terms actually mean? Are they intentionally ill-defined and ambiguous to veil unambiguous intentions? How is it possible that in 1999 a term like *gender mainstreaming* became a "guiding principle" of German politics, yet over a decade later, barely anyone among the population knows what the term really means? As Marguerite Peeters writes, "It is not the governments, but non-state minorities who have played a central role from beginning to end in the revolutionary process. They were at once spearheads, pioneers, experts, lobbyists, awareness-raisers, consensus-builders, facilitators, partners, social engineers, operational agents, watchdogs and champions of the new ethic."[3] She goes on to say, "The legitimate authority of governments is in effect redistributed to interest groups which are not only without legitimacy but also often radical. Moreover, it is in the logic of the partnership principle to claim ever more political power for the 'partners,' to the detriment of legitimate power holders."[4] They present

3. Peeters, *Globalization*, 28.
4. Ibid., 29.

themselves as "experts," but are really lobbyists for small radical minorities who assert their own interests at the expense of the public welfare.

As radical minorities, feminists and homosexual activists played a central role in pushing the new ethic forward. These minorities' interests—the dismantling of sexual norms—can be exploited for the strategic purpose of worldwide population reduction. In the name of freedom, new "rights" have been proclaimed and propagated to undermine religious traditions: the right to free love, the right to contraception, the right to abortion ("I have the right to control my own body!"), the right to artificial fertilization, the right to freely choose one's sexual orientation, rights of children against their parents. At the core of it all is the right of the autonomous individual to free choice. The term "freedom" is truncated, divorced from truth, responsibility, the good of others, and the common welfare. Selfishness makes the autonomous individual easily seduced by these new rights.

To instill the public consciousness with the new ethic, the UN has held world conferences to establish a new vision of the world. These conferences on the major issues of the Third Millennium are key events for bringing about the global paradigm shift:

- Bucharest 1974: Population
- New York 1990: Children
- Rio 1992: Environment; 2012, Rio +20
- Vienna 1993: Human rights
- Cairo 1994: Population
- Beijing 1995: Women; 2010, Beijing +15

Population Control

The central concern of the United States, as the most powerful country in the UN, was and still is reduction of the world population. Its cornerstone is the Kissinger Report of 1974.[5] It was a turning point for a new population-reduction strategy.

In 1974, Henry Kissinger, National Security Advisor to President Nixon and a friend of the Rockefeller family, drew up National Security Study Memorandum 200 (NSSM 200), which was held strictly confidential at the time. It bore the subject line "Implications of Worldwide Population Growth for U.S. Security and Overseas Interests." Kissinger worked closely with John D. Rockefeller III's Population Council. In this

---

5. Henry Kissinger, "Security Study Memorandum 200: Implications of Worldwide Population Growth for U.S. Security and Overseas Interests," National Security Council, http://www.population-security.org/11-CH3.html (accessed December 27, 2014).

strategic document, Kissinger claimed that American national security depended on the introduction of population-control measures in underdeveloped countries.

One of the UN's most important partners for this global strategy has been the International Planned Parenthood Federation (IPPF). At the first UN conference in 1974, in Bucharest, the IPPF was already part of the US delegation. However, the conference didn't succeed as planned, because the Vatican, together with the Soviet Bloc countries and the Third World, exposed its "contraceptive imperialism."

The US didn't shy away from coupling its development aid to programs for abortion and sterilization. The operative organization is the United Nations Population Fund (UNFPA—formerly the United Nations Fund for Population Activities). For example, in cooperation with Peruvian dictator Alberto Fujimori, the UNFPA had 300,000 poor women in Peru sterilized without their consent and often even without their knowledge. In China, the UNFPA contributed significantly to the introduction of the brutal one-child policy.[6]

It was not enough to blackmail countries by bundling development aid with abortion and sterilization programs, because that evoked too much resistance. Strategies had to be found to portray the programs as humanitarian aid to needy countries. Linguistic sleight of hand was needed to make the US's "contraceptive imperialism" seem like a humanitarian response to the urgent needs of women in poor countries with high birth rates.

Terms like *health, freedom of choice, women's empowerment, unmet needs, quality services,* and *reproductive health* are clichés used to market the strategy of population reduction. Every woman on Earth should be able to *choose* how many children she would like to have by being provided with *reproductive health services* through the United States and UN agencies. This term is a Trojan horse for contraceptives, "safe" abortion, and sterilization.

The trick is to use ambiguous, positive-sounding words to push clear objectives that cannot otherwise attract consensus. Who can argue with reproductive health if it means "a state of complete physical, mental and social well-being"? The definitions quoted below from the action plan, the final document of the 1995 UN World Conference on Women, in Beijing, show the obfuscation:

6. Douglas A. Sylva, *The United Nations Population Fund: Assault on the World's Peoples* (New York: The International Organizations Research Group, 2002), 50.

> Reproductive health therefore implies that people are able to have a satisfying and safe sex life and that they have the capability to reproduce and the freedom to decide if, when and how often to do so. (Section 94)[7]

Could this mean that the woman obtains free choice in her reproductive potential through abortion?

> Bearing in mind the above definition, reproductive rights embrace certain human rights that are already recognized in national laws, international human rights documents and other consensus documents. (Section 95)

What human rights documents are they talking about?

> Reproductive health eludes many of the world's people because of such factors as: inadequate levels of knowledge about human sexuality and inappropriate or poor-quality reproductive health information and services [. . .]. Adolescents are particularly vulnerable because of their lack of information and access to relevant services in most countries. (Section 95)

Does "services" mean abortion services, and does "lack of information" among "vulnerable adolescents" imply a call for sex education on the Western model?[8]

> The human rights of women include their right to have control over and decide freely and responsibly on matters related to their sexuality, including sexual and reproductive health, free of coercion, discrimination and violence. (Section 96)

Does a woman's freedom to decide extend to number of sexual partners, sexual orientation, and abortion?

The big breakthrough for "reproductive rights" came at the 1994 UN Population Conference in Cairo. In the run-up to the conference, advertisements like this appeared: "The Pope forbids birth control—millions

---

7. United Nations, *Report of The Fourth World Conference on Women* (1995), http://www.un.org/esa/gopher-data/conf/fwcw/off/a--20.en (accessed December 27, 2014).

8. Seventeen years later, in June 2012, at the UN conference on sustainable development (Rio +20), delegates succeeded in removing the terms *reproductive health* and *population dynamics* from the final document. Both terms work as a Trojan horse for abortion and population control. It was a remarkable setback for the United Nations Population Fund and International Planned Parenthood (http://www.c-fam.org/fridayfax/volume-15/abortion-propo- nents-admit-defeat-at-rio-conference.html).

starve." This accusation was modified in 2011 against Pope Benedict XVI: "The Pope forbids condoms—millions die of AIDS."[9] Al Gore, US vice-president at the time, was one of the major players at this conference. He proclaimed to the world that all of the Third World's problems stemmed from overpopulation, which in this sense means a lack of birth control and abortion.

Besides the Islamic countries, he had one main antagonist, who was Pope John Paul II. The pope put all of his authority and influence behind stopping the global abortion agenda, which each year takes the lives of more than 40 million unborn children. But the pope's message didn't make much headway when rivaled against the billions the UN and American foundations had placed behind the cause, along with their worldwide media campaigns.

Depending on the political leanings of US presidential administrations, this policy continued with greater or lesser impetus and more or less money. Presidents Ronald Reagan and George W. Bush supported prolife policies, while President Bill Clinton joined Al Gore in throwing his weight behind anti-life policies. However, no president has fought so radically for the feminist-homosexualist agenda as Barack Obama, with his first secretary of state, Hillary Clinton (see Chapter 10). At the International Conference on Population and Development on January 8, 2010, Secretary Clinton announced a new Global Health Initiative. In her address, Clinton said, "In addition to new funding, we've launched a new program that will be the centerpiece of our foreign policy, the Global Health Initiative, which commits us to spending $63 billion over six years to improve global health by investing in efforts to reduce maternal and child mortality, prevent millions of unintended pregnancies, and avert millions of new HIV infections, among other goals. This initiative will employ a new approach to fighting disease and promoting health."[10]

The world's super-rich are behind the population control programs. In May 2009, such multi-billionaires as David Rockefeller, Bill Gates, Ted Turner, George Soros, Michael Bloomberg, and Warren Buffett met in New York. They agreed that this world's greatest problem is overpop-

9. On his trip to Africa in 2009, Pope Benedict XVI told journalists that AIDS "is a tragedy that cannot be overcome by money alone, that cannot be overcome through the distribution of condoms, which even aggravates the problems." He said that the real solution lies in "spiritual and human awakening" and "friendship for those who suffer." This launched a storm of indignation in media and politics.

10. Hillary Rodham Clinton, Remarks on the 15th Anniversary of the International Conference on Population and Development, Washington, DC, 2010, http://www.state.gov/secretary/20092013clinton/rm/2010/01/135001.htm (accessed August 20, 2012).

ulation. Because the world has too many poor, they wanted to ensure there are fewer of them—with reproductive health services as the means. For this purpose, they founded The Good Club.[11]

With capital of $36.3 billion, the Bill and Melinda Gates Foundation focuses its global program on the objective of population reduction in poor countries. Bill and Melinda Gates have helped fund production of the low-cost system Sinoplant II.[12] The medication is a Chinese version of Jadelle, which is implanted under the skin and can keep a woman sterile for up to five years.[13]

On July 11, 2012, billionaire Melinda Gates joined the British government in London to put on a Family Planning Summit. At this "conference of donors," the rich nations made 2.1 billion euros available for financing contraception and sterilization programs for women and girls in poor countries. The implementation partners are the International Planned Parenthood Federation (IPPF), the world's largest abortion organization, and the United Nations Population Fund (UNFPA).

In May 2011, the UNFPA published new population growth estimates. They claimed that by 2050 there would be 9.31 billion people on earth, and in 2100, 10.1 billion—and that now is the time to decrease their numbers.[14]

Steven Mosher, president of the Population Research Institute, said that the UNFPA's claims that women are demanding contraceptives are "simply not true" and that women were actually "crying out" for better healthcare for themselves and their families. "Their cries are ignored by the population controllers at the UNFPA and elsewhere, however, who are bent not upon saving lives, but upon reducing the number of people on the planet [. . .]. The UNFPA and other population control organizations are loath to report the truth about falling fertility rates worldwide, since they raise funds by frightening people with the specter of over-population. They tell us that too many babies are being born to poor people in developing countries. This is tantamount to saying that only the wealthy should be allowed to have children, and is a new form of

---

11. Paul Harris, "They're Called the Good Club—and They Want to Save the World," *The Guardian*, May 30, 2009, http://www.theguardian.com/world/2009/may/31/new-york-billionaire-philanthropists (accessed December 27, 2014).

12. Bill & Malinda Gates Foundation, *Annual Letter* 2012, http://www.gatesfoundation.org/who-we-are/resources-and-media/annual-letters-list/annual-letter- 2012 (accessed December 27, 2014).

13. "Jadelle," http://www.rxlist.com/jadelle-drug.htm (accessed December 27, 2014).

14. Given the interests of the UN and the United States, it is hard to decide which estimates are reliable.

global racism. We should stop funding population control programs, and instead turn our attention to real problems like malaria, typhus, and HIV/AIDS."[15]

UN World Conference on Women in Beijing, 1995

One year after the UN population conference in Cairo, the organization held its 1995 World Conference on Women in Beijing. These conferences are prime examples of the "shift of power to the unelected," as Marguerite Peeters has called them. While in representative democracies political power is transferred through elections and controlled by legislatures, global governance works through collaboration of international bureaucracies with non-governmental organizations (NGOs). These are often special interest groups of radical minorities that are financed by opaque fund transfers from globally active foundations. They call this "participative democracy."

The UN women's conference in Beijing was controlled by radical feminists. Their long-term strategic goal was to replace the word "sex" with the term "gender." A new term was necessary to achieve three objectives:

- "Substantive equality" of men and women
- Deconstruction of male and female sexual identity
- Deconstruction of "normative compulsory heterosexuality"

In her book *The Gender Agenda,* Dale O'Leary describes in detail how the world women's conference was strategically and manipulatively bulldozed by radical feminists.[16] The conference was prepared and held by the Women's Environment and Development Organization (WEDO) and the International Planned Parenthood Federation (IPPF). Anti-life groups were favored with accreditation, while groups advocating protection of life and family received none. Anyone who represented the complementarity of man and woman, motherhood as a special vocation for women, or the family, was marginalized. O'Leary describes the methods:

- Falsified translations
- Defamation of "fundamentalists"

---

15. Rebecca Millette, "UN Population Projections Prompt Calls for Population Control" (May 9, 2011), https://www.lifesitenews.com/news/un-population-projections -prompt-calls-for-population-control (accessed December 27, 2014).

16. Dale O'Leary, *The Gender Agenda: Redefining Equality* (Lafayette, Louisiana: Vital Issues Press, 1997).

- Changing the voting rules
- A last-minute extension of the conference by one day[17]

The reason is that delegates from poor countries couldn't afford to rebook their flights, so they could be excluded from the final voting. Thus, despite serious objections from the Vatican and the Muslim delegations, the Beijing action platform was adopted "unanimously."

In the end, the coalition for families distributed a flyer with the title *We Do Not Consent*. "The Platform of Action which will leave the Conference of Beijing is a direct attack on the values, cultures, traditions and religious beliefs of the vast majority of the world's people in both the developing and developed world. . . . The document doesn't respect human dignity, seeks to destroy the family, totally ignores marriage, minimizes the importance of motherhood, seeks to impose depraved sexual attitudes, promotes homosexuality, lesbianism, sexual promiscuity, and sex for children and seeks to destroy the authority of parents over the children."[18] The family coalition did not prevail.

Abortion as a "Human Right"?

Under the umbrella of the UN, which was still drawing moral authority from the Human Rights Convention, the cultural revolutionary strategists set about converting the action platform from the Beijing conference into strategies and binding international treaties, and thus into social reality.[19]

But they had a problem: they had succeeded in pouring old wine into new skins, associating the old goal of population control, now called *gender mainstreaming* and *reproductive health*, with lofty values such as *freedom of choice, human rights*, and *health*. Nonetheless, they had not achieved the goal, which was declaring abortion to be an internationally recognized human right. There was no consent supporting the final document, because the Vatican, along with majority Catholic and Muslim countries, had mounted massive resistance. Now it was time to find

---

17. Christl Vonholdt, "Dale O'Leary, Die Gender Agenda Teil 1," Deutsches Institut für Jugend und Gesellschaft, Bulletin no. 13 (Spring 2007), 4–17.

18. Dale O'Leary, *The Gender Agenda* (Lafayette: Vital Issues Press, 1997). See also: *Nachrichten aus dem Deutschen Institut für Jugend und Gesellschaft*, no. 13 (Spring 2007), http://www.un.org/documents/ga/conf177/aconf177-20add1en.htm (accessed December 27, 2014).

19. Douglas A. Sylva and Susan Yoshihara, "Rights by Stealth: The Role of UN Human Rights Treaty Bodies in the Campaign for an International Right to Abortion," International Organizations Research Group, White Paper no. 8 (2009), http://c-fam.org/en/white-papers/6581-rights-by-stealth-the-role-of-un-human-rights-treaty-bodies-in-the-campaign-for-an-international-right-to-abortion (accessed December 27, 2014).

opportunities to put pressure on national governments to implement the strategies of "reproductive and sexual health."

How was it possible to create a new international right—to derive from the human right to life a "human right" to kill? How could abortion be declared a human right and member states be forced to go along with it? How was it possible to get around the resistance from sovereign states and their people? How could this all be done under the light of legitimacy?

The Networker Conference in Glen Cove

The answer was simple: by networking. "Global players" are brought together so that, unseen and uncontrolled, they can pull for the team. This happened in 1996, in Glen Cove, New York. At the roundtable were high-ranking representatives of the UN Population Fund (UNFPA), UN High Commissioner for Human Rights (UNHCHR), and UN Division for the Advancement of Women (DAW) along with people from selected NGOs, such as the International Planned Parenthood Federation (IPPF) and the Center for Reproductive Rights (CRR), who are among those with the most influence on the UN. The idea was to drive a population reduction strategy forward, even though not one of the UN's treaties defining human rights mentioned "abortion" or "reproductive rights." These treaties had been carefully negotiated, word for word, by legitimate representatives of sovereign countries. Monitoring bodies had been formed to oversee implementation of human rights in the member states. They include:

- The Human Rights Committee (HRC)
- The Convention on the Elimination of Discrimination Against Women (CEDAW)
- The Convention on the Rights of the Child
- The International Covenant on Civil and Political Rights

In Glen Cove, it was agreed that the treaty-monitoring bodies, also called compliance committees, would be used for converting "soft norms" into "hard laws." The monitoring bodies were to further develop, update, and reinterpret the binding treaties. Persistent repetition was to create the false impression that reproductive and sexual health rights were binding components of the human rights treaties already in existence.

Examples of the human rights committee's reinterpretations include:

- The right to freedom of movement was used to derive a right to travel abroad for an abortion.
- The right to privacy was used to derive a right to make decisions

about pregnancy and abortion.
• The right to freedom of expression legitimized the right for females of any age to receive information on "reproductive health services," contraception, and sex education.[20]

A network of entities was established to keep a relay going: the UN agencies, UN programs, monitoring bodies, and NGOs. The monitoring bodies are flush with skills and financial resources. While their members are appointed by the member states, they are no longer answerable to them. The core of the strategy is the right of committees to demand reports from the individual states on implementation of what the human rights treaties allegedly call for.

The committees can field complaints from individuals and independently conduct investigations in member states. The countries must then draw up reports on what measures they have taken to remedy the situation.

The NGOs' influence on the treaty-monitoring process is constantly growing. NGOs act as watchdogs at the national level to monitor implementation of the committees' recommendations. The countries are even challenged to integrate local NGOs into the process. NGOs deliver shadow reports to the committees, such as to the Convention on the Elimination of Discrimination against Women (CEDAW). Another NGO, The Center for Reproductive Rights (CRR), has 45 full-time employees and an impressive network of other NGOs and donors. The CRR is financed by the UNFPA and annually receives another $10 million from foundations.

UN institutions and nationally active NGOs ignore the democratic decision-making processes of sovereign states and together exert massive pressure on "hard countries" who are not willing to implement the gender bundle of abortion, sexualization of youth, and LGBTI rights. These include Malta, Lithuania, Namibia, Uganda, Hungary, and, recently, Finland. The NGOs' lobbyists provide the committees with the arguments and strategies for converting the "right to life" into the "right to abortion." Reducing maternal mortality does not require improvements in obstetrics, hygienic conditions, and aftercare. Instead, the ban on abortion must be lifted, so that "women's health" can be promoted through "safe abortion" ("reproductive health services"). There is no binding international law establishing a right of women to kill their unborn children. Nonetheless, this is constantly claimed, and pressure is brought forth.

---

20. Ibid., 15.

This is done through confusion of ideas, obscureness of strategy, working in the background, defaming opponents—most of all the Vatican—and marching ahead step by step according to the varying conditions of each country. In a country where abortion is forbidden, first there is a fight to legalize therapeutic abortion in strictly limited cases. For this, isolated mediagenic cases are used to conform to the model: a 9-year-old is raped by her father and has a crisis pregnancy. Who could be so heartless as to deny the poor girl an abortion?

Sometimes it is effective to have well-credentialed lawyers from the NGOs fight a case as far as the country's supreme court or the European Court of Human Rights. The high court then imposes on the member states and lower courts a new legal interpretation that undermines or even reverses the previously valid law (see Chapter 5).

Ideological seduction, pressure on national politicians, linking financial aid to "reproductive health" programs, children's sex education, distribution of condoms, media propaganda, and all sorts of cultural activities create the climate that makes the next step possible.

Krisztina Morvai, a Hungarian member of CEDAW, has openly accused the treaty-monitoring bodies of regularly overstepping their mandate to push for controversial social objectives. These include the right to abortion, legalized prostitution, promotion of sex education for children and youth, promotion of contraception for young girls, and distribution of free condoms in developing countries.[21]

After World War II, the United Nations was a light of hope for the people of the world. Now it is the spearhead of the cultural revolution.

21. Krisztina Morvai, "Respecting National Sovereignty and Restoring International Law: The Need to Reform UN Treaty Monitoring Committees," briefing at UN headquarters (New York, September 6, 2006). Quoted in "Rights by Stealth."

5

Totalitarian Access:
The Yogyakarta Principles

Humankind suffers from a fatal delayed ignition. It doesn't understand
anything until the next generation.

Stanislaw Jerzy Lee

THE YOGYACARTA PRINCIPLES (YPs) are a detailed manual for implementing gender ideology worldwide: free choice of gender, sexual orientation, and identity. The 29 "Principles" will be discussed here in depth because they are a key document for understanding the freedom-threatening goals of the global sexual revolution. A group of "renowned human rights experts," having no official authorization or legitimation, formulated these principles in 2007 at a conference in Yogyakarta, Indonesia. In March of that year, they presented them to the public at the UN building in Geneva to lend them a glow of authority. The YPs are a "new tool for activists." They are furnished with a 200-page handbook called *An Activist's Guide to the Yogyakarta Principles,* which translates the Yogyakarta Principles into political action. The *Activist's Guide to the Yogyakarta Principles* takes international human rights treaties to be "living instruments. . . . Just as international human rights law is a living, evolving instrument, so too the Yogyakarta Principles is a living document. The scope of the Principles will expand."[1]

The wording of the international human rights treaties was negotiated with extreme care by representatives of member states, but anyone who thinks they're binding has another thing coming. In the eyes of the

---

1. *An Activist's Guide to the Yogyakarta Principles*, August 2010, https://iglhrc.org/sites/default/files/Activists_Guide_Yogyakarta_Principles.pdf (accessed January 21, 2015).

Yogyakarta Principles' authors, human rights are merely a tool for enforcing the "principles" worldwide. The *Activist's Guide* is a concrete set of instructions for activists. It shows them how cultures that have completely different social and legal standards regarding the LGBTI agenda can be revolutionized using the YPs as an instrument.

In Germany, all political parties other than the Christian Democrats have committed themselves to implementing the Yogyakarta Principles. The key to their enforcement is admitting "sexual identity" into the constitution as an anti-discrimination criterion. Other countries that have jumped on the YP bandwagon include Argentina, Brazil, Denmark, the Netherlands, Norway, Sweden, Switzerland, the Czech Republic, and Uruguay. US president Barack Obama and his former Secretary of State Hillary Clinton have thrown their weight behind the homosexualization of the culture. The principles demand that *all countries of the world* take totalitarian measures to change their constitutions, laws, social institutions, education systems and their citizens' basic attitudes in order to enforce and legally compel acceptance and privileged status for homosexuality and other non-heterosexual identities and behaviors.

Each of the 29 principles appears below the heading: "THE STATES SHALL embody the principles . . . in their national constitutions or other appropriate legislation. . . ." Then the detailed cultural revolutionary demands follow.

The text of the Yogyakarta Principles clearly exhibits (1) the goals, (2) the methods of obfuscation, and (3) the enforcement methods of the global implementation of the LGBTI agenda. It is good to know the plan behind the changes we see happening at our moment in history.

The Goals of the Yogyakarta Principles

The word *principle* comes from Latin *principium* and means "beginning" or "origin." It represents a legal foundation from which other laws or rules can be derived. However, the Yogyakarta Principles are not really principles, but 29 arbitrary "rights" based on reinterpretation and "further development" of human rights; they amount to a call for privileged status for non-heterosexual minorities at the expense of the majority's rights and civil liberties. The document's central concepts are "sexual orientation" and "gender identity," and are defined in its preamble as follows:

UNDERSTANDING 'sexual orientation' to refer to each person's capacity for profound emotional, affectional and sexual attraction to, and intimate and sexual relations with, individuals of a different gender or the same gender or more than one gender.[2]

This definition does not exclude *any* type of sexual preference or activity, not even pedophilia (sex with children), incest (sex between blood relatives), polygamy, polyandry, polyamory (sex with more than one person), or zoophilia (bestiality, sex with animals).

> UNDERSTANDING 'gender identity' to refer to each person's deeply felt internal and individual experience of gender, which may or may not correspond with the sex assigned at birth, including the personal sense of the body (which may involve, if freely chosen, modification of bodily appearance or function by medical, surgical or other means) and other expressions of gender, including dress, speech and mannerisms.[3]

One's sexual identity, then, is not defined by objective biological and neurological differences for which there is ample scientific proof, but should be a question of *feeling* and an arbitrary subjective decision. This is the cornerstone of gender theory intent on "subversion of identity" (Butler); that is, the dissolution of the given binary structure of human existence.

Each of the "principles" is introduced by a general statement. Each statement is followed by demands that, according to the human rights experts, *all* countries *must* enforce.[4]

Acceptance of non-heterosexual sex behavior (LGBTI)[5]

The definitions of "sexual orientation" and "gender identity" show that the YPs' authors have separated sexuality from its inherent end: the joining of a man and woman in marriage, and procreation. Full equality is to be established for all types of "sexual orientation and identity." Principle 2 says:

> Everyone is entitled to enjoy all human rights without discrimination on the basis of sexual orientation or gender identity . . . whether or not the enjoyment of another human right is also affected. Discrimi-

---

2. International Commission of Jurists (ICJ), "Yogyakarta Principles: Principles on the Application of International Human Rights Law in Relation to Sexual Orientation and Gender Identity," March 2007, http://yogyakartaprinciples.org/ (accessed January 21, 2015).

3. Preamble, The Yogyakarta Principles.

4. P3-F means: Principle 3, Demand F. If no capital letter appears after the principle, the introduction is indicated.

5. LGBTI stands for lesbian, gay, bi-, trans- and intersexual.

nation on the basis of sexual orientation or gender identity includes any distinction, exclusion, restriction or preference based on sexual orientation or gender identity which has the purpose or effect of nullifying or impairing equality before the law or the equal protection of the law, or the recognition, enjoyment or exercise, on an equal basis, of all human rights and fundamental freedoms.

In plain language: All moral criteria regarding how people deal responsibly with the power of sexuality are classified as "discrimination." People's essential moral distinction between right and wrong, good and evil, is to be forbidden as applied to sexuality. Human rights that may stand in the way, such as freedom of religion and freedom of conscience, are considered subordinate. People are no longer allowed to preach, teach, or be raised to believe that the purpose of sexuality is the bond of love between a man and a woman and the creation of children, even though stable heterosexual relationships are essential to the existence of society.

Dissolution of binary sexual identity

According to the definition of "sexual orientation" and "gender identity," it is a matter of *feeling*—that is, of a person's arbitrary, purely subjective self-definition—what one's gender is. The *Activist's Guide* adds: "Requiring a person to subscribe to a particular identity group would only perpetuate the oppression that the rights are seeking to combat."[6]

Identity refers to a person's stable identifying characteristics. However, feelings and emotions are unstable. Biology, medicine, brain research, hormonal research, psychology, sociology and other sciences make precise statements about the differing characteristics of man and woman, to the point that each individual cell of a man's or woman's body is masculine or feminine. According to the YPs' authors, all claims of inalienable differences between men and women are based on "prejudices and stereotyped roles for men and women" (Preamble). The YPs are intended to wipe out these "prejudices" worldwide.

Because the YPs say that a person's identity is not determined by biological sexual characteristics but by his arbitrarily chosen "sexual orientation" and "gender identity," there are not just two genders, but as many as there are "sexual orientations." There are no longer men and women, but queer men, lesbian women, bisexual, transsexual, intersexual men and women as their own "genders." Because there is a small

---

6. *Activist's Guide*, http://www.ypinaction.org/files/02/85/Activists_Guide_English_nov_14_2010.pdf (accessed October 6, 2015).

group of people who suffer from the unfortunate fact that they cannot identify with their biological gender (transsexuals) or were born with ambiguous biological sexual characteristics (intersexuals), the YPs use this as a pretext to upend the values deeply rooted in humanity and in the legal system, and even to ignore the clear results of research.

However, gender ideology gets tangled up in an obvious contradiction: On the one hand, a person's gender is to be flexible and changeable, but on the other hand, every non-heterosexual orientation is supposed to be an unchangeable identity. To implement this contradictory image of man, the YP authors demand that:

- No status, such as marriage or parenthood, may be invoked as such to prevent the legal recognition of a person's gender identity. (P3)
- [States shall] take all necessary legislative, administrative and other measures:
- To fully respect and legally recognize each person's self-defined gender identity. (P3-b)
- To ensure that procedures exist whereby all State-issued identity papers which indicate a person's gender/sex—including birth certificates, passports, electoral records and other documents—reflect the person's profound self-defined gender identity. (P3-c)
- To ensure the right of all persons ordinarily to choose when, to whom and how to disclose information pertaining to their sexual orientation or gender identity. (P6-f)

In plain language: Let's say that a married father of three children is overcome by the feeling that his real identity is that of a woman. He has the gender information removed from his birth certificate, driver's license, and passport and from then on wears women's clothing. According to the YPs, his wife would be guilty of "discrimination" if she found this reason for divorce. In P24-C, it says that "the best interests of the child shall be a primary consideration." Did the authors of the YPs ask children how they would feel if their father suddenly dressed like a woman?

Or consider this case: A woman who is really a man marries a man without telling him about his/her altered sexual identity. After the wedding he/she changes his/her mind about his/her sexual identity and goes back to being a man. Is it "discrimination" if the man sues for fraud?

It is astounding that "experts on human rights" can make such demands without perceiving that they are ridiculous. But even more astounding is that international organizations, governments and political parties have made the goals of such tiny minorities their own.

Homosexual "marriage" with adoption rights

"Everyone has the right to found a family, regardless of sexual orientation or gender identity. There are many different types of families. No family should suffer discrimination because of one of its members' sexual orientation or gender identity" (P24).

No definition is given as to what "family" means. However, the criteria for family that applied in all cultures since time immemorial—the marriage of a man and a woman giving birth to biological offspring—was done away with. Absolutely any amalgamation of people of any—mutable—gender is to be called "family" and recognized, protected, and provided with social services by the state. The participants are to have status as "next of kin" (P17-H). This is in stark contrast to Article 16 of the *Universal Declaration of Human Rights* (1948). Once again, Article 16 states:

1. Men and women of full age, without any limitation due to race, nationality or religion, have the right to marry and to found a family.
2. The family is the natural and fundamental group unit of society and is entitled to protection by society and the State.

To do away with this concept of family, the institution of marriage has to be redefined. Even though at first, for tactical reasons, only the "registered partnership of same-sex couples" was demanded, P24-E clearly states:

[States shall] ensure that any entitlement, privilege, obligation or benefit available to different-sex married or registered partners is equally available to same-sex married or registered partners.

The sterility of same-sex relationships is to be remedied artificially through "access to adoption or assisted procreation (including donor insemination)" (P24-A).[7] "[States shall] take all necessary legislative, administrative and other measures to ensure that [. . .] the best interests of the child shall be a primary consideration, and that the sexual orientation or gender identity of the child or of any family member or other person may not be considered incompatible with such best interests" (P24-C).

Because the parents' constitutionally guaranteed right to raise their children could be an obstacle to implementing the LGBTI agenda, it is demanded that

[States shall] ensure that a child who is capable of forming personal views can exercise the right to express those views freely, and that

---

7. Cf. *Google Baby*, film on artificial child-production through surrogate mothers, www.youtube.com/watch?v=pQGlAM0iWFM (accessed September 20, 2015).

such views are given due weight in accordance with the age and maturity of the child. (P24-D)

In plain language: A child's right to his biological parents is inverted to a right of adults with "flexible" sexual orientation and identity to a child, which they can produce through anonymous methods of reproduction. Once arbitrariness is actually promoted to the status of law, there would be no more possibility of protecting child welfare. For example, if a father who has just decided he is homosexual or is really a woman enters a partnership with another person of flexible gender, custody for children from a previous marriage could no longer be refused on the grounds that these new sexual relationships are detrimental to the welfare of the child.

Marriage and family will be dissolved. In their place, arbitrary relationships between two or more people of any gender are to be recognized as "marriage" and "family" and benefit from government subsidy.

Privileges for LGBTI people

The YPs claim that they are the application of existing human rights to people with "diverse" sexual orientations, i.e., those deviating from heterosexuality. In reality they involve the creation of new legal provisions for the deregulation of sexual norms which are to be imposed on sovereign states.

The YPs demand special rights for LGBTI activism. "The right to freedom of opinion and expression" (P19) and "the right to freedom of peaceful assembly and association" (P20) "must not be restricted" by otherwise generally applicable notions of "public order, public morality, public health and public security."

In "A Brief Commentary on the Yogyakarta Principles," Dr. Jakob Cornides, an expert on international law, remarks:

> It should be noted that, if YP 20 [were] accepted, associations, assemblies and demonstrations promoting the LGBT lifestyle would be the *only* ones not being subject to any restriction of public order and morality; it would give them unlimited freedom to insult or provoke persons not sharing their views or opposing the promotion of their agenda. This kind of privilege is completely unacceptable in a democratic society; to accept it would mean to give up democracy in exchange for the LGBT agenda. Once more it seems that the primary purpose of the YP is not to protect human rights, but to seek privileges.[8]

8. Jakob Cornides, "A Brief Commentary on the Yogyakarta Principles," 2009, http://works.bepress.com/jakob_cornides/20 (accessed January 21, 2015).

By definition, human rights apply to everyone on earth at all times. There are many groups and minorities on this earth who suffer human rights violations. Wherever this happens, states, international organizations and courts are called on to monitor adherence to human rights, even, of course, when the human rights of LGBTI people are violated.

The YP authors owe an explanation as to why specifically minorities defined by non-heterosexual behavior should receive special care from the state through newly created laws, measures and monitoring institutions. This is, in fact, privileged status.

The UN and EU are selective in their eagerness to protect groups of people against discrimination. Today, persecuted religious minorities do not receive a fraction of the attention that international institutions pay to discrimination based on sexual orientation. Currently, Christians are the most persecuted group in the world. Entire countries in the Middle East, Africa, and Asia are being depopulated of Christians, who are deprived of decent living conditions, whose churches are set ablaze, and whose faithful are expelled or persecuted even to the point of death. But, in contrast to the comparatively small minority of LGBTI people, there are no UN or EU programs for protecting Christians.

Methods of Obfuscation

It should be clear by now that the LGBTI agenda is not about "tolerance" and application of human rights to sexually defined, smaller and smaller minorities, but about giving privileges to non-heterosexual minorities at the expense of the majority's freedoms. If the global LGBTI network called their goals what they are, the agenda would have no chance, because special privileges for LGBTI people are rejected by the great majority of the world's population of all continents, cultures, and religions, who have varying but always restrictive heterosexual norms, acknowledge clear, indissoluble differences in the sexual identities of men and women, and hold marriage and family to be high cultural goods that make an irreplaceable contribution to the welfare of all.

The success of the worldwide sexual revolution therefore requires obfuscation until the point of no return, when all opposition can be suppressed. The obfuscation is done in three ways:

- Through presumption of false authority and legitimacy.
- Through use of undefined, ambiguous terms.
- Through the false pretense of accord with existing international law.

Presumption of false legitimacy

As shown at the beginning, the authors of the Yogyakarta Principles lack any official legitimation or authorization through official bodies of the United Nations. However, high-ranking Yogyakarta activists appear on behalf of the UN. Such false legitimacy allows nations to be pressured if they do not share this new image of mankind and do not wish to enshrine it in their legal system.

Manipulation of terms

The YPs' central terms are *sexual orientation* and *gender identity*. If the demand is made that all human rights treaties and all countries' national legal systems must be oriented toward these benchmarks, it should be objectively and scientifically ascertainable what constitutes a specific "sexual orientation." However, the definition of sexual orientation makes subjective feelings the basis for rights and privileges. There are no exclusion criteria for forms of sexuality that *still* appear unacceptable today. Their public and legal acceptance is already being promoted by lobbying groups using the same methods as the homosexualist movement and who lobby on behalf of rights to pedophilia, incest, and polyamory.

The YPs legitimize their far-reaching demands for privileges for defined minorities by using terms that indicate lofty values but have been hollowed out by ideology. Sexual orientation and gender identity are explained as "integral to each person's dignity" (P9). Equality of what is unequal is represented as justice, but in reality it is injustice. Any differentiation and resulting treatment of LGBTI people unequal to that of heterosexuals in marriage and family law is considered "discrimination," which must be prosecuted. (Confusion of concepts is covered in detail in Ch. 8.)

The false pretense of accord with international law

Principle 27 demands "the right to promote human rights." Closer examination shows that this is about protection of cultural revolutionary activism. That is, everyone has "the right to develop and discuss new[!] human rights norms and to advocate their acceptance." So this is not about asserting existing human rights, but about asserting minority interests that are represented as "human rights norms." Among other things, the YPs demand that states shall

- "Ensure a favorable environment" for these activities. (P27-A)
- Combat any opposition to "human rights defenders." (P27-B)
- Guarantee "access to, participation in, and communication with,

national and international human rights organizations and bodies."
(P27-C)
• "Ensure the protection of human rights defenders, working on
issues of sexual orientation and gender identity, against any violence,
threat, retaliation, *de facto* or *de jure* discrimination, pressure, or any
other arbitrary action perpetrated by the State, or by non-State
actors." (P27-D)

Jakob Cornides hits the nail on the head: "The rights they seek to promote are no human rights, but the slogans of a pressure group."[9] For the
state to provide protection from discrimination by the state requires a
monitoring entity that is above the state. This function is already performed by the monitoring bodies of the UN and the European Union
Fundamental Rights Agency in Vienna, which the member states can
barely control.

Methods of Implementation

As Edward Bernays, the inventor of mass manipulation and nephew of
Sigmund Freud, knew: "We are dominated by the relatively small number of persons . . . who understand the mental processes and social patterns of the masses. It is they who pull the wires which control the
public mind." These are the methods of "conscious and intelligent
manipulation":

• Hollowing out national sovereignty through treaty-monitoring
bodies and NGOs.
• Securing financial resources in the millions from the UN, EU, and
individual states for LGBTI organizations.
• Litigating court test cases at all levels in the name of human rights.
• Changing the population's fundamental values.
• Enacting social and legal sanctions against opposition.

Hollowing out national sovereignty

At the end of the document, the Yogyakarta activists provide 16 "additional recommendations" (marked A through P) for implementing the
cultural revolution based on the Yogyakarta Principles. Those called to
action are not the democratically legitimate representatives of sovereign
governments, but the UN High Commissioner for Human Rights (A),
the UN Human Rights Council (B), NGOs, (D, J), the Treaty-Monitoring Bodies, regional and sub-regional intergovernmental organizations

9. Ibid.

with a commitment to human rights (H), regional human rights courts (I), humanitarian organizations (K), professional organizations, the educational sector (M), commercial organizations (N), the mass media (O), and governmental and private funders (P). This describes the global network that is poised to create the new gender environment.

The United Nations' treaty-monitoring bodies play a special role in putting through the LGBTI agenda. As previously mentioned, the members are not elected democratically, but delegated by the member states, and are not accountable to the governments of their countries of origin. They carry the authority of the UN and demand that the governments of sovereign states be accountable for implementing human rights as the delegates interpret and "further develop" them. In this way, influence is exerted on the legislation of individual states, even to the point of demanding changes to their constitutions. Meanwhile, relevant local NGOs are brought into the process and deliver "shadow reports."

Financing of LGBTI organizations by the UN and EU

Funds by the tens and hundreds of millions flow to the LGBTI agenda through official UN and EU sub-organizations and private foundations (Rockefeller, Ford, Bill & Melinda Gates, etc.). This is obscured as part of their official budgets. The International Lesbian, Gay, Bisexual, Trans and Intersex Association (ILGA) is more than 60-percent funded by the European Commission, supplemented by contributions from billionaire George Soros and two other large donors.[10] The European Commission also regularly uses tax money to fund projects of the world's two largest abortion organizations, Marie Stopes International and International Planned Parenthood. This is camouflaged as "sexual and reproductive health," even though the EU's definition of the term explicitly excludes abortion.[11]

Test cases in the name of human rights

Under the heading "Strategize the Yogyakarta Principles,"[12] the first point asks: "Is there an issue around which a legal strategy can be built in the context of which the human rights principles laid out in the Yogyakarta Principles can play a supportive role?" To pursue such a strategy, it is recommended that one "engage with the UN system, via

---

10. *Activist's Guide.*

11. This was uncovered in a report from *European Dignity Watch*: http://www.europeandignitywatch.org/de/day-to-day/detail/article/revealing-report-on-funding-of-abortion-in-eus-development-aid.html (accessed October 3, 2015).

12. *Activist's Guide.*

the Universal Periodic Review, shadow report to treaty bodies, in coalition with others, making contact with Special Rapporteurs, etc."[13] It is obviously assumed that the UN system is LGBTI-friendly. Such cases are then brought to the European Court of Human Rights (ECHR) and the European Court of Justice (ECJ) with the well-founded hope of finding a sympathetic judge.[14]

Change in the population's fundamental philosophy

Public demonstrations

Demonstration marches are organized in the capitals of the Western world, such as Christopher Street Days, where gross obscenities are displayed to the public, and politicians march in the front row. As shown above, the YPs' authors demand that the rights to freedom of assembly and association not be limited by "notions of public order, public morality, public health and public security" (P20).

Media influence

P19 demands the right "to seek, receive and impart information and ideas of all kinds, including with regard to human rights, sexual orientation and gender identity, through any medium and regardless of frontiers." In addition, the YPs demand that States shall take all necessary legislative, administrative, and other measures to:

- Ensure that the outputs and the organization of media that is State-regulated is pluralistic and non-discriminatory in respect of issues of sexual orientation and gender identity. (P19-B)
- Ensure that the exercise of freedom of opinion and expression does not violate the rights and freedoms of persons of diverse sexual orientations and gender identities. (P19-E)

In "Further Recommendations" (O) the mass media are requested to

Avoid the use of stereotypes in relation to sexual orientation and gender identity, and promote tolerance and the acceptance of diversity of human sexual orientation and gender identity, and raise awareness around these issues.

13. Ibid.
14. LGBT test cases at the European Court of Human Rights in recent years include: Schalk and Kopf vs. Austria, Kozak vs. Poland, Courten vs. UK, Schlumpf vs. Switzerland. LGBT test cases at the European Court of Justice include Maruko vs. VddB, Römer vs. City of Hamburg, and others.

In plain language: Limitless agitation through all media across all borders; LGBTI quotas on public TV; a ban on all statements that LGBTI people feel violate their self-defined rights and freedoms; conversion of the mass media into LGBTI propaganda institutions.

Implementation of the LGBT Agenda in the school system
In P16, the "Right to Education" demands that

> [States shall] ensure that education methods, curricula and resources serve to enhance understanding of and respect for, inter alia, diverse sexual orientations and gender identities, including the particular needs of students, their parents and family members related to these grounds. (P16-D)

In plain language: School curricula and training of caregivers and teachers must be focused on changing the mindset of children and teenagers, so that they perceive any form of non-heterosexual behavior as "normal" and equal and can "choose" between various sexual orientations and gender identities.

Training the bureaucracy
If the vast majority of humanity did not believe that fertility-based sexuality between people of the opposite sex is right, and that sexuality between people of the same gender is wrong, things would look pretty grim for the survival of humanity. For advocates of evolutionary theory, prioritization of heterosexuality in a society's value system must be both a theoretical and practical necessity.

However, the YP authors see it as the state's job to employ "programs of training and awareness-raising" to change this belief among the vast majority of the world's population, especially among these groups:

- the police (P7)
- judges, judicial staff, prosecutors and attorneys (P8)
- prison staff (P10)
- employers (P12)
- social workers (P15)
- "teachers and students at all levels of public education, professional bodies, and potential violators of human rights" (P28-F)

In plain language: All occupational groups must promote the YP agenda. If there is suspicion that they are "potential violators of human rights," they are subjected to "programs of training and awareness-raising."

Social and legal sanctions against opposition

Curtailment of freedom of contract

> [States shall] take all necessary legislative, administrative and other measures
> • to eliminate and prohibit discrimination on the basis of sexual orientation and gender identity in public and private employment, including in relation to vocational training, recruitment, promotion, dismissal, conditions of employment and remuneration. (P12-A)
> • to ensure adequate housing, including protection from eviction. (P15)

In plain language: An employer, such as the Catholic Church or a private school, is not allowed to refuse employment to a teacher or caregiver because the applicant is an active homosexual or a man in woman's clothing. The same applies to landlords.

Curtailment of freedom of speech

As mentioned previously, LGBTI people's freedom of speech and freedom of expression are to be exempt from general views of "public order" and "public morals," while the rest of the population's freedom of speech and expression must not hurt the feelings of LGBTI people (P19). Once again, Jakob Cornides:

> Quite obviously, this 'interpretation' of 'human rights' is not only wrong, but outright dangerous: It calls into question the equality of all before the law, undermines democracy, directly affects the rights of those not supporting the LGBT agenda, and betrays the totalitarian mindset of the YP drafting panel. . . . If accepted, this clause will have devastating effects on the freedom of opinion and expression, reaching far beyond the special purposes of the YP. If the particular interests of the LGBT rights movement supersede concerns of public order and morality, any other pressure group may legitimately make the same claims. The notions of public order and public morality would therefore be completely undermined by this clause.[15]

Suppression of non-compliant information

The LGBTI lobby considers research into the causes of homosexuality (LGBTI) and availability of therapeutic assistance for those suffering from their sexual tendencies to be "discrimination" and attempts to

---

15. Cornides, "A Brief Commentary on the Yogyakarta Principles."

suppress them, even when the affected person wishes to access such help. They demand that

> [States shall] ensure that any medical or psychological treatment or counseling does not, explicitly or implicitly, treat sexual orientation and gender identity as medical conditions to be treated, cured or suppressed. (P18)

The interest groups use intimidation, defamation and campaigns against therapists, speakers they dislike, and undesirable conferences to suppress any information about the possibility of altering LGBT orientation and behavior. The causes for non-heterosexual proclivities are not to be scientifically researched, and the message that sexual tendencies can be changed should be suppressed (see Ch. 10, 152). In September 2012, California became the first US state to pass a legal ban on "reparative" or "conversion" therapy for minors with unwanted homosexual orientation (Senate Bill 1172). Almost a year later, the governor of New Jersey signed a similar bill into law,[16] and other states may follow. This is not only an unconstitutional curtailment of scientific freedom, but also of a person's freedom to access information and therapy if they suffer from their non-heterosexual orientation.

Criminalization of opposition

The last principle, 29, is titled "Accountability." Readers will be disappointed if they think this is about accountability of LGBTI people and activists toward the overall society. Among the demands:

> Everyone whose human rights, including rights addressed in these Principles[!], are violated is entitled to have those directly or indirectly[!] responsible for the violation, whether they are government officials or not, held accountable for their actions in a manner that is proportionate to the seriousness of the violation. There should be no impunity for perpetrators of human rights violations related to sexual orientation or gender identity. (P29)

- [States shall] establish . . . monitoring mechanisms. (P29-A)
- Ensure that . . . those responsible are prosecuted, tried and duly punished. (P29-B)

---

16. Martha T. Moore, "N.J. Gov. Christie Signs Ban on Gay Conversion Therapy," *USA Today,* August 19, 2013, http://www.usatoday.com/story/news/politics/2013/08/19/chris-christie-gay-conversion-therapy-new-jersey/2671197/.%20http://narth.com/2012/04/narth-statement-on-califortnis-sb-1172-sexual-orien-tation-change-efforts/ (accessed January 23, 2015).

• Establish independent[!] and effective institutions and procedures to monitor the formulation and enforcement of laws and policies to ensure the elimination of discrimination. (P29-C)
• Remove any obstacles preventing persons responsible for human rights violations based on sexual orientation or gender identity from being held accountable. (P29-D)

In plain language: independent, effective state institutions must be established for enforcing and monitoring the Yogyakarta Principles—a type of autonomous LGBTI police. All obstacles to criminalizing the opposition must be removed. What is being demanded here is the suppression and criminalization of any type of opposition to the elevation of the choice of one's gender and sexual behavior to a universal norm, and the establishment of a surveillance state to enforce it.

Toolbox for LGBTI Activists

The *Activist's Guide to The Yogyakarta Principles* (AG) is a revolutionary toolbox for LGBTI people for changing the values and legal bases of sovereign states. Central to this is the "language of human rights," which demands "rights" rather than fulfillment of "needs."[17] The toolbox contains strategic instructions:[18]

• Challenge oppressive legal standards.
• Develop new government policy.
• Seek a more responsive government.
• Educate the public.
• Build a movement.

Internet links connect globally active organizations:

• Human Rights Watch
• International Planned Parenthood
• Centre for Reproductive Rights ILGA
• The "UN system"

Effective application of the YPs is explained through success stories and "best practices" in countries on every continent (Section 3, pp. 87–135). They exemplify the LGBTI agenda's adaptability to different cultural conditions. Each of the strategic actions depicted stresses the central significance of the Yogyakarta Principles. A selection:

17. Ibid.
18. Ibid.

In *Nepal,* a Supreme Court ruling on recognition of transgendered women (a "third gender") constituted a "sweeping victory." The ruling serves throughout the world as a precedent for legal recognition of sexually defined minorities.

In *India,* a coalition of activists for HIV/AIDS prevention, children's rights, women's rights, and LGBTI groups used "pride marches, public events with VIPs, media campaigns, and court proceedings to achieve decriminalization of consensual homosexual sex."

In the *Netherlands,* which was the first country to legalize homosexual "marriage," activists succeeded in obtaining legal recognition of "chosen gender identity" without medical intervention.

In *China*—similar to the American Psychiatric Association's historic 1973 decision (see chapter 10, 152)—homosexuality was no longer listed in the Chinese Classification of Mental Disorders (CCMD-3), and thus no longer considered an illness. This was welcomed as the basis for all further societal changes. It is seen as disappointing that the new CCMD "continues to state that homosexuals experiencing distress due to their sexual orientation (ego-dystonic homosexuality) need mental health services."[19]

In *Brazil,* the government program Brazil without Homophobia was implemented in 2004.

In *Sweden,* one of the most advanced LGBTI countries, LGBTI rights were systematically integrated into development assistance policies by the International Development Cooperation Agency, even through direct financing of LGBTI organizations in cooperating countries.

In *New Zealand,* access to health services for gender reassignment were improved, and it was made easier to change one's gender in identification documents. "Trans people" can demand that no gender be listed in their passport at all.

In *Venezuela,* the Union Affirmativa, an LGBTI NGO, held training for 800 police officers and 120 jurists in 2006.

In *Poland,* the ban on homosexual parades and "homosexual propaganda in schools" was lifted. In 2001, a campaign against homophobia was initiated. It works with a traveling exhibition titled *Berlin-Yogyakarta,* which shows "the horrors of the persecution of homosexuals during the Nazi regime, and the hope represented by the Yogyakarta Principles as evidence of progress toward rights for LGBTI people."

In *Lebanon,* ground was broken with a weekly magazine and book

19. Ibid.

featuring the life testimonies of "lesbian, bisexual, queer, and questioning women."

At the end of the *Activist's Guide* is stated what may actually drive the culture revolution: "When you undertake activities discussed in this Guide, not only do you create change, but you become a valued part of the international human rights system that operates for the benefit of all people."[20]

There are influential individuals who formulated the *Yogyakarta Principles*, and there are influential individuals and NGOs that drive its global implementation with help from UN and EU institutions. In every country there is a small minority of non-heterosexually oriented people to whom prospects for life are offered: They are supplied with money, education, jobs, and juridical support and can gain power and influence in the international network of the global sexual revolution. Countries that see marriage and family as the foundation for a vital society should become familiar with the attack strategies of the global Cultural Revolution.

20. Ibid.

6

The European Union
on the Gender Bandwagon

[Since the fall of the Soviet Bloc totalitarian regimes] there remains the legal extermination of human beings conceived but unborn. . . . Nor are other grave violations of God's law lacking. I am thinking, for example, of the strong pressure from the European Parliament to recognize homosexual unions as an alternative type of family, with the right to adopt children. It is legitimate and even necessary to ask whether this is not the work of another ideology of evil, more insidious and hidden, perhaps, intent on exploiting human rights themselves against man and against the family.

Pope John Paul II[1]

The EU and the New Gender Person

IN 2006, former Soviet dissident Vladimir Bukovsky held a lecture in Brussels in which he warned of a new totalitarianism promoted by the European Union.[2] He feared that, against the will of the people, the EU was developing into a super-state similar to the Soviet Union, and he saw a massive lack of democracy in its structure.

As a man who had spent 12 years incarcerated in Soviet prisons, work camps, and psychiatric institutions, he had observed the transition to the modern world and may have been haunted by ghosts of totalitarianism where they didn't actually exist. However, he could also have been very perceptive of hard times ahead that the general public did not see because Europeans had been used to 60 years of prosperity and liberal democracy and thought this unusual situation would last forever.

---

1. Pope John Paul II, *Memory and Identity* (New York: Rizzoli, 2005).
2. Paul Belien, "Former Soviet Dissident Warns for EU Dictatorship," *The Brussels Journal* (February 2006), http://www.brusselsjournal.com/node/865 (accessed December 28, 2014).

Is there something in this warning of totalitarianism, and if so, what? Without a doubt, the EU has made many things easier for us, so far. We can change our residence without long, complicated bureaucratic procedures; work abroad; have our pension claims recognized across borders; and much more. But what tendencies can be observed at the EU level regarding the image of man and protection of personal freedom? The EU's strategic agenda seems aimed at a new image of man that shakes the foundations of the previous social order. All of the EU's decisions involving gender mainstreaming, sexual orientation, gender identity, gender diversity, anti-discrimination, homophobia, and same-sex "marriage" come under this sphere. (They also include bioethical questions that are not the topic of this book). All of these terms are new, and they designate something new: a new ethics in the field of gender and sexuality, and hence a new legal and social order.

Marriage and family constitute a political realm that, based on the *principle of subsidiarity*, is reserved to the member states, according to the EU constitution.[3] The principle of subsidiarity—a core element of Catholic social teaching—states that higher institutions are only to govern what cannot be governed at a lower level. However, 50 years after the European Union was born of the European people's yearning for peace after World War II, it has developed into a power apparatus that enables influential lobbyists to establish the new "gender person" as the norm at the European level and to penalize opposition. The labyrinthine structures of the European Commission and the European Parliament, with their sub-organizations and enormous bureaucratic machine, give favored NGOs privileged access for wielding influence and pushing through their agenda. For example, the LGBTI organization ILGA gets almost 70 percent of its funding from EU taxes, yet still has the status of an independent nongovernmental organization claimed to represent the interests of "civil society." Human rights ("fundamental rights") are exploited for creating a new image of human gender, and those rights are constantly being reformulated, expanded and manipulatively interpreted.

3. Treaty Establishing the European Community (EU treaty), Art. 5: "The Community shall act within the limits of the powers conferred upon it by this Treaty and of the objectives assigned to it therein. In areas which do not fall within its exclusive competence, the Community shall take action, in accordance with the principle of subsidiarity, only if and in so far as the objectives of the proposed action cannot be sufficiently achieved by the Member States and can therefore, by reason of the scale or effects of the proposed action, be better achieved by the Community. Any action by the Community shall not go beyond what is necessary to achieve the objectives of this Treaty."

Exploitation of Human Rights

The first worldwide document on human rights is the United Nations' 1948 *Universal Declaration of Human Rights*. It protects the dignity of people, the marriage of a man and a woman, and the family.

The European Convention on Human Rights (ECHR), adopted in 1950 by the Council of Europe, must be signed by every state that joins the Council of Europe. In 1950 there were 27 member states, and by 2012 there were 47. Soon the EU will join as an individual member of the ECHR. Compliance is monitored by the European Court of Human Rights (ECHR). The Convention also protects marriage between a man and a woman, saying that men and women of marriageable age have the right to marry and to found a family, according to the national laws governing the exercise of this right (Art. 12).

In the year 2000, the EU adopted a new human rights document: The Charter of Fundamental Rights of the European Union. Here, Article 9 contains an inconspicuous but significant modification to family law: "The right to marry and the right to found a family shall be guaranteed in accordance with the national laws governing the exercise of these rights."

The ECHR already reserves the right to govern marriage and family law for national states. What's new is that men and women are no longer mentioned. According to this, marriage and family are institutions unconnected with male-female relationships. This opens the door to legal implementation of homosexual "marriage." Article 21 of the Charter of Fundamental Rights of the European Union also introduces "sexual orientation"—a new and undefined concept—as a criterion for discrimination. Human rights activists use this as the legal basis for eliminating or suing over any perceived unequal treatment or refusal of privileges to people with a non-heterosexual orientation.

The prerequisite for these changes was the 1999 Amsterdam Treaty. One year before the Charter of Fundamental Rights went into effect, the term "sexual orientation" was adopted as a criterion for protection against discrimination for the first time—a deviation from all previous human rights treaties and a deviation from the constitutional traditions of the member states. Since then, the battle has been ignited for adopting the criterion of "sexual orientation" in the member states' constitutions, with the institutions of the European Union and their considerable financial resources adding fuel to the flames.

How did LGBTI lobbyists succeed in anchoring "sexual orientation" in the treaties? Maciej Golubiewski sheds light on that in his work "Europe's Social Agenda: Why is the European Union Regulating Morality?":

Isabelle Chopin, an activist of the International Lesbian and Gay Alliance (ILGA), had started an initiative called the Starting Line Group. She and her colleagues frequently spoke at the EP (European Parliament) in favor of inserting homosexual rights into the Amsterdam Treaty. They succeeded. Then, around the time of the passage of the anti-discrimination directives, Chopin and her colleagues were invited by the EC to create a European branch of ILGA with EC money taken from the "community action program" created to implement the directives in the member states. The anti-discrimination unit charged with coordinating the implementation of the directives has been funded with 200 million dollars over the next seven years, with 20 million earmarked for specific projects involving research and NGOs. ILGA is officially listed on the DG Employment, Social Affairs and Equal Opportunities (EMPL). It is important to note that ILGA is involved in continuous lobbying for legal reforms leading to the adoption of "gay marriage" laws in the member states. Given the fungibility of money, [this means that] the money ILGA receives from the EC can potentially be spent on promoting initiatives illegal in many EU member states.[4]

Activities of Some General Directorates (GD)

A small selection of activities conducted in the Commission's various General Directorates (similar to ministries) includes:

- Employment, Social Affairs and Equal Opportunities (EMPL).
- Development of anti-discrimination legislation in Europe (together with the GD of Justice).
- A Europe-wide campaign called "For diversity. Against discrimination, equality between women and men," furnished with 290 million euros for six years.
- Awarding of an anti-discrimination prize for journalism.
- Development and Cooperation—EuropeAid (DEVCO), financed by NGOs promoting "reproductive rights" (contraception, abortion, sex education) in developing countries (Marie Stopes International and International Planned Parenthood).
- Health and Consumers (SANCO) promotes "reproductive rights" in the EU member countries.
- Education and Culture (EAC) works through the European Youth

---

4. Maciej Golubiewski, "Europe's Social Agenda: Why is the European Union Regulating Morality?," *Center for Family and Human Rights*, March 2008, http://c-fam.org/white_paper/europes-social-agenda-why-is-the-european-union-regulating-morality/ (accessed December 28, 2014).

Forum with organizations that change young people's sexual and religious values.
• Justice (JUST) steers all activities in the realms of human rights and discrimination. It battles "homophobia" and "discrimination on the grounds of sexual orientation."

What is questionable here is the interplay between the Commission and the nongovernmental organizations that pose as "legitimate" representatives of the "civil society," partly thanks to magnanimous financing from the Commission. They influence all steps of the political process, formulation and implementation of laws, and monitoring and accompanying activities aimed at changing the culture. Through "civil dialogue," NGOs are integrated into the legislative process; and, through "community action programs" armed with millions in EU money, they handle implementation in the individual countries.

The European Youth Forum (EYF), financed with millions of euros from the EU, campaigns on the "European and international level" for the rights of youth, "youth empowerment," "gender equality," and "safe sex." It battles discrimination based on age and "sexual orientation," and especially discrimination due to an intersection of age and "sexual orientation."[5] A sub-organization is the International Lesbian, Gay, Bisexual, Transgender and Queer Youth and Student Organization (IGLYO). The EYF collaborates with abortion organizations like International Planned Parenthood and Marie Stopes International.

One of EYF's community action programs is called TRIANGLE. TRIANGLE stands for "Transfer of Information against Discrimination of Gays and Lesbians in Europe," and the project links young people to the homosexual scene. An official cooperation partner in Germany is the government of the state of Nordrhein-Westfalen, which backs a school project for battling homophobia.[6]

The EYF's goals are clear from the letter they fired off to EU President Barroso on April 27, 2010.[7] The signatories[8] were alarmed because the Lithuanian parliament had passed an amendment to the youth protec-

5. http://www.youthforum.org/european-youth-forum/ (accessed January 10, 2015).

6. http://www.schule-der-vielfalt.de (Schule der Vielfalt, accessed January 10, 2015).

7. "European Youth Forum 2013–2014 Report," *European Youth Forum*, http://www.youthforum.org/index.php?option=comcontent&view=article&id= 670%3Ayfj -writes-to-barroso-freedom-of-expression-for-all-should-be-safeguarded &catid=25%3Anews& Itemid =30&lang=en (accessed December 28, 2014).

8. Tine Radinja, President, European Youth Forum (YFJ); Simon Malievac, Chairperson of IGLYO; Lukas Kaindlstorfer, member of Organizing Bureau of European School Student Unions (OBESSU); and Vytautas Valentinavicius, Chairperson, Tolerant Youth Association (Lithuania).

tion act[9] that opposes "promotion of homosexual relationships" with the justification that "homosexual, bisexual and polygamous relationships damage the physical and mental health of youth." The signatories fear that "such a law could aggravate stereotypes and prejudices against lesbian, queer and bisexual people in school. . . . We, the young people of Europe, believe that further steps must be taken to eliminate discrimination for any reason, including sexual orientation and age in order to achieve de facto equality in Europe."

The EU was up in arms about tiny Lithuania's breaking away from gender mainstreaming. The European Parliament passed two resolutions in 2009 to torpedo the democratic decision of a member state's parliament. The decision was changed, but not completely relinquished. The EU shows no respect for member states' self-determination regarding marriage and family, although marriage and family are not under the purview of the EU and interference with national regulations violates the principle of subsidiarity. As Golubiewski sums up: "the EU has become a playground for lobbyists and interest groups who realize that by skillfully exploiting an already wide jurisdiction of the EU institutions they can advance and expand their agenda throughout Europe."[10]

The European Court of Justice (ECJ), headquartered in Luxembourg, and the European Court of Human Rights (ECHR), an institution of the Council of Europe located in Strasbourg, play an important role in strategic litigation. They pass down human rights judgments with repercussions for all case law in the member countries.

The Fundamental Rights Agency and the European Institute for Gender Equality

Newly founded EU agencies gather data and monitor implementation of the newfound human rights. The Fundamental Rights Agency (FRA), founded in Vienna in 2007, has an annual budget of 20 million euros, and has 80 employees. Its primary issues include battling homophobia and discrimination based on "sexual orientation" and opposing "Islamophobia." Another group, the European Institute for Gender Equality (EIGE), was also founded in 2007, in Vilnius, Lithuania. Up to the year

9. Detrimental Effect of Public Information (as last amended on December 22, 2009), No. XI, 594. Available in English at http://www3.lrs.lt/pls/inter3/dokpaieska.show doc_l?p_id=363137.

European Parliament resolution of September 17, 2009 on the Lithuanian Law on the Protection of Minors against the Detrimental Effects of Public Information, available at http://www.europarl.europa.eu/sides/getDoc.do?type=TA&reference=P7-TA-2009-0019 &language=EN (accessed January 2015).

10. Golubiewski, "Europe's Social Agenda," 11.

2013 it has had a budget of 52.5 million euros. It defines its mission like this:

> The European Institute for Gender Equality (EIGE) is an autonomous body of the European Union, established to contribute to and strengthen the promotion of gender equality, including gender main-streaming, in all EU policies and national policies. It is also dedicated to fighting against discrimination based on sex, as well as to raising EU citizens' awareness of gender equality . . . there is still a clear and demonstrated democratic deficit with regard to women's involvement in EU policymaking . . . the European Union is only half way towards a gender-equal society.[11]

As EIGE Director Virginija Langbakk explains:

> Being a comparatively small EU agency, the Institute seeks to attract the best possible competence from the outside by creating working groups of experts in certain areas—we will rely on their support for the development of future activities. [. . .] We have already entered into a dynamic cooperation with our newly created journalists' task-force. The taskforce will advise us on the most effective ways to communicate our messages and reach audiences around Europe.[12]

In plain language: the EU used 52.5 million euros to set up still another center that will work closely with the European Commission, the EU parliament, relevant NGOs, and a journalistic taskforce to use "best practices" in all spheres of politics to influence the attitudes of EU citizens by "raising awareness."

The EIGE and FRA appear to be activist centers with an expansive interpretation of their mandate. They are equipped with financial resources on a scale that makes it realistic to impose their cultural revolutionary goals on the 500 million residents of the EU's member states.

The European Parliament and the Council of Europe Go LGBTI

The European Parliament and the Council of Europe regularly pass resolutions and laws that aim to impose new morality in the areas of sexuality and family. The magic word for conjuring up solid majorities is "homophobia." Anyone opposing the legislation is a homophobe, racist,

---

11. "In Brief," The European Institute for Gender Equality, http://eige.europa.eu (accessed December 28, 2014).

12. http://www.europarl.europa.eu/sides/getDoc.do?pubRef=-//EP//TEXT+TA+P6 -TA-2006-0273+0+DOC+XML+V0//EN (accessed October 6, 2015).

sexist, and an enemy of human rights in general. What politician is willing to be stigmatized in this way? Recent decisions include:

EU Parliament

- Resolution on Respect for Human Rights in the European Union (A4-0223/1996 and 1999). This calls on all member states that still have restrictive homosexuality laws to change them.
- Resolution on Women and Fundamentalism (March 13, 2002, 2000/2174[INI]). This puts pressure on countries that are or want to become members to legalize abortion.
- Resolution on Homophobia in Europe (P6_TA [2006]0018, January 18, 2006). This resolution calls on the states to prosecute "homophobia" and provides for monitoring by EU courts. "Homophobia" is defined as "an irrational fear of and aversion to homosexuality and to lesbian, gay, bisexual and transgender (LGBT) people based on prejudice and similar to racism, xenophobia, anti-Semitism and sexism." Thus, "irrational fears" are to be criminalized.
- Resolution on the Increase in Racist and Homophobic Violence in Europe (June 15, 2006).
- Resolution on the Fight against Homophobia in Europe (2012/2657[RSP] 24.05.2012). "Homophobia" is again equated with racism, xenophobia and anti-Semitism, and the EU Commission is called on to fight against it. Discrimination is "often hidden behind justifications based on public order, religious freedom and the right to conscientious objection" (Section B). The resolution pressures member states to legalize same-sex "marriage," even though this matter lies fully outside the EU's authority. This resolution was prepared by an LGBTI intergroup of the European Parliament and was pushed through the parliament using a strategic ambush maneuver.[13]

Council of Europe

- Resolution on Discrimination on the Basis of Sexual Orientation (2010). The demands are nearly identical to those in the EU Parliament's resolution against homophobia.[14]
- Resolution on How Marketing and Advertising Affect Equality between Women and Men (2008/2038[INI]). "Gender-stereotyped"

13. "EP Pressures Member States To Legalise Same-Sex Marriage," European Dignity Watch, last modified May 2012, http://www.europeandignitywatch.org/de/day-to-day/detail/article/ep-pressures-member-states-to-legalise-same-sex-marriage.html (accessed January 10, 2015).

14. "Parliamentary Assembly," Council of Europe, http://assembly.coe.int/Mainf.asp?link=/Documents/AdoptedText/ta10/ERES1728.htm (accessed January 10, 2015).

images (such as housewives' activities) in TV advertising and other media, especially those for the young, are to be stopped, because they are "sexist" and "degrading."[15]

All other measures for changing deep-seated conceptions in the culture were acknowledged by the EU on the initiative of ILGA Europe's May 17, 2005 Europe-wide "International Day against Homophobia." There is a history to this: On May 17, 1990, the World Health Organization (WHO) removed homosexuality from its diagnostic codes. In 2010, the president of the Council of Ministers and the European Parliament, and the vice-president of the General Directorate for Justice, issued a joint declaration damning "homophobia."

J.C. von Krempach, EU insider and author of many articles on human rights in the EU, describes the worldwide umbrella organization ILGA in this way:

> ILGA is an international gay rights lobby, which organizes all the major "Gay Pride" manifestations around the world and promotes an extremist agenda (full recognition of same-sex marriage everywhere around the globe, adoption rights for gay people, social benefits to reward being gay, gagging order legislation against possible opponents such as Christians and Muslims…). Very notoriously, the self-described "human rights advocacy group" was several times denied accreditation consultative status at the UN ECOSOC, given that several of its Members openly promoted the legalization of pedosexuality.[16]

Today the EU, Tomorrow the Whole World

To implement the LGBTI agenda in member states and non-member countries, on June 8, 2010, the Working Party on Human Rights approved the "Toolkit to Promote and Protect the Enjoyment of all Human Rights by Lesbian, Gay, Bisexual and Transgender (LGBT) People."[17] It is the toolbox necessary for global enforcement of the LGBTI agenda through the EU human rights groups.

15. "European Parliament resolution of September 3, 2008," Europäisches Parlament, http://www.europarl.europa.eu/sides/getDoc.do?pubRef=-//EP//TEXT+TA+P 6-TA-2008-0401+0+DOC+XML+V0//DE (accessed January 10, 2015).

16. "The EU Lobbies Itself on Gay Rights: Is ILGA-Europe an 'Unofficial' EU Agency?," http://www.turtlebayandbeyond.org/2011/homosexuality/the-eu-lobbies-itself-on-gay-rights-is-ilga-europe-an-unofficial-eu-agency/.

17. "Toolkit to Promote and Protect the Enjoyment of all Human Rights by Lesbian, Gay, Bisexual and Transgender (LGBT) People," Council of the European Union, 2010, http://www.consilium.europa.eu/uedocs/cmsUpload/st11179.en10.pdf (accessed December 28, 2014).

The document "seeks to enable the EU to proactively react to cases of human rights violations of LGBTI people and to structural causes behind these violations." The "promotion and protection of human rights" is declared a goal of EU foreign policy, for which the "financial instruments available both through the EU institutions and the Member States" are to be used.

The Council Working Group on Human Rights (COHOM) will update this Toolkit at least every three years after its adoption. COHOM will also promote and oversee further mainstreaming of the LGBTI issues within the EU's external action and actively disseminate this Toolkit and promote its implementation by the EU Member States, the European Union External Action Service, the European Commission and the European Parliament. Some of those tools include:

- Exchange of information on "best practices."
- Sending political support messages.
- Making it easier to obtain information and finances.
- Promotion of external activities by local LGBTI organizations, by, for instance, setting up debates and seminars on relevant issues and including LGBTI aspects.
- Support for cultural events, conferences and social projects.
- Submitting the proposal that UN special correspondents, EU special emissaries, and relevant representatives of the Council of Europe, the Organization for Security and Cooperation in Europe (OSCE), and regional human rights committees meet as part of their visits to local NGOs that promote protection of LGBTI people's human rights.
- Calling on local groups to record information on the situation for LGBTI people in their alternative reports to regional human rights organizations and UN committees.
- Recording such information in the documents that the UN Human Rights Council uses as part of its system of regular, general inspections.
- Collaboration with international institutions.
- Involving members of the civil society in side groups run parallel to the conventions of multilateral committees to gain a hearing for issues affecting the human rights of LGBTI people.

The Organization for Security and Cooperation in Europe, an amalgamation of 56 countries of Europe, Central Asia and North America, maintains an Office for Democratic Institutions and Human Rights (ODHIR). In 2003, the EU Council of Ministers assigned it to take over the LGBTI anti-discrimination agenda. For this purpose, the Tolerance and Non-Discrimination Information System (TANDIS) was established. TANDIS is a coordinating point for worldwide networking of LGBTI activists and provides them with necessary information, such as:

- Information from specialized institutions of OSCE countries.
- Pages with information on country initiatives, legislation, and specialized entities, and statistics pages with information on key topics.
- Country reports and annual reports from government organizations.

A TANDIS country report of this type is the annual report on Hate Crimes in the OSCE Region.[18] In close collaboration with state authorities and civil society organizations, local LGBTI NGOs collect data on hate crimes in OSCE member countries. The definition of "hate crime" can be found on the OSCE website LEGISLATIONLINE. The definition includes the following:

> The crime must have been committed with a bias motivation. . . . "Bias motivation" means that the perpetrator chose the target of the crime on the basis of protected characteristics. . . . While legislation that specifically addresses bias-motivated crime tends to enhance the criminal justice response, it is also important to note that the occurrence of these crimes does not depend on the existence of specific legislation.[19]

For an act to qualify as a hate crime, it need not be proven that "hate" was the motive. Instead, it must be established that the crime has been committed and that the motive was a type of bias. For an act to be recorded in the annual report as a "hate-motivated incident," it need only be shown that there was a "manifestation of intolerance," because this is an early sign of "escalating patterns of violence."

So this is no longer about objectively ascertainable crimes that any person is protected from by generally applicable law—it is legal prosecution of *motives for manifesting intolerance*. They are reported to state authorities by the affected person himself, and appear in the OSCE annual report without examination.

For the 2009 report, nineteen countries provided information. The number of reported cases varies. Portugal reported one; German, 164;

18. "Tolerance and Non-Discrimination Information System," TANDIS, http://tandis.odihr.pl/?p=about (accessed January 10, 2015).

19. "Hate Crimes in the OSCE Region: Incidents and Responses: Annual Report for 2009," OSCE, last modified November 2010, http://www.osce.org/odihr/73636 (accessed December 28, 2014).

Sweden, 1,060; and the United Kingdom, 4,805. How can it be explained that a country like the United Kingdom, which pursues a radical anti-discrimination policy, has far more hate crimes to report?

How are we to evaluate the warnings of Vladimir Bukowsky, who has had long exposure to totalitarianism? He is by far not the only one to complain of an "incurable lack of democracy," especially in relation to management of the European financial crisis. Here we are dealing only with the efforts of the European Union to deconstruct marriage and the family and enforce the new gender ideology. The EU puts all its institutional, financial and cultural strength behind this objective.

It is probable that many countries mainly seek entry to the EU for economic reasons. These countries may not be aware that the possible economic advantages come at the price of forced overthrow of their values and morals. In a resolution of May 21, 2013, the EU Parliament makes it quite clear what the EU expects of those states that want to become EU members, i.e. Croatia, Serbia, Macedonia, Albania, Bosnia-Herzegovina, Kosovo, and Montenegro. They are to adopt gender mainstreaming measures, such as:

• To fight against gender stereotypes and all forms of discrimination.
• To raise the participation of women in politics and employment through quotas.
• To implement gender equality measures and especially gender mainstreaming policies concerning non-discrimination as regards sexual orientation and gender identity.
• To address lingering homophobia and transphobia in law, policy, and practice, by legislating on hate crimes, police training, and anti-discrimination legislation.
• To adopt legislation and policies that ensure universal access to reproductive health services and promote reproductive rights.[20]

With the EU's debt crisis, even the economic advantages have become uncertain. It may be that the effects of both processes—deregulation of the finance markets and deregulation of sexual norms—will reinforce each other and destabilize the political structure in Europe.

---

20. "Hate Crimes," Legislation Online, http://www.legislationline.org/topics/topic/4 (accessed December 28, 2014).

7

Case Studies
of the Gender Revolution

You can free things from alien or accidental laws, but not from the laws
of their own nature. You may, if you like, free a tiger from his bars; but
do not free him from his stripes. Do not free a camel of the burden of his
hump: you may be freeing him from being a camel. Do not go about as a
demagogue, encouraging triangles to break out of the prison of their
three sides. If a triangle breaks out of its three sides, its life comes to a
lamentable end.

G. K. Chesterton, *Orthodoxy*[1]

The Gender Package

GENDER MAINSTREAMING is a high-priority goal at every level of
politics. At the same time, there is barely a citizen who can make head
or tail of the term—a strange situation in democratic societies.

At first, it seems like it is using "the politics of equality" to eliminate
discrimination against women that allegedly still exists. Over the past 15
years, equal opportunity officers have been deployed at all levels of society. Their task is to move the gender relationship between men and
women to the advantage of women, abolish "stereotypes" and "sexist"
roles of men and women, and to fight for "empowerment" of women
through quota regulations. As has already happened in France, quotas
are to be set for women's participation on corporate boards. This is justified by enforcement of "substantive equality" of men and women.

But gender mainstreaming is about much more than equality of men
and women. It involves manufacturing equality through *"deconstruc-*

---

1. Gilbert Keith Chesterton, *Orthodoxy* (1908; reprt., New York: John Lane Company, 1921), 86.

tion" of *the binary hierarchical gender order* to arrive at *a diversity of genders with equal value and equal rights*.[2]

The gender package includes

- full equality (equivalence) of men and women.
- deconstruction of male and female sexual identity.
- the battle against heterosexual normativity, which means to provide full legal and social equality—or, in fact, privilege—to all non-heterosexual ways of life.
- abortion as a "human right," packaged as *reproductive rights.*
- sexualization of children and teenagers through sex education as a mandatory subject.
- material deprivation and impoverishment of the family.

Policy and a large number of special interest groups are lined up on many fronts, but they work together. You will seldom hear an equal opportunity officer limit "rights" to abortion or the LGBTI movement.[3]

Political Implementation of Gender Mainstreaming

The revolution began at the very top and has now reached down to the microstructure of society. Here are the most important stages of gender mainstreaming/LGBT implementation in Germany:

1985	Third UN World Conference on Women in Nairobi: Gender mainstreaming is introduced as a political strategy.
1994	Sweden: Gender mainstreaming is introduced at all levels of policy.
1995	Fourth UN World Conference on Women in Beijing: The term "gender mainstreaming" is enforced and chosen as a guiding principle of the UN. The *Beijing Platform for Action* is signed by 189 states. It declares *gender justice* a constituent element of democracy and obligates all countries to implement a state policy on women's equality and gender.
1996	Norway makes gender mainstreaming a cross-departmental task for all government ministers.

---

2. Das Gender-Manifest, ed. by Genderbüro Berlin (www.gender.de) and Gender-Forum Berlin (www.genderforum-berlin.de). http://www.Gender-Mainstreaming.org/manifest (accessed October 6, 2015).

3. Das Gender-Manifest.

1998	The European Commission publishes its first gender mainstreaming progress report.
1999	Gender mainstreaming is embedded into EU employment guidelines.
1999	The Amsterdam Treaty comes into force. Articles 2 and 3 of the European Community Treaty obligate member states to implement an active equality and non-discrimination policy.
1999	A decision of the German cabinet declares gender mainstreaming a "guiding principle and cross-cutting political issue." [a]
2003	The "Gender Competence Center" (GCC) opens at Humboldt University in Berlin to support "gender mainstreaming in all political arenas, initiating research, assembling knowledge and educating experts."
2007	The project "Gender Aspects in Advanced Education" (*Gender-Aspekte in der Fortbildung*) is to integrate gender mainstreaming into Germany's higher education system. The strategy of "gender budgeting" is adopted.
2010–2013	"Action Plans against Homophobia" become part of national policy.
2013–2014	In federal states with a left wing/green government, public education at all age levels and in all subjects is geared toward teaching acceptance of LGBTI lifestyles.

a. After the German federal government's cabinet decision made gender mainstreaming the "guiding principle" of politics, corresponding laws were quickly passed in the German federal states.

The Gender Manifesto

The Gender Manifesto issued by a network of academic gender activists—all of them women—in Germany shows how quickly the delusion of allegedly non-existent male/female gender identity gained entry to social policy. Published in 2006, the Gender Manifesto deals with "quality development in Gender Training and Consultancy." To the amazement of the manifesto's authors, this had reached a scale that "was unthinkable in the mid-90s." "Advisors, trainers and coaches now make a living training and advising institutions of all types in gender issues."

In so doing, they ran into the "gender paradox," which, according to Judith Butler, was only a transitional stage on the path to full abolishment of binary gender identity: that gender mainstreaming is still being sold in policy as "equality" of men and women. This general understanding of gender mainstreaming is maintained because it can count on public acceptance. In 150 years of the battle for women's emancipation, we have become accustomed to thinking of men as perpetrators, and women as victims who need the state's help to achieve equality. This opens up the financial spigots, but at the price of "affirming gender duality," which gender ideology is intended to destroy. In the Gender Manifesto, "the prevailing gender order, which for instance associates a body defined as female with certain personal attributes and behavior patterns classified as feminine and with a necessary focus on men as regards desire" undergoes a "fundamental critique." "This critique is based on the observation of numerous social genders and of different ways of desire. This has also shown that 'sex' is also a by-product of socio-cultural construction." Thus, as Butler's eager disciples say, a body is not feminine; this is just a "socio-cultural construction." Personal characteristics and behaviors cannot be derived from it, not even desire for the opposite sex. There aren't just two, but many genders.[4] This is how the paradox is resolved in practice: under the pretext of equality and justice, even more *equivalency* is manufactured between men and women until the genders are no longer distinguishable.

The signers of the Gender Manifesto don't hide their objectives; their motto is "using gender to undo gender." It is about "overcoming the unequal social gender order" through its "deconstruction." They stand against "common theoretical assumptions as well as fundamentalist religious or socio-biological determinist approaches" that hold to "pre-discursive factors such as the will of God or genetic determination." The signers describe this perfect freedom in this way: "A diversity of genders of equal value, designed individually and renegotiated based on companionship and solidarity. . . . Where gender duality was, there shall diversity of genders be."

In plain language: anyone who thinks there is a divine purpose for man and woman is a religious fundamentalist. Whoever finds it significant that a body's cells are defined as genetically male or female, or that

---

4. On indissoluble gender differences, see Louann Brizendine, *The Female Brain* (New York: Morgan Road Books, 2007); Lise Eliot, *Pink Brain, Blue Brain: How Small Differences Grow into Troublesome Gaps—And What We Can Do About It* (New York: Houghton Mifflin Harcourt, 2009); and Susan Pinker, *The Sexual Paradox: Men, Women and the Real Gender Gap* (Scribner: New York, 2008).

men's and women's brains show considerable differences, is a biological, sexist fundamentalist and therefore a dangerous enemy of freedom, because he opposes loosening "the ties, relations and attachments of the bipolar hierarchical gender order."

The German Ethics Council and the "Third Gender"

One important stage victory was the German Ethics Council's 2012 statement on intersexuality. The process is a prime example of collaboration among international networks for enforcing the global cultural revolution. This method is used by UN sub-organizations internationally.

The UN Committee on the Elimination of Discrimination Against Women (CEDAW) demands reports from member states' governments on topics that CEDAW chooses for publication in its country reports. In 2010, CEDAW was interested in how UN member states dealt with intersexual and transsexual people.[5] CEDAW sent the German federal government a request to "enter into dialog with nongovernmental organizations of intersexual and transsexual people to reach a better understanding of their concerns and to take effective measures for protecting their human rights" and "to submit a written report of the measures implemented." The federal government met this request by asking the German Ethics Council to issue a statement.[6]

The Ethics Council spent two years questioning 200 affected individuals and 30 scientists, and presented its statement on intersexuality on February 23, 2012. It came to the following conclusions:

1. To avoid "a negative attribution in the sense of an illness or disorder" and to leave it open as to "whether there is a third gender," the Ethics Council uses the term "differences of sex development" (DSD).
2. The Ethics Council considers it an "unjustifiable intervention into the right to privacy and the right to equal treatment" if people with DSD were forced to be assigned the category "male" or "female" in the birth register. Therefore, a category "other" should be introduced. However, until a maximum age, to be determined, no entry at all should be made, and the entry would be changeable at any time.
3. People with a gender of "other," the Ethics Council majority believes, should have the right to a registered civil union, which had

---

5. Transexuality is a mental disorder involving gender identity when biological gender is unambiguous. It is listed in the official diagnosis list as a mental illness (ICD-10). Intersexuality designates people with ambiguous biological gender characteristics, previously called hermaphroditism.

6. Letter of federal minister Annette Schavan to president of Deutsche Ethikrat, Prof. Dr. Edzard Schmidt-Jortzig, of December 20, 2010. The author has a copy of the letter.

previously been possible only for same-sex partners. "Moreover, some members of the Ethics Council recommend opening the possibility of marriage."

4. The last sentence of the statement reads: "It should be considered whether a gender entry in the birth register is even necessary."[7]

Thus the German Ethics Council constructed a "third gender" to suit the requirements of about 8,000 people whose biological gender characteristics are ambiguous.[8] If the federal government follows the recommendation, future forms will provide the option to choose "male," "female," and "other," which could cause irritation to Germany's other 80,000,000 people—even to the point of making heterosexual gender identity ambiguous and uncertain, which is what the gender activists are aiming at.

One tool for deconstruction is situational ethics: extreme cases that tug at people's heartstrings are turned into guidelines for fundamental decisions that overturn the whole society's value system. Life is certainly difficult for a person and his parents when there is a biological gender anomaly and the person does not know whether he is a man or a woman. It is right to search for a reasonable way to ease this person's life situation. But why infringe on the male-female gender order, on which society is based, just to create the appearance of improving things for 0.01 percent of the population and to fulfill the wishes of all the organized minorities who are using this group for their own purposes? If it is the unfortunate fate of a few thousand people to have no clear gender identity, why demand total deconstruction of male and female identity as a remedy? If there is a "third gender" to which "gender justice" forbids denial of marriage or demands "the right to a child," then the entire "queer" diversity of genders will claim these rights for themselves.

CEDAW scores a goal! The triumphant team consists of CEDAW, the German federal government, the Ethics Council and the activist NGOs.

Whoever believes there is a limit to the overthrow of moral values should note the latest decision of the Deutscher Ethikrat (German Ethics Council). On September 24, 2014, the council decided that the law that criminalizes incest should be repealed, and consensual incest, relationships between siblings from age 14 and over, should be allowed, if the siblings live away from their family.

7. Deutscher Ethikrat, *Stellungnahme Intersexualität,* February 23, 2012, 178, http://www.ethikrat.org/dateien/pdf/stellungnahme-intersexualitaet.pdf (accessed October 6, 2015).

8. This is the German government's estimate. The special interest organizations speak of much higher numbers.

Society Gets Gendered

Wherever you look—politics, the media, universities, foundations, the courts, business, schools, daycare—gender mainstreaming is the path to postmodern progress. It is the ruling ideology that no one can oppose without being shunned and defamed. No one dares subject gender ideology to "stress testing": to determine its consequences and fitness for the future. Instead, every law is examined for "gender budgeting," as to whether it contributes to mainstreaming gender ideology. A paper from the Berlin senate states that "Introduction is done top-down, i.e. the political head of an organization commits to the introduction of gender mainstreaming and decides how the processes can be guided and evaluated."[9] In less than two decades, gender mainstreaming has become the ruling ideology to which allegiance must be paid. Whoever asks questions is silenced with accusations of "discrimination." If you go along with it, you get to the top. It is rewarded with money, a career, power and a tailwind from the media.

Alignment of politics with the LGBTI agenda was stated in a rather subdued manner at the turn of the millennium and concealed behind the terms *equality, equity* and *freedom of choice*. A decade and a half later, it is being openly implemented in the socio-political strategies of government coalitions in Europe. An example is the coalition contract between the governing Social Democrat and Green parties in 2010 in North Rhine-Westphalia. It states:

> We are for a tolerant Nordrhein-Westfalen—lesbians, gays, bisexuals and transgender people are born equal in dignity and rights. . . . Eliminating discrimination will be a comprehensive task for the new state government. Complete equality of marriage and registered domestic partnerships will be implemented immediately. At the federal level, we will work for the for full equality for domestic partnerships, particularly in tax and adoption rights, for opening up marriage and for insertion of the characteristic sexual identity into Article 3 of the German constitution. We will set up an action plan against homophobia for lesbians, gays, bisexuals and the transgendered. We will finance lesbian and gay elder care and youth employment.[10]

The German constitution prescribes that marriage and family are under the special protection of the state. Yet here, marriage and family

---

9. Quoted by Günter Bertram, "Gender-Mainstreaming, das unbekannte Wesen," *MHR Mitteilungen des Hamburgischen Richtervereins,* Nr. 1/2011, March 15, 2011.

10. http://www.nrwspd.de/db/docs/doc_30009_201252317330.pdf (accessed October 6, 2015).

are not even mentioned. Instead, Article 3.3 of the constitution is to be extended with the term "sexual orientation" as an anti-discrimination criterion. If that succeeds, courts may be forced to take all further steps for overturning sexual norms—at the cost of parents' rights to rear their own children, civil liberties, religious freedom, and the basic democratic order.

Turning Science into Ideology

What "Dialectical Materialism" once was to universities under Communist dictatorships, gender ideology is today to Western universities, where the next generation of academics is being prepared to take leading positions in society.

Dr. Michael Bock, professor of criminology at the University of Mainz, was formally reprimanded by his employer in February 2007 for a critical article on gender mainstreaming and feminism. He was threatened with disciplinary and criminal consequences if it was ever published. What he wasn't allowed to say was this:

> Gender mainstreaming differs from traditional feminist politics in that the gender aspect is to penetrate all policies in all individual actions. . . . The claim to put a society "on track" in this way through a comprehensive, uniform formal principle of politics is known to us from the totalitarian regimes of the 20th century. It involves bringing not only the entire apparatus of state, but also associations, organizations and other social groups effectively on board with the policy of renewal. The total will to subordinate the entire social reality to a uniform principle or to penetrate it with this principle is the reason these regimes are called "totalitarian." It indicates the extreme opposite of a liberal concept of the state, according to which people can unfold freely in their social existence up to the limits by which the state guarantees the freedom of other individuals.[11]

At colleges and universities, the field of *gender studies* is firmly established. In 2014, there were more than 200 chairs for gender/queer studies, nearly all held by women, and around thirty interdisciplinary gender institutes. It is a booming job market and "probably the only discipline of the humanities that enjoys uninterrupted job growth. However, gender research and gender studies are not just going on in academic institutions specially established for the purpose. They are

---

11. Michael Bock, *Gender-Mainstreaming als totalitäre Steigerung der Frauenpolitik,* Kellmann-Stiftung.

firmly established in humanities chairs, especially in sociology, political science, history and literature, and are expanding far beyond disciplinary boundaries."[12]

All types of sexual practices are researched at universities by those who practice them, and they are implemented in strategic concepts for changing society. "Many gender researchers and especially queer researchers make it no secret that the subject of their research reflects their sexual interests. Thus, queer researchers deal 'scientifically' with themselves, which means with their scene as defined by sexual identities and practices."[13]

Gender Studies, Women's and Gender Research, Trans-Disciplinary Gender Studies, and *Queer Studies* are the signs on doors at the university centers for training academic gender activists. What the Frankfurt School established as a program—using science as a tool for subverting the existing social order—has now become the normal state of affairs. Science's ideal of truth and objectivity is given up, and the claim to being scientific is misused to force society's acceptance of all types of "queer" sexual practices. This is financed by a gush of money taken from taxpayers who still don't know what the word *gender* is being used to mean.

Gender Conferences

In late October 2010, Germany's Federal Agency for Civic Education (Bundeszentrale für politische Bildung, or BpB) held its third gender conference, on the topic "The Flexible Gender: Gender, Happiness and Crisis Times in the Global Economy." The BpB is a government institution originally founded to teach Germans to be good citizens of a democracy. Its publications land on legislators' desks, in higher educational institutions and in schools.

In this first lecture, BpB president Thomas Krüger campaigned for protection from discrimination against so-called "neo-genders": "bisexuals, fetishists, BDSM practitioners, the bi-gendered, transvestites, the transgendered, the trans-identified, e-sexuals, intersexuals, polyamorists, asexuals, objectophiles and the agendered."

In July 2009, the tax-financed Heinrich Böll Foundation held a one-week conference entitled "Gender Is Happening." Henning von Bargen, head of the foundation, explained the program: "Porn will be on the table this week—or at least the question of how it can exist without fall-

---

12. Ferdinand Kraus, "Feministinnen erforschen sich selbst," *Handelsblatt*, September 19, 2007.
13. Ibid.

ing into the trap of customary gender representations. Professional politicians will discuss how they would like to rewrite the German constitution and what leeway the current legislative situation grants or denies to queer lifestyles."[14]

Politicians, professors and representatives of LGBTI NGOs spoke for a week on topics like these:

- From the Constitution to a Gender-Justice Constitution
- Queer Lifestyles: Does the law reflect the needs of the social movements, or does it torpedo them...?
- Language Discrimination and Privilege
- From Hardcore Porn to Post-Pornography
- Toward an interconnection of sex work and drug use, a field of work that society still stigmatizes
- Toy, toy, toy: Sex toys and their history
- Gender is not binary. "In this workshop, participants can have fun learning and trying all possible gender representations.... Gender is not an inner truth, but something that drives us to madness, and that we must drive to madness, so that we can be senselessly happy. Because: Every gender is *drag*."

Justice Gets Gendered

In 2007, the Austrian federal justice ministry held training for judges (the female form of the noun was used for both sexes) on the topic of "Justice and Human Rights." The gathering was star-studded, with well-known judges, politicians, attorneys, professors, and media figures in attendance. Since many of the speakers, including jurist and homosexual activist Helmut Graupner,[15] were internationally active, the strategies discussed included those used in other countries also. The consensus at the conference was that the legal system must be "gendered" using the human rights as a tool, that is, adapt it to the diversity of sexual lifestyles.

In his keynote speech, Graupner called for lowering the minimum age for homosexual consent to 14, for protection of pornography under the laws on freedom of information and communication (European Convention on Human Rights, Art. 10), and making same-sex partnerships equivalent to civil marriage. For him, anything else is "sexual

---

14. Heinrich Böll Stiftung, Gunda Werner Institut, Gender is Happening, Conference, Berlin, July 6–11, 2009, http://www.gender-happening.de. (Program of 2009 no longer available on the internet.)

15. Dr. Helmut Graupner, born 1965, is a lawyer in Vienna and a European activist for the rights of homosexual, bisexual, and transgender women and men.

apartheid." In Art. 9 of the European Charter of Fundamental Rights, man and woman were eliminated as the subject of marriage, and the same was to be done in the constitutions of European Union member states. "This would give us a carbon copy at all levels of government, because federal legislators have the authority to determine marriage law."[16] Thomas Hammarberg of Sweden was also invited for the edification of the judges and attorneys. Since 2006, he had been the Council of Europe's Human Rights Commissioner and was previously the general secretary of Amnesty International. He spoke of "the key role of the judiciary in the system of protecting human rights." Hammarberg fights for the "human right" of transgender people to freely choose the "gender of their choice." For this, he deconstructs the concept of gender identity: "The concept of 'gender identity' opens the possibility of understanding that the gender assigned to an infant at birth must not necessarily correspond to the *innate* gender identity that the grown child develops."[17] Thus, Hammarberg states that the gender "assigned" at birth is not inborn, but the gender the grownup "develops" is inborn. The two don't have to coincide. Because people who live with this dilemma must have justice, the Council of Europe human rights commissioner calls for "rapid, transparent procedures for changing the name in personal documents" (surgical or hormonal transformation is not to be a prerequisite), state health insurance coverage of the cost of elective therapy and surgery, and the right to continue marriage after "sex change," because this allegedly serves the well-being of children. Hate crimes laws are to be passed and the Yogyakarta Principles imposed.

This Austrian ministry of justice trains judges, attorneys, and politicians to enforce this agenda. This is the ideological *input* that the public doesn't know about when they are surprised by the *output* in the form of laws and court decisions that strive to abolish society's order based on two genders.

Gender Mainstreaming in K through 12 [18]

Since 2001, "Girls' Days" have been held on the initiative of the German Federal Ministry for the Family. Participation increased from 1,800 girls in 2001 to 123,000 in 2010. The goal is to overcome "gender stereotypes"

---

16. *Schriftenreihe des Bundesministeriums für Justiz*, vol. 134 (Wien-Graz: Neuer Wissenschaftlicher Verlag, 2007).

17. Thomas Hammarberg, "Human Rights and Gender Identity" (speech, Strasbourg, France, July 29, 2009), https://wcd.coe.int/ViewDoc.jsp?id=1476365 (accessed October 6, 2015).

18. For more, see Ch. 12.

in the choice of educational programs and to steer girls into technical professions. The Federal Minister for Families from 2009 to 2013, Kristina Schröder, came up with the obvious idea to also introduce a "Boys' Day" for steering boys into social and communicative professions that women previously preferred, such as daycare, teaching kindergarten or elementary school, and eldercare.

Germany's nationwide center for coordinating Girls' and Boys' Days is the Competency Center for Technology, Diversity and Equal Opportunity in Bielefeld.[19] For the Center, it is clear that "the traditional role models of the man as 'sole breadwinner' and the woman as housewife and mother increasingly seldom reflect reality." Because these "traditional gender roles" are doggedly ingrained, girls and boys must be provided with "gender-sensitive choices" for life planning without "neglecting the diversity within gender groups." Thus political measures for social engineering are used to create new social realities; propagation of the radical agenda is then justified by adjusting to these newly created "realities."

At first sight, Girls' and Boys' Days are associated only with dissolution of "stereotypical gender roles" to bring about "substantive equality" between men and women. The sexual components are not immediately visible. However, the Federal Family Ministry's project is in the hands of a competency center for "diversity," which means LGBTIQ diversity within gender groups.

Like the Girls' and Boys' Days, the Gender and School[20] project was initiated and financed by the education ministry of the north German state of Lower Saxony. Under the menu item "Gender in teaching/practice" specific teaching instructions can be found, such as the suggestion that a nylon stocking on a boy's leg brings life to coeducation and that girls and boys are to "be given the chance to develop their individual repertoire of behaviors through the diversity of their inherent potentials." Furthermore, gender pedagogy is to "free" children from "stereotypical assigned gender." The example of a "gender-sensitive" preschool to remedy people's fixation on binary gender roles comes from Vienna. It is called *Fun and Care*. The website presents it in this way:

> From birth on, children learn to comply with their gender roles. We therefore strive to observe in boys and girls the extent to which they have already been socialized into society's expected roles. We con-

19. www.http://www.kompetenzz.de; www.neue-wege-fuer-jungs.de.

20. Niedersächsisches Kultusministerium (Federal Ministry for Education of Lower Saxony), *gender und schule,* http://www.genderundschule.de/index.cfm?8D8DEC7F9327 CFB39927478A08B94D03 (accessed October 6, 2015).

sciously want to broaden the girls' and boys' scope of action and thereby create truly equal opportunity (in regard to capabilities and skills, choice of profession, partnership, child-rearing, etc.). If children do not collect gender-atypical knowledge early, when they grow up it is often difficult for them to find alternatives to a given role, even if they want to.[21]

How does this work in practice? Little girls are guided to play soccer (not traditionally a girls' sport in Europe), to assert themselves physically, to shout and to box. They are especially supported in the areas of technology, wood and metal shop, and computers.

On the other hand, boys learn massage and personal hygiene (cosmetics) to acquire a positive perception of the body, to be careful and nurturing toward others, to practice losing, and to enjoy slipping into feminine roles, such as dressing like a princess or polishing their nails. They are to be encouraged to be good fathers in playing with dolls and good househusbands in domestic activities.

However, this targeted ambiguity of children's gender identity is no liberation, but an ideological abuse of dependent children. People come into the world as girls and boys through the merging of a woman's egg cell and a man's sperm cell. Because children are not shaped only by their genes, but also by what they see, experience and imitate, through "triangulation" with mother and father, each child develops an identity as a man or woman and identifies with his or her biological gender. This gives them their identity, a permanent feeling of what they are. To lack a clear sense of whether one is male or female is a sign of a mental disorder.

What was once a joke has become a reality. The joke goes like this: A married couple has a baby. Grandma calls, very excited, and asks, "Which is it?" The father answers, "We'll let the child decide that." In May 2011, a report came through the media that a Canadian couple actually did this. The father, David Stocker, and the mother, Kathy Witterick, told no one the sex of their child, whom they named *Storm*.[22] After the child was born, the couple sent an e-mail to friends and relatives, saying: "We've decided not to share Storm's sex for now—a tribute to freedom and choice in place of limitation, a stand up to what the world could become in Storm's lifetime." They seem to have set a precedent.

---

21. http://www.funandcare.at (accessed October 6, 2015).

22. http://www.thestar.com/life/parent/2011/05/21/parents_keep_childs_gender_se cret.html (accessed October 3, 2015).

Gender Mainstreaming and Political Parties

These are highlights of the gender revolution that is consummated in a strange fog of concealment and ubiquity. Because it is a global strategy, news comes every day from every country and continent reporting of new breakthroughs and dam bursts.

If policy were still focused on the general welfare and not on enforcing the interests of a tiny minority at the expense of the majority, the state would have to call up a national action plan for the family in which men and women are prepared for parenthood and children can grow into healthy, capable adults. Without a doubt, society can live and survive without homosexual couples and partnerships. But it will cease to develop successfully if men and women do not open their lives to children and accept responsibility for them for a lifetime. The political strategies that touch the very core of the living conditions of citizens and future generations are not openly discussed, whether in the legislature or in the media. Voters in Europe should know that when they vote for a leftist, green, or liberal party, they're voting for the gender agenda, which is tolerated by the Christian parties.

8

Political Rape of Language

The reality of the word in eminent ways makes existential interaction happen. And so, if the word becomes corrupted, human existence itself will not remain unaffected and untainted.

Josef Pieper[1]

These new words do not designate actual things, in any case, not things that exist, but they name non-existent things with words that are not true but are meant to be effective.

Helmut Kuhn[2]

The Corruption of Words

ONE'S PERCEPTION and understanding of the world happens through language. Adam's special position among all creatures is shown by his giving names to all the animals. But, even while doing that, he still had no one he could talk to. For this reason, God placed a woman by his side, whom he greeted with joy: "This one, at last, is bone of my bones and flesh of my flesh" (Gen. 2:23).

Normally, we learn language from our mothers, whose intonation is already familiar to us in the womb before we are even born. Later, she repeats words again and again until we understand that this sound means that object, and until we can form the sounds ourselves. We soon learn to give names to feelings, and still later to abstract ideas and perceptions. What a miracle!

Language exists to express something about reality and to communicate it to others. We have not made the reality nor the linguistic vessels

---

1. Josef Pieper, *Abuse of Language: Abuse of Power* (San Francisco: Ignatius Press, 1992), 15.
2. Helmut Kuhn, "Despotie der Wörter: Wie man mit der Sprache die Freiheit überwältigen kann," in *Sprache und Herrschaft*, ed. Gerd-Klaus Kaltenbrunner (München: Herder, 1975), 12.

to hold it in. Does the speaker strive to bring both into accord, so that the vessel contains the truth? Or does the speaker deliberately use language to represent reality differently than it is? The latter of the two is called lying.

And manipulation can be a refined form of lying. Let's say someone wants another person to change his thinking and behavior *without even noticing it.* Terms are turned into false labels that misrepresent the contents of the package. When political rulers do this, we call it propaganda. *Pravda,* a newspaper whose title means "truth," was the official mouthpiece of the Communist dictators of the Soviet Union. An even subtler form of manipulation is to alter the grammatical structure of the language in order to change society. Feminists and gender activists have made this method their own.

Poets do something much different: they use language's existing vessels in such a way that they become transparent and allow a new perception of reality. They reverently take these vessels in hand and place them in a new location, in new surroundings, coax out their sound and rhythm, and give us a look behind the backdrop of the stage of life. The poet's expressive force does no violence to the language, but gives words the full power of reality.

Every political regime develops its own language; it turns words against reality to make people submit. A system of false, corrupted words is called an ideology. It is a system of thought that serves the interests of a minority. It hides behind a fog of an era's "values" to gain acceptance. Everyone wants to look good, and when one's plans benefit only himself and do damage to others, he hides them behind highly popular words and values: a wolf in sheep's clothing. The sheep that run with the herd either never notice it, or don't see it until the wolf's wicked jaws are making a meal of them. Friedrich Hegel, who, along with Plato, exposed sophistic word-contortionists, said: "You need not have advanced very far in your learning in order to find good reasons even for the most evil of things. All the evil deeds in this world since Adam and Eve have been justified with good reasons"[3]—and the help of lovely words.

Because reality always changes, so does language. But it evolves slowly, according to mysterious laws. "The ear for speech is conservative. It doesn't like what it's not used to," writes Dieter E. Zimmer in his amusing book *On Trends and Madness in the New German Usage.*[4] Zimmer

---

3. Quoted in Pieper, *Abuse of Language,* 8–9.
4. Dieter E. Zimmer, *Über Trends und Tollheiten im neudeutschen Sprachgebrauch* (Zürich: Haffmans Verlag, 1986), 9.

discusses "movements and madnesses" that come about in the widest imaginable variety of ways—through contact with other cultures, immigration, new technical means of communication, and changes in values and attitudes.

The last item in that list is what interests us here. Terms are thrown out, emptied of meaning, perverted, outlawed, forbidden, and arbitrarily invented. As Josef Pieper has said, words become corrupted when they are used as instruments of power. "Whoever [in speaking to another person] is not committed to the truth—such a person, from that moment on, no longer considers the other as a partner, as equal. In fact, he no longer respects the other as a human person. . . . [The other person] becomes an object to be manipulated, possibly dominated."[5] "Perversion of the relationship to reality" and "perversion of communicative character" make the word unsuitable for dialog. In this process, four qualities can be distinguished:

- Terms that express traditional values are made suspicious and discarded. Example: Chastity.
- Terms with positive connotations are given new content and then exploited. Example: Diversity.
- New terms are invented for transmitting new ideologies. Example: Polyamory.
- New terms are introduced to smear opponents. Example: Homophobia.

The mudslide affecting all sexual norms over just a half century—from the pinnacle of esteem for monogamy to the depths of "sexual diversity"—can't help but affect the language. Words that express a society's values carry an emotional charge, whether of approval or rejection, esteem or contempt. This emotional charge contributes to social stability. If these values change, the terms take on what the French call a *haut goût*, that is, a slight taint of decay, a gamey taste that was once popular but is no longer desirable. They ultimately become stigmatized or even completely taboo. Terms that describe the world from a Christian view now have a *haut goût*, even for Christians, and are being scrapped. This goes both for terms that describe a positive reality and for those describing a negative one:

Truth, virtue, morality, tradition, virginity, chastity, purity.
The devil, sin, vice, fornication, perversion.

---

5. Pieper, *Abuse of Language*, 21.

These terms oriented people with regard to right and wrong and were taught through one's upbringing. Those who use them now arouse suspicion. Who still says that children must be raised to be virtuous (by adults who practice virtue!), that a person requires moral discernment to strive toward virtue, or that virtue is even worth striving for? That virginity is a precious wedding gift, that chastity is respect for a person's dignity, that chastity gives one a radiant beauty? That evil is an active force, that sin separates one from God, that one vice opens the door to the next, that self-education is necessary for cultivating the sex drive, or that there are behaviors that pervert what is natural?

Key Terms Affected by Ideology[6]

Important terms whose content philosophers have disputed since time immemorial—and whose fulfillment in society is a measure of its humanity—are transformed into false labels promoting ideologically based social change.

Values

Many get on their soapbox complaining about the loss of "values." But which values? A value is something good. If there is something good, there must also be something evil. If not, the term "value" is just a hollow shell. When the term is not qualified further, it assumes there is societal consensus about what is good and what is evil. If that were so, we would have a common foundation of values. This sort of consensus largely depends on how we understand man, what he is, and what place he occupies in the order of the world. The guiding concept of gender mainstreaming—absolute individual freedom with no bounds or obligations—makes such a consensus increasingly impossible. There are still people who consider it necessary to distinguish between good and evil. They feel that a society without such a consensus will crumble, but for them there is a new swear word: "fundamentalist!"

Freedom

Gender mainstreaming, and the new "gender person" who is to be created by it, cannot be understood unless the concept of freedom behind it is clarified. Today we commonly understand freedom as: "I can do what I want." When freedom is reduced to personal whim, it is cut loose from the truth. However, recognition of the truth is necessary to choose the

---

6. Cf. Joseph Ratzinger, *Values in a Time of Upheaval* (New York: Crossroads Publishing, 2006).

good. A concept of freedom reduced to subjective whim also releases one from responsibility for the consequences of one's own decisions and actions. However, cutting freedom loose from truth and responsibility does not lead to more freedom but to less, because it can be achieved only at the expense of others. Man becomes a wolf to man, to paraphrase Thomas Hobbes.[7] This is true not only for the community, but also for man's inner freedom. If he does not orient his freedom toward comprehensible nature—that is, to truth—he will be controlled by his desires. Not to accept that people were born man or woman in a preexisting reality is not freedom, but a denial of the obvious truth regarding humanity.

Tolerance

One powerful plea for tolerance is Voltaire's *Treatise on Tolerance*. Voltaire wrote the following sentence to René Descartes: "I do not agree with what you have to say, but I'll defend to the death your right to say it." Tolerance means to put up with something, even if I disagree with it. It does not mean to call everything good or to make no distinction between good and evil. While the Enlightenment philosophers used the term "tolerance" to defend freedom of religion and conscience against absolutist rulers, the same term is used today to try to bury freedom of religion and conscience. Now the mere assertion that truth exists is considered "intolerant"—regardless of whether one uses love or violence to gain recognition for one's conviction. Jesus Christ himself imparted the most radical principle of tolerance to his disciples: *Love your enemies.* The current concept of tolerance has strayed very far from that. It is no longer about truth and the conviction that it is not to be forced, and that falsehood must be tolerated. It is about eradication of truth.[8] Over two centuries after Voltaire, tolerance has become the battle cry of relativism.

Justice

The question of justice and the equitable state has occupied philosophers and theologians ever since the time of Plato and Aristotle. Justice is one of the four cardinal virtues. The cry of the disenfranchised has resounded through all epochs. It is always about a *balance of interests* in the social fabric of individuals and institutions through rights and obligations, give and take. The universally valid legal principle is: *Treat same*

7. 17th-century English philosopher.
8. Cf. Gabriele Kuby, "Sind Märtyrer intolerant?" in *Kein Friede ohne Umkehr: Wortmeldungen einer Konvertitin* (Laudes Verlag, Eggstätt, 2002). Available through femedienverlag, Kisslegg.

as same and different as different, and everything to each accordingly; or in Latin: *Suum cuique*, to each his own. This principle is constantly threatened by exertion of power by the powerful who do not submit themselves to the law, but submit the law to their own whim.

Radical feminists and LGBTI activists demand *gender equality*. They claim that justice means the state forcing "substantive equality" between men and women according to the ideal of "Women in the boardroom, men in the kitchen, and children in the crib." They claim that justice means each person having a free "choice" of his gender and "sexual identity." They claim that justice means the "right" of lesbians, homosexuals, and the transgendered to "marry" and produce children by using biotechnology.

This is not a just *balance* of interests, but special interest politics that aims to use state power to force the wishes of a minority at the expense of the general public. Now, what is unequal—that is, objectively different—must be treated as equal. To do otherwise would be called inequality. This means reversal of the principle of justice that our legal system is built on.

Equality

Equality is presented as the fulfillment of justice. As already stated, though, justice requires that equal things be treated as equal and unequal things as unequal, and that everything be handled fairly. This is a universal legal principle that the German constitutional court has stated as a guideline for handling the principle of equality: "The general principle of equality in Art. 3 paragraph 1 of the constitution calls for things that are substantially equal to be treated as equal, and things that are substantially unequal to be treated as unequal."[9] If unequal things are treated as the same, the result is injustice.

Thus the crucial question is what the significant characteristic is, the *tertium comparationis*, by which two objects or people are compared, so that their sameness or differentness can be determined. Are four-legged mammals and people the same, and must they be treated the same because they reproduce by the sex act? Or are they different because the animal is bound by instinct while the person has free will and reason, so that they must therefore be treated differently for justice to be done? It is crucial that a significant criterion be chosen for determining equality and inequality. What is the significant criterion for demanding equal

---

9. Bundesverfassungsgericht, Judgement of the First Senate of November 17, 1992.

treatment of heterosexual and homosexual partnerships in regard to marriage? Is marriage constituted by sexual attraction between two people, or by the ability to create offspring and thus form a family?

Discrimination

Discrimination is *the* key concept for legitimizing the battle to change the value system. The word is used to claim that it is unjust to distinguish between differing realities. The concept exploits collective guilt from historical discrimination—especially that based on race—to advance the interests of people of non-heterosexual orientation now. Are annual gay pride marches in Western capitals, homosexuals in top political positions, millions in government subsidies to lobbying groups, equal opportunity officers in every government agency, and implementation of the LGBT agenda in the educational system evidence of discrimination?

The term "discrimination" in its new incarnation is defined very vaguely. However, its usage makes one thing clear: *any* unequal treatment of heterosexuals and non-heterosexuals is classified as discrimination. Evaluative distinctions between different sexual behaviors can no longer be made, even though sexual behavior greatly affects successful development of the individual and the common good of society.

Discrimen is the Latin word for "distinction" or "difference." The person endowed with free will must distinguish between right and wrong, good and evil, to handle his freedom in such a way as to succeed in his own life and not to bring harm to his fellow human beings. For the person who knows that he is answerable to God, this distinction between good and evil is essential for his eternal salvation. If he is forbidden to make this distinction—and it is prohibited for him to pass on the criteria for doing so to the next generation—then religious freedom is *de facto* banned. Christian culture is destroyed at its roots.

To distinguish between good and evil is not to discriminate against people. Every person, regardless of his sexual orientation, is equal in dignity, and every person enjoys legal protection against libel, harassment, and exclusion.[10] Judging a person's behavior, however, is not an offense against his dignity, but makes possible coexistence, which cannot happen without moral principles.

---

10. Cf. Jakob Cornides, "Fiat aequalitas et pereat mundus? How 'Anti-Discrimination' is Undermining the Legal Order," in Gudrun Kugler (ed.), *Exiting a Dead End Road: A GPS for Christians in Public Discourse* (Wien: Kairos Publications, 2010), 157.

Diversity

Since people have legitimately become concerned about endangered species, *diversity* has been a positive term. Maintaining biodiversity is a goal worth striving for. For some years now, the term has been used excessively by the LGBT community to give legitimacy to all types of sexual practices, as if their "diversity" were desirable and essential to the common well-being of society. A positive term has been hijacked for the purpose of changing negative views of deviant sexual behavior and to eliminate "compulsory heterosexuality." This also includes eradication of the word *deviant*, because it assumes that heterosexuality within a committed relationship is the norm from which all other orientations and identities deviate. This norm is to be crushed.

Sexism

It is no small undertaking to convince people that their gender as man or woman is irrelevant to their identity. To accomplish this, such binary identity has to be associated with negative terms and made offensive. Once the derogatory terms have been established in the sensitivities of the majority, they replace discussion.

Sexism is one such feminist battle cry and is often uttered in close proximity to the word *racism*. Related forms, such as *sexist*, are derived from it. The suffix "*-ist*," as found in *racist, Islamist, Communist, classist,* and *fundamentalist*, indicates an absolutization of ideals that must be enforced, even if it takes violence to do so. At first, the term *sexism* was used to condemn a system in which men treated women as sex objects. However, it is a victory for gender mainstreaming when any observation of differing gender characteristics or their positive complementarity is stigmatized as "sexism." Differing tasks and roles between men and women are denigrated as "stereotypes" that must be eliminated by political authorities. The ideology of "socially constructed" gender differences has proven resistant to research results in biology, medicine, sociology, psychology and brain science, which are describing ever more precisely the differences between men and women and the causes of these differences.

Homophobia

The term *homophobia* is a neologism coined in the late 1960s by psychoanalyst and homosexual activist George Weinberg to make people who reject homosexuality appear mentally ill. A *phobia* is a neurotic fear that is treated therapeutically, such as fear of spiders (arachnophobia), crowds (agoraphobia), enclosed spaces (claustrophobia), the number 13 (triskaidekaphobia), etc. With the keen insight of a psychoanalyst,

Weinberg intended to show that people who feel revulsion toward homosexuality actually just fear their own homosexual inclinations. Thoughtful rejection of the homosexual lifestyle for anthropological, psychological, medical, social or religious reasons was condemned with the blanket term "homophobia" and thus classified as a neurotic fear. Needless to say, insulting or even violent forms of rejection are stigmatized in people's everyday interactions, including, of course, against people with homosexual tendencies.

In regard to homosexuals, the Catholic Church must oppose the dissolution of Christian anthropology and the sexual morality derived from it if it is to preserve its deposit of faith. The Catechism of the Catholic Church (CCC) tells believers that "They must be accepted with respect, compassion and sensitivity. Every sign of unjust discrimination in their regard should be avoided" (CCC 2358). St. Augustine's words on the issue have become a proverb: Love the sinner, hate the sin.[11]

Marriage and Family

The terms *marriage* and *family* have been stripped of their universal meaning, namely that of a permanent, publicly recognized bond between a man and a woman and their offspring. Today a "wide range of families"[12] are represented as equivalent, including patchwork families, single-parent families and "rainbow families," starting with kindergarten picture books in which a prince marries a prince. However, these are broken families, and in most cases the happy facade conceals great suffering among those affected, and long-term negative effects—especially on the children.

Parent 1 and Parent 2

In the rage to eradicate "sexist stereotypes," the *mother* is to disappear from the language. In June 2010, Swiss socialist Doris Stump, a member of the Council of Europe, submitted a petition that women in the media no longer be depicted as "passive, inferior beings; mothers[!] or sex objects"—and she is not alone in this mindset. Scotland's National Health Service demands that the designations "Mom" and "Dad" be banned from kindergarten, because they discriminate against "same-sex parents." The 192-page *Leitfaden zum geschlechtergerechten Formulieren im Deutschen* ("Guidelines for gender-neutral wording in German")

---

11. This shows a deep-seated difference between Christianity and Islam. Christians categorically reject persecution of homosexuals as it is practiced in many Muslim countries in the name of Sharia law.

12. Cf. *Yogyakarta Principles*, Principle 24.

from the Swiss Federal Chancellery[13] recommends replacing "father" and "mother with "gender-abstract" terms, such as "the parent." Hillary Clinton, US Secretary of State from 2009 to 2013, had intended to do the same thing on passport forms and other documents, using "Parent 1" and "Parent 2" instead of "Mother" and "Father." The reason: "These improvements are being made to provide a gender neutral description of a child's parents and in recognition of different types of families," according to the State Department website. After strong criticism, however, Clinton had to work out a compromise. The forms are now to read, "Mother or parent 1" and "Father or parent 2."[14]

Why should the first word that comes out of an infant's mouth be purged from the language? No person—not even a feminist—could fight for the abolition of mothers if they were not born of one. Even Parent 1, Elton John, and his partner, Parent 2, had to get a surrogate *mother* to fulfill their wish for a child. Shouldn't the person to whom every human being owes his life be honored?[15] Nevertheless, because homosexual "parents" feel discrimination when Mom and Dad are talked about, political potentates have set about "cleansing" the language.

Feminist State Incursion into the Language

In the 1970s, feminists discovered grammar as a means of changing society. At the University of Constance, Luise F. Pusch and Senta Trömel-Plötz were among the founders of "feminist linguistics." They complained: "Our language does us violence, because masculine forms have priority. This creates a worldview in which women are not present."[16]

Let's try to follow Trömel-Plötz's argument: language is an instrument for "imparting psychological violence." Psychological violence leads to physical acts of violence, such as "bombs, armies and war." If we remove violence from our language, we will prevent war. *He* who so far does not feel that *he* has been done violence must be "sensitized" to it. For example, in the sentence just stated, both sexes are addressed using masculine personal pronouns, which makes women "invisible." While

13. Swiss Federal Chancellery in collaboration with the Zürich University of Applied Sciences, Gender-Neutral Language, *Leitfaden zum geschlechtergerechten Formulieren im Deutschen*, fully revised second edition, 2009.

14. "Passport Change Will Be Inclusive," *Washington Post*, January 9, 2011.

15. For a humorous recognition of motherhood watch https://www.youtube.com/watch?v=HB3xM93rXbY (accessed October 3, 2015).

16. Senta Trömel-Plötz, *Gewalt durch Sprache: Die Vergewaltigung von Frauen in Gesprächen* (Frankfurt a. M., 1984), http://www.gleichsatz.de/b-u-t/begin/troml1.html (accessed October 3, 2015). Unless otherwise noted, the quotes from Trömel-Plötz come from this text.

in the English-speaking world, feminist attempts to change the language have focused more on gender neutrality—using gender-neutral professional titles and pronouns, for example—in the German-speaking countries the focus has often been on women's visibility instead. This will be seen in the discussion below.

Because "we use language to construct our reality . . . , language is a tool of power and can become a tool of violence." For the Swiss newspaper *Neue Züricher Zeitung* to use the term "women's lib" instead of "the women's liberation movement" in a headline strikes Trömel-Plötz as an example of "sexist language." The accusatory term "sexist" was used in 1984 with the secure feeling that this condemnation would strike a positive chord in women and pique the guilt feelings of men, so that any linguistic definition would be superfluous. Trömel-Plötz opines that this kind of sexism paves the way to various genocides:

> Besides the language of sexism, other examples include violence by the powerful, violence by the eloquent, the language of the persecution of Jews, the language of white racism, the language of Indian oppression, the language of militarism, which involved defining a group of people as inferior in order to limit their rights, massively discriminate against them, persecute them, incarcerate them and wipe them out.[17]

That is the chain of crimes against humanity, affecting women—all women always and everywhere—if they have been subject to "sexist" linguistic violence.

For this reason, in 1980, Ms. Trömel-Plötz and her colleagues Guentherodt, Pusch, and Hellinger established "Guidelines for Non-Sexist Use of Language" (Richtlinien für einen nicht-sexistischen Sprachgebrauch) to which the German-speaking nations began to adhere. It reads, "Language is sexist when women and their achievements are ignored, when women are only described dependently and subordinately to men, when women are shown only in stereotypical roles and their interests and abilities beyond the stereotype are denied, and women are humiliated and ridiculed through condescending language."

Mind you, it is not what people intend to say in their language that linguistic feminists find reprehensible, but the language itself in its grammatical structure. This brings us to the "generic masculine"—one of the main targets of feminist attack. Because group designations that gather people into a specific category (voters, students, readers) are almost always masculine in German, "the language does us violence,

17. Ibid.

because the masculine forms have priority." This builds the bridge from racism to the generic masculine.

But is it true? Before being sensitized by Trömel-Plötz and her cohorts, did people actually feel "raped" when they were addressed as "students," "citizens," as "dear readers," or "listeners" in their language's overarching masculine form? Over the last twenty years German speakers have gotten so used to the masculine and feminine forms being paired up that it strikes them as a sign of patriarchalism when women are not addressed with gender doublets such as these: *Liebe Bürger und Bürgerinnen* ("dear male and female citizens"), *Studenten und Studentinnen* (male and female students), *Christinnen und Christen* (female and male Christians), *Terroristinnen und Terroristen* (female and male terrorists), *Faschistinnen und Faschisten* (female and male fascists), *Sexistinnen und Sexisten* (female and male sexists).

Wait… those last three were a mistake! Only positive terms are to be paired, not negative ones like *terrorists* and *fascists*. Women want to be shown in a good light, and if they might not be, they would rather stay invisible. This is why the ban also extends to such pejorative terms as the feminine terms in German for *battle-axe*, *bitch*, and *airhead*. Men do not call for bans on words for *wimp*, *jerk*, or the various derogatory terms denoting machismo. But are all women good and all men bad? Are all women in Western society really victims and the men perpetrators?[18]

Authorities at the national and international level have made feminist concerns their own and issued binding manuals that keep speakers constantly on pins and needles for fear of violating a politically correct regulation. Such guidelines range from flyers[19] to the 192-page tome mentioned above. The recommendations of the German UNESCO commission for non-sexist use of language appeal to all "who use the German language professionally, whether at schools or universities, in the parliament, in the media or in official agencies. They appeal to the

---

18. Translator's note: The German suffix "-in" in such terms designates the feminine form. In English, terms like "sculptress," "actress," and "seamstress" have tended to fade in favor of the traditional masculine forms "sculptor," "actor," and "tailor," which are applied to people of both sexes. In some cases, new terms are coined to cover both genders, such as "server" to replace "waiter" and "waitress" or "firefighter" to include both genders. Current German custom differs, however, because the focus is on women's visibility instead of gender fairness. Such designations have to come in pairs upon each mention. It would be as if in English, theaters did not call both men and women "ushers" but said "ushers and usherettes" every time a mixed group of such employees was addressed, and indeed every time the job title was mentioned.

19. https://www.kreis-euskirchen.de/kreishaus/downloads/Flyer_geschlechtergerec hte_Sprache.pdf (accessed October 3, 2015).

creatresses and *creators* of learning and teaching materials, nonfiction, radio and television scripts, dictionaries, encyclopedias, speeches and lectures, advertising copy and newspaper and magazine articles of every kind."[20]

No longer are we allowed to talk the way our mouths are accustomed to. Everyone has to learn feminist German as a second language, so that he/she or s/he, or they, constantly show that he/she, s/he or they are on the right side, that is, on the side of victims and the oppressed—in other words, on the side of women.

A lot of linguistic nuance is lost in the process. The bizarre, artificial, forced nature of this language betrays the spirit at work behind it. As a result, it is hard to resist making fun of this bombastic feminist war against the language, but that would be ignoring the seriousness of the attack. Because of feminism's victorious march through institutions, people everywhere are kowtowing to the guidelines the activists have hatched, including public authorities, universities and the media. Students are forced to write their exams in "gender-neutral language" (even female students who do not subscribe to its values), and the Protestant churches are squandering millions to ruin Scripture through creation of a falsified "Bible in fair language." Everyday language has become a fun house of political correctness that no one can find his way out of—or less offensively *his/her*, or maybe *their*, way out of. And this is exactly the purpose of the strategy: the feminist worldview is imposed on people through the language to usher in a brave new world of invisible men.

20. Marlis Hellinger and Christine Bierbach, *Eine Sprache für beide Geschlechter: Richtlinien für einen nicht-sexistischen Sprachgebrauch* (Bonn: German UNESCO Commission, 1993).

9

Pornography—Completely Normal?

It is a large, unethical human experiment, and why it goes unhindered is a mystery to me.

Prof. Klaus Beier
Head of the Institute of Sexology and Sexual Medicine,
Charité University Hospital, Berlin[1]

The New Global Scourge

THE MEDIA age has brought new, lasting injury to the human psyche: images of evil. They settle in, unleash uncontrollable forces, occupy thoughts, fantasies and dreams, and affect people's behavior.[2] And most people are not aware of it. People have strict standards for the purity of water, air, and food, but they consume without reservation the most wretched pornographic filth, dreadful violence, and hair-raising horror as "entertainment." While the body has mechanisms for excreting poisons, the soul does not. Man has no power over his memory: images burn into the mind forever. This is reported by every pornography addict who fights to free himself of the obsession.

The term *pornography* is a coinage derived from the ancient Greek, a combination of *fornication* and *writing*. Thus, pornography represents fornication in writing. Until the invention of photography, it was limited to words and drawings that were not widely distributed. But today the media are at its service: sound recordings, photos and videos are distributed around the world over the Internet and through cellphones.

Before Germany's reform of criminal law, it was forbidden to distribute "lewd writings" in that country. However, in 1973, this term was

---

1. *Frankfurter Allgemeine Zeitung*, May 29, 2010.
2. Cf. Gabriele Kuby, "Vergiftung durch Bilder," in *Kein Friede ohne Umkehr: Wortmeldungen einer Konvertitin* (Laudes Verlag, Eggstätt, 2002). Available through fe-medienverlag Kisslegg.

changed to "pornography," and its distribution was legalized to anyone older than 18 years. Extreme pornography, involving violence or sex with children or animals, remained prohibited, but since then all of this has become available to any man, woman, or child through computers and cellphones with just a few clicks. Violation is subject to fine or up to a year in prison, but, being hard to catch, people accessing the material from their homes can easily ignore these penalties.

Germany's 1973 deregulation of pornography was preceded by an intense national debate that was finally won by those who believed that "mature adults" should not be subject to such restrictions. Besides, it was claimed, pornography use would decrease along with the thrill of the forbidden once the products were sold over the counter instead of under it.[3]

The Scandinavian countries led the way in pornography production. In 1969, the German news-magazine *Der Spiegel* (No. 50) wrote, "According to official estimates, in the past year Germans bought about a half billion deutsche marks of pornography—books, magazines, films and phonograph records." Legislators found this a convincing reason to adapt the law to "reality" and strike down the pornography ban.

However, the appetite of "mature adults" for pornography has proven to be insatiable. If you Googled the letters "XXX," a common symbol for pornography, on September 11, 2014, for instance, with the filter "English," you would have gotten about 1,150,000,000 hits. That is about 16 percent of the world population. The word "sex" in English gets about 4 billion hits.

Pornography is everywhere, and accessible to anyone of any age over the Internet. A Huffington Post headline on April 5, 2013 stated that "Porn Sites Get More Visitors Each Month than Netflix, Amazon and Twitter Combined."

In addition to that, there are hundreds of millions of porn video rentals at home and in hotels—with the bill kept strictly confidential.

---

3. Obscenity law in the United States is more complex than the European situation presented here, because it is largely based on local legislation and court rulings. The definition of what is obscene is based on "community standards" and "redeeming social value" or the lack thereof. Federal prosecutions wax and wane with the willingness of presidential administrations to bring violators to court, and the yardstick of "community standards" can change as the media and the Internet make the public more inured to sexual material. For a good basis for US obscenity rulings and prosecutions, refer to the website of the Public Broadcasting Service show *Frontline*, which includes an overview of court rulings. See http://www.pbs.org/wgbh/pages/frontline/shows/porn/prose-cuting/overview.html (accessed October 6, 2015) and a video documentary: http://www.pbs.org/wgbh/pages/frontline/shows/porn/view/ (accessed October 6, 2015).

Pamela Paul, who published the pioneering 2005 book *Pornified: How Pornography Is Transforming Our Lives, Our Relationships, and Our Families,* reported in 2010 that "Today, the number of people looking at pornography is staggering. Americans rent upwards of 800 million pornographic videos and DVDs (about one in five of all rented movies is porn), and the 11,000 porn films shot each year far outpaces Hollywood's yearly slate of 400." Four billion dollars a year is spent on video pornography in the United States. One in four Internet users looks at a pornography website in any given month. Men look at pornography online more than they look at anything else. And 66% of 18–34-year-old men visit a pornographic site every month."[4]

The child pornography market is booming the fastest. Every day, there are approximately 116,000 online searches for child pornography.[5] It is estimated that 2 million children worldwide have been offered on the web or depicted in sexualized violence. According to the annual report of ECPAT (*End Child Prostitution, Pornography and Trafficking of Children for Sexual Purposes*), in the European Union alone, several hundred thousand children are trafficked every year.[6] Many thousands of children are abducted and never seen again. This traffic in children serves the Internet supply and demand.

A few decades ago, pornography was almost exclusively consumed by grown men, limited to print media, videos, and films in "adult" movie theaters. Now, however, new communications media offer a wide array of active and passive interaction options: uploading and sharing porno videos, sex chats, webcam sex, telephone sex, and erotic computer games.

Today, however, an estimated one-third of porn consumers are women. It is estimated that 41 percent of all women in the United States look at pornographic websites at least once a month and that 10 million women do it regularly.[7]

For young people, especially adolescent boys, pornography consumption is now commonplace. Boys are significantly more likely than

4. P. Paul, "From Pornography to Porno to Porn: How Porn Became the Norm," in *The Social Costs of Pornography: A Collection of Papers* (Princeton, NJ: Witherspoon Institute, 2010).

5. J.S. Carroll, et al., "Generation XXX: Pornography Acceptance and Use Among Emerging Adults," *Journal of Adolescent Research* 23, no. 1 (2008): 6 et seq.

6. http://www.ecpat.net/EI/Publications/Annual—Reports/ECPAT—Annual—Report12008-2009.pdf. (accessed January, 2015).

7. Corinna Rückert, *Frauenpronographie: Pornografie von Frauen für Frauen. Eine kulturwissenschaftliche Studie* (Frankfurt: Peter Lang, 2000), quoted in Thomas Schirmacher, *Internetpornografie* (Holzgerlingen: Hänssler-Taschenbuch, 2008), 18.

girls to have friends who view online pornography. In one study, 65% of boys ages 16 and 17 reported that they had friends who regularly viewed and downloaded internet pornography.[8] Young people who have friends who consume pornography are more likely to do so themselves. In the era of smartphones, parents and caregivers can no longer protect children from pornography. These numbers make clear what legalization of pornography in the Western world has wrought with the help of the digital media revolution: in just a few decades, pornography has gone from suppression to obsession. While 50 years ago, a kiss on the lips was all that was shown on screen, today we are bombarded all day with images of sexual activity that have just one purpose: to sexually stimulate the viewer and prompt him to buy products of all types, from cars to tabloid newspapers to sexual services—and to increase TV ratings. There is barely a movie anymore that does not turn the viewer into a sexual voyeur. The Encyclopedia Britannica defines voyeurism as "human sexual behavior involving achievement of sexual arousal through viewing the sexual activities of others or through watching others disrobe." Since this occurs publicly at every movie theater and privately in front of computer screens, this perversion is now everyday behavior. The perversion itself is no longer stigmatized, but the actual word *perversion* is.

Pornography is saturating all of society, all classes, all professions, all age groups. Unlike food addictions or anorexia, pornography addiction is not visible on the addict himself—at least not at first glance. But one can't rely on one's own perception. As pornography researcher Tabea Freitag[9] told the author, "From my experience with those affected, I can say that on many of them you can't see it at all. You wouldn't think it possible that someone with a kind, gracious look in his eye at the same time consumes the hardest, most violent pornography."

The pornification of our world has catastrophic consequences for individuals, the family, children, and youth: the whole society. Pornography has social costs for those involved at the primary level (consumers and producers, be they men, women or children) and secondary level (usually women and children). Mary Eberstadt and Mary Anne Layden have summarized the social costs of pornography. They say:

8. National Survey of American Attitudes on Substance Abuse IX: "Teen Dating Practices and Sexual Activity," *The National Center on Addiction and Substance Abuse at Columbia University* (August 2004): 23.

9. Tabea Freitag, *Fit for Love? Praxisbuch zur Prävention von Internet-Pornografie-Konsum* (Hannover: Fachstelle Mediensucht, 2013).

Research and data suggest that the habitual use of pornography—and especially of internet pornography—can have a range of damaging effects on human beings of all ages and of both sexes, affecting their happiness, their productivity, their relationships with one another, and their functioning in society.[10]

The Degradation of Perpetrator, Victim and Consumer

What are people doing when they look at porno movies? They watch strangers engaged in sex acts, people who are degrading and humiliating themselves by publicly using their bodies as a tool of lust, allowing themselves to be filmed so that multitudes of strangers can get sexually aroused over them. This body is that of a still-living person who was once born as an innocent baby, has a father and mother, a memory, feelings; a person who feels joy and sadness, has a soul and a yearning for happiness and love, although perhaps barely any remaining hope of fulfilling these aspirations. The person must typically be drugged or given alcohol to be able to do at all that she is paid for—and they are often coerced. She may be one of many millions of victims of the traffic in women, girls and children from poor countries, from which criminal gangs extract billions, using them as prostitutes to sate the sex addiction of millions of men in rich countries, whether live or on screen.

Do people who sit at the screen seeking sexual excitement ever stop to think that it could be their own daughter, sister, wife, mother or even their own son, brother or husband before the camera? Given the high mortality rate in the porn industry, do they stop to think that the object of their lust may already have tragically died? Why do pornography consumers not realize that these are *human beings* through whose degradation and humiliation the consumers degrade and humiliate themselves?

And it is not only the woman who ends up degraded and humiliated. The man degrades and humiliates himself no less, because he is also a person of flesh and soul who has reduced himself to an animal impulse and slides into an ever-deeper abyss through the abuse of his human freedom. To think that only the female victim is degraded when men do them sexual violence is a throwback to ancient times, when a distinction was made between the perpetrator and the victim, and the active party was respected and the passive party despised, although both participate in each act.

Even the consumer just watching "totally normal" soft porn on the

---

10. Mary Eberstadt and Mary Anne Layden, *The Social Costs of Pornography: A Statement of Findings and Recommendations* (New Jersey: The Witherspoon Institute, 2010), 10.

screen degrades himself and reduces himself to an animal's drive for physical gratification. He is driven by a craving for ever-newer, stronger stimuli, because the intensity decreases the more he views pornographic images and thus is caught in the cycle of addiction. The drive becomes a slave driver, robs him of his freedom, and forces him into behaviors that destroy his life and that of fellow human beings. And the longer it goes on, the worse it gets. Weren't people talking about "mature adults" whose freedom shouldn't be limited by a pornography ban? How "free" are the millions of pornography addicts? How "mature" are they?

Yet our society considers this completely "normal." When it comes to child pornography—the exploitation of children and babies to sate the inscrutable sexual desires of some grown-ups, first live during recording and then hundreds of thousands of times by users—there is still a legal prohibition, but often as half-hearted as the hapless attempts of politicians to stem its distribution on the Internet.

Pornography is Addictive

People's basic, life-sustaining behaviors are secured by *drives*. Humans want to live, humans want to eat, humans want to pair sexually. The sex drive ensures the continued existence of humanity. Systematically suppressing the reproductive function of sexuality causes the population to die out—a process that has already begun in most European nations. Unfortunately, instinct-driven behaviors can derail and lead to pathological behaviors ranging all the way to addiction.

Child and adolescent therapist Christa Meves has been warning for four decades of the spiritual and social destruction that inevitably occurs when sexuality is detached from the anchor of morality. In her 2011 book *Wohin? Auf der Suche nach Zukunft* ("Where to? In Search of the Future"), she describes the instinctive purpose of the sex drive in this way:

> In the preliminary phase [it is about] finding one's identity, and after sexual maturity about copulation with a person of the opposite sex for the purpose of creating offspring and thus the propagation of the human species. . . . If the purpose of this drive is not achieved in a satisfactory manner . . . the danger arises that the drive will become dominant in such a way that it—even unconsciously—becomes detached from the purpose of the drive. This can open the dangerous path to addiction.[11]

11. Christa Meves, *Wohin? Auf der Suche nach Zukunft* (Bad Schussenried: Kopp Verlag, 2011), 65 et seq.

If we soberly examine our society, we can see that all types of addictions are spreading like an epidemic: alcohol, drugs, overeating, undereating, gambling, the Internet, sex and pornography. Addiction is a loss of freedom. The person is caught in a vicious circle of a search for gratification through a means that provides the false appearance of gratification, only to throw him into even greater need and dependence. What he thinks he needs for his well-being destroys him and others. The drive develops a life of its own, becomes a tyrant, and makes the person a slave to gratification of the drive. Meves continues:

> When completely detached from its objective of procreation, the disturbed sex drive causes sexual addiction involving an abundance of varieties and vicarious satisfactions that may include any sort of perversion. A particular danger for young males is easily accessible pornography on the Internet. Masturbation soon becomes addictive, leading to a search for stronger stimulus, so that even the danger of sex crime looms: torture, rape, finally even to the urge to abuse children to achieve that vicarious satisfaction.

Although with a few mouse clicks both young and old can access images and depictions of behavior that were once taboo, it has now become taboo to frankly state the destructive consequences of pornography consumption for the individual, the marriage, the family, and the entire society. It must not enter the public consciousness that pornography destroys life-sustaining relationships and addicts people in the clinical sense. This is the result of an abundance of studies that have looked into the effects of pornography.[12]

Dr. Victor Cline is a psychologist and psychotherapist who, by his own reckoning, has treated approximately 300 sex addicts, delinquents, and victims of sex abuse. He concludes from his therapeutic experience that pornography consumption has a causal relationship to obsession and crime. Dr. Cline describes the process as consisting of four stages:

1. *Addiction*

The first change to happen was an addiction effect. The porn consumers got hooked. Once involved in pornographic materials, they kept coming back for more and still more. The material seemed to provide a very powerful sexual stimulant or aphrodisiac effect, followed by sexual release, most often through masturbation. The por-

---

12. Complete references to scientific sources can be found in Pamela Paul, *Pornified: How Pornography is Transforming Lives, Our Relationships, and Our Families* (New York: Henry Holt and Company, 2004).

nography provided very exciting and powerful imagery, which they would frequently recall to mind and elaborate on in their fantasies.

Once addicted, they could not throw off their dependence on the material by themselves, despite many negative consequences such as divorce, loss of family, or problems with the law (as with sexual assault, harassment or abuse of fellow employees).

2. *Escalation*

The second phase was an escalation effect. With the passage of time, the addicted required rougher, more explicit, more deviant, and "kinkier" kinds of sexual material to get their "highs" and "sexual turn-ons." It was reminiscent of individuals afflicted with drug addictions. Over time there is nearly always an increasing need for more of the stimulant to get the same initial effect.

3. *Desensitization*

The third phase that happened was desensitization. Material (in books, magazines or film/videos) which was originally perceived as shocking, taboo-breaking, illegal, repulsive or immoral, though still sexually arousing, in time came to be seen as acceptable and commonplace. The sexual activity depicted in the pornography (no matter how antisocial or deviant) became legitimized. There was increasingly a sense that "everybody does it" and that this gave them permission to also do it, even though the activity was possibly illegal and contrary to their previous moral beliefs and personal standards.

4. *Acting Out Sexually*

The fourth phase that occurred was an increasing tendency to act out sexually the behaviors viewed in the pornography that the porn consumers had been repeatedly exposed to, including compulsive promiscuity, exhibitionism, group sex, voyeurism, frequenting massage parlors, having sex with children, rape, and inflicting pain on themselves or a partner during sex. This behavior frequently grew into a sexual addiction which they found themselves locked into and unable to change or reverse—no matter what the negative consequences were in their life.[13]

Those who start using pornography generally aren't aware that looking at pornographic images can quickly lead to a clinical addiction. And

---

13. http://www.catholicnewsagency.com/resources/life-and-family/pornography/pornographys-effects-on-adults-and-children/ (accessed August 20, 2015).

if adults aren't aware of it, then children and teenagers certainly aren't either. After they stumble upon it—perhaps it confronts them un-prompted through their cellphones or computer screens—children real-ize at some point that they have been caught. The addict does what he doesn't want to do, and doesn't want to do what he does. To feel "good" temporarily, he has to damage himself. And he becomes blind to damage he may inflict on others.

It starts with the "discovery" that they can seemingly escape unpleas-ant feelings, such as those of frustration, anxiety, loneliness, or inferior-ity. The real problem isn't solved, so momentary relief is sought again and again, temporarily to bring on a feeling of pleasure or dull a feeling of pain. The dose has to be increased; the addictive behavior takes over more and more of the person's life, and begins to destroy those support structures that still exist—marriage, family and friends. If the addict tries to escape the cycle, he suffers withdrawal symptoms that he may no longer have the strength to endure.

At the beginning there may be the power and will to tough it out through the unpleasant feelings and to seek a positive solution. With addictive consumption, the suffering is much greater, the consequences are more devastating, but the will submits to the addiction again and again and is much weaker than at the beginning—a dynamic similar to falling into debt.

Pornography addiction is among the substance-independent addic-tions, such as gambling addiction, workaholism and anorexia. Strangely enough, however, these induce biochemical processes in the brain simi-lar to those of substance-dependent addictions. The brain's self-reward system starts to break down, atrophies due to excessive use, so the dose has to be increased. The frontal lobes—which are responsible for dis-cernment—start to shrink.

Modern brain research shows that the brain is actually changed through pornography addiction. Author and researcher Norman Doidge states that

> Pornography, by offering an endless harem of sexual objects, hyper-activates the appetitive system. Porn viewers develop new maps in their brains, based on the photos and videos they see. Because it is a use-it-or-lose-it brain, when we develop a map area, we long to keep it activated. Just as our muscles become impatient for exercise if we've been sitting all day, so too our senses hunger to be stimulated. The men at their computers [addicted to] looking at porn [are] uncannily like the rats in the cages of the NIH, pressing the bar to get a shot of dopamine or its equivalent. Though they [don't] know it, they [have]

been seduced into pornographic training sessions that [meet] all the conditions required for plastic change of brain maps.[14]

In addition, during sex, the binding hormone oxytocin is released. This biochemical mechanism, which anchors the primary life-relationships of man and wife, mother and child, deep in the psyche, becomes perverted: The masturbating pornography consumer bonds with the anonymous sex partners on the Internet, and interest in his own wife and children wanes.[15]

Signs of addiction include:

- The inability to quit voluntarily.
- The declining effect of the same sort of sexual activities, and therefore the need for stronger stimuli.
- A constant preoccupation with sexual thoughts, images and desires.
- Withdrawal symptoms when attempting to quit.
- More and more time wasted. Social, professional and family obligations and leisure activities neglected.
- The behavior continues despite its destructive effect on the addict's own psyche, family and work.

The research studies agree that the pornography consumer finds himself on a slippery slope to ever-more abnormal sexual practices. He has to up the dose, and thereby increasingly loses moral inhibition. The reason: *The "substance" of the addiction is the breach of taboo itself.* When a taboo has been broken and habituation has occurred, the "substance" loses its effect.

So far, the international diagnostic classifications (ICD and DSM) have contained no recognized diagnosis for pornography addiction. As therapist Tabea Freitag says,

The existence of this addiction is frequently denied. That is why those affected seldom appear in the rehabilitation system, very few are treated, and they barely cause any expense. Because therapists and doctors have not been sensitized to it, when addicts actually dare to overcome the shame barrier and put their trust in a doctor, most of them are waved off. Diagnostic recognition is what is needed, but there is massive opposition to it.[16]

14. Norman Doidge, *The Brain That Changes Itself: Stories of Personal Triumph from the Frontiers of Brain Science* (London: Penguin Books, 2007), 108.

15. Donald L. Hilton, Jr., "Slave Master: How Pornography Drugs and Changes Your Brain," *Porn Harms* (2010), www.pornharms.com (accessed January 26, 2015).

16. Tabea Freitag, private communication, June 26, 2012.

Heaven and Hell

Let us consider the true, proper nature of sexuality. Fundamentally, sexuality can express the most tender, most heartfelt, and deepest union between a man and a woman. Driven and enabled by mutual love to the risk of devotion and lifelong commitment, the two give themselves up to an event that transcends their conscious powers, each going beyond the limits of the ego to open up to one another. They experience this simultaneously both as a revelation of their own and the other person's uniqueness and of the nature of the opposite sex. In this way, a new person can come into being—a child, which is received in awe by man and woman as the embodiment of their love. For religious people, it can be a deep experience of God to be taken over in this way by something greater, something that transcends the self. Fidelity to the person with whom one experiences the happiness of mutual devotion and mutual personal intimacy is a precondition and unconditional demand of the soul.

On the other hand, pornography means complete separation of sexual function from the person, thus making sexuality anonymous. Those who use it reduce themselves and the other to an object of lust and are driven ever deeper into degradation, humiliation, violence, perversion and obsession. With time, all limits can disappear—even children and infants can be victimized in this hell of unleashed sexual greed.

In a relationship of love between a man and woman, the man's greater, hormonally conditioned tendency toward aggression can be pacified through the woman's receptivity. This requires mutual devotion and respect for the opposite sex as a unique "you." In today's culture, feminism drives women to battle with men for power, and vilifies masculine strength as violent, evil and threatening. This throws the complementarity of strength and receptivity—of power and love—off its rails. Could it be that pornography is the dark side of feminism? The outward-reaching sexual power of the man finds no secure home in the woman, but becomes wild and violent, and subjugates and humiliates the woman.

A feminist culture brings about women who don't need men, and who, if they want to have a child, buy the seed from a sperm bank. Men no longer see a reason to use their greater power to protect women or to employ it responsibly and energetically as fathers. They have both lost one another—the man has lost the woman, and the woman has lost the man. And the children have lost their father and mother.

Pornography's Destructive Consequences

Pornography violates the dignity of a person and does severe and lasting harm at the spiritual, physical, and social levels. When pornography is consumed, the user gradually changes his attitudes toward sexuality. Men become cooler toward women, stop respecting them, and become more willing to use force. The user starts to consider deviant sexual practices to be "normal." He develops the "rape myth" that claims that "women really want it." The desire for a permanent relationship, family and children wanes.

Effects on marriage and family include the following:

- Emotional distance from the partner.
- Inability to love. Loss of normal affective expressions of emotion such as benevolence, friendship, caring and tenderness.
- Decreased intimacy in marriage and less sexual satisfaction, even to the point of impotence.
- Confronting the partner with perverse sexual requests.
- The partner perceives pornography use as emotional infidelity.
- Infidelity through cybersex, chat, the telephone, webcam and prostitution.
- Loss of interest in spouse and children.
- Affairs and promiscuity.
- The risk for children of running across pornographic material or walking in on a parent during pornography use.
- Separation and divorce.

Effects on children and youth include:

- Establishing a view of sexuality as satisfaction of drives.
- Developing a degrading image of women.
- The earlier the exposure to pornography, the greater the probability of addiction.
- The earlier sexual intercourse begins, the higher the risk of sexual diseases.
- Pornography becomes mainstream youth culture. Pressure on boys to perform sexually; cosmetic operations for girls.
- Promiscuity, hooking up, and deviant sexual practices are taken as normal and worthy of emulation.
- Insecurity and dissatisfaction with one's own sexuality.
- Pressure from the peer group to engage in sex, even to the point of cyberbullying[17] and sexual attacks.

17. *Cyberbullying* is harassment and humiliation of a person through the internet, often including distribution of nude or sexual photos against the person's will. *Sexting* is

- A lowered threshold for sexual violence.
- Marriage and family lose their leading role in planning the future.

The Baltic Sea Study, a large, representative study of youth conducted in 2007, shows two things: 1) far more boys than girls are heavy pornography users (10.5 percent of boys see pornography daily, 29 percent more than once a week, but only 1.7 percent of girls); 2) there is a significant difference between daily and occasional users, among both boys and girls. The heavy users show three to six times the rate of sex with animals, sex with children, and sexual violence. They are three times more likely to commit sexual abuse or rape, and they are more likely to want to try themselves what they have seen.

Tabea Freitag says the following:

> The results show that sexual abuse and consumption of child pornography has not been just a matter of a few pedophiles for a long time. In fact, free access to deviant content has fostered a new class of perpetrators who are in a constant search of a greater kick and consume pornography depicting orgies, rape and sex with children. The material can turn this new type of user's fantasies into desires that he may act out.[18]

Getting Out

Those who started out too weak to listen to their consciences may learn from their suffering. If they look for help, it is there: online programs that help defeat the habit, self-help groups such as anonymous 12-step programs, and therapeutic assistance.[19] Behind every addiction, there is a longing for something essential to life. In order for this longing to be discovered and fulfilled, the addict must seek help in renouncing his need for immediate gratification. As with every vice, every addiction, the first thing required is the personal will to take up the battle for one's own freedom and do whatever it takes to win.

---

sending sexually explicit text messages, sometimes including erotic photos. The word is a combination of "sex" and "texting."

18. Tabea Freitag, "Internet-Pornografiekonsum bei Jugendlichen: Risiken und Nebenwirkungen," in C. Möller (ed.), *Internet- und Computersucht: Ein Praxishandbuch für Therapeuten, Pädagogen und Eltern* (Stuttgart: Kolhammer, 2011).

19. Morality in Media's *Porn Harms* website (http://pornharms.com/#resources) has dozens of links to resources and programs for those seeking help with pornography issues, not only users, but also victims, parents, and others. The site lists secular programs and programs for people of various religions.

Excursus: Popular Music

Even popular music plays a crucial role in encouraging misguided sexuality. Anything goes—the crasser the offense against sexual norms, the more successful the music tends to be. And this isn't just an American phenomenon. German rapper "Sido" (Paul Würdig) glorifies anal and oral rape—even against one's own mother. His songs sell by the millions. He has published his diary in the German pornographic teen magazine *Bravo*, has appeared on talk shows, emceed major TV broadcasts, and was a juror on a popular Austrian talent show in 2011. However perverse and increasingly satanic the content may be, the media turn the "artists" into stars, because nothing hauls in the money like violating taboos.

The trend in pop music from dissolution of sexual standards to satanic content was described to me in the following report by a student who had observed the scene:

> From what I see and hear the pop music industry propagating, disintegration of sexual standards was just a step in the moral destruction of youth. I watched what was modern a few years ago, and one can see that for decades popular music has become more and more sexualized. Now pedophilic allusions and promotion of degrading sexual practices—even rape—have become routine. In my opinion, there have never been so many occult influences among "mainstream artists."
>
> Lady Gaga's appearances are now obviously occult rituals, and she doesn't seem to want to hide it. People have criticized her for promoting gender mainstreaming ideology and lack of sexual restraint. But this is standard for the music industry. In the late 1980s and 1990s, people like Madonna were already involved in it. After 2000, the trend was more toward hip-hop and R&B, which has little to do with gender ideology, but is more about pornography and glorifying violence. The new pop music, which sounds like the '90s again, sucks everything into itself. Since Lady Gaga arrived, the occultism has become more and more open. It is also disconcerting how often weapons and the military appear in the latest music videos.
>
> In addition, trances and dreams are repeated themes. It is about not knowing what is real. The new stars, like Lady Gaga or Beyoncé, have one or more alter egos that represent their bad side. I think it is now about actually leading young people to satanic worship and dehumanization.
>
> For several weeks, Lady Gaga's song "Born This Way" was No. 1 on the German music charts. The song begins with the verse, "It doesn't matter if you love him or capital H-I-M. A different lover is not a sin.

Believe capital H-I-M (hey, hey, hey)." What does H-I-M mean? There is a moderately popular rock band with that name. In their case, H-I-M stands for "His Infernal Majesty." In my opinion, there has never been anything like this in mainstream pop music before. In the music video, Gaga gives birth to a race of people and also appears as a zombie or some type of mutant. In another video, she plays Mary Magdalene, who has fallen in love with Judas and convinces him to betray Jesus. Jesus and the apostles are a biker gang. The video is full of occult symbols.

There is a strong trend toward Satanism that is not just aimed at a specific youth subculture like Goths or EMOs but has reached the mainstream. Any attempt to protect minors seems to fail completely.

In discotheques, I see how many young girls imitate these singers' dance and clothing styles and sing along with the lyrics. This turns the whole thing into a huge super-ritual that starts over again every weekend. Maybe I'm exaggerating, but I have the feeling that now that Christianity has been eliminated, a new cult is being ushered in with its own ritual gestures and symbols.

Any attempt to protect minors seems to fail completely, and you don't hear any objection anymore. I don't know any journalists or other people who have influence on public opinion. I suspect they know how dangerous this trend is and maybe know people who talk about this issue in public.

M.F.

Everyone Looks the Other Way

The alarming facts are not alarming anybody. A book by Siggelkow and Wolfgang Büscher, *Deutschlands sexuelle Tragödie: Wenn Kinder nicht mehr lernen, was Liebe ist*[20] ("Germany's Sexual Tragedy: When children no longer learn what love is"), prompted a short debate in 2008. As directors of a foundation for children and youth, the authors report on the sexual deviance that is very widespread among both the underclass of Germany's large cities and the upper classes. Children watch porn with their parents, mothers have sex with their umpteenth boyfriend with the door open, girls willingly submit themselves to mass rape, otherwise known as gang bangs.

Sex educators make children "porn competent" during obligatory sex education classes. There they learn that their penis doesn't need to be a foot long, that they don't have to have 10 orgasms one after the other,

---

20. Bernd Siggelkow and Wolfgang Büscher, *Deutschlands sexuelle Tragödie: Wenn Kinder nicht mehr lernen, was Liebe ist* (Asslar: Gerth Medien, 2008).

that women actually don't enjoy rape, and that they can say "no" if they don't feel like engaging in a gang bang!

Surely politicians, the UN, the EU and national governments feel called to protect the populace from a worldwide sex industry that makes an estimated $97 billion[21] and that:

- Degrades, humiliates and enslaves its actors.
- Drives increasing human trafficking for prostitution and pornography.
- Generates demand for prostitution.
- Addicts consumers.
- Destroys families.
- Alienates parents from children and children from parents.
- Undermines parental authority.
- Teaches children and youth an image of sexuality that is hostile to women, marriage and family.
- Lowers the birth rate, because uncontrolled sexual desire stifles the desire for children.
- Prepares the way for sex crime.

If national governments and the European Union can fight against people hurting themselves with tobacco use, why not against pornography addiction, which devastates not only the body, but the entire person, and has even worse effects on society? There is no rational answer, but we can ask two questions: 1) What role does pornography play in the lives of stressed-out politicians and journalists? And 2) Could it be that the forces aiming to destroy the family and make individuals easy to manipulate are consciously using pornography as a means to that end?

Why is the issue just pornography and not protection of the youth and children who lose their lives in this murderous machinery? Is it OK for someone over 18 to satisfy his sexual desires with dehumanizing sex depicted on the screen, to become addicted, to ruin his marriage and family, and to lose his job? Adults *do* set examples for young people, whether good or bad. If a son finds his father's porn, or catches him masturbating in front of the computer screen, what lesson does the son receive? How much respect does he still have for his father?

As soon as there is talk of a ban, a loud cry ensues. The defenders of "freedom" come on the scene. However, it has been shown that wherever the state has lifted criminal sanctions against behavior that objec-

21. Chris Morris, "Porn Industry Feeling Upbeat about 2014," *NBC News*, January 14, 2014, http://www.nbcnews.com/business/business-news/porn-industry-feeling-upbeat-about-2014-n9076 (accessed December 29, 2014).

tively harms the common good—behavior caused by strong subjective drives—it spreads like wildfire. Such as abortion. Such as pornography. Laws have an orientation function and provide the skeletal frame for a society's binding values. The flesh on this frame consists of tight-knit communities through which people internalize these values, such as the family and—decreasingly—the church.

Parents who want to raise their children to be responsible adults who are capable of commitment, so that they can succeed in life and will want to and can become parents themselves, find their children exposed to a sexualized environment that they can no longer protect them from. Access to the Internet can barely be monitored anymore. In addition, there is the massive sexual pressure among peers and the forced sexualization of children and teenagers through obligatory "sex education" in the schools (see Chapter 12).

Patrick F. Fagan, a senior fellow at the Family Research Council, thinks strong family relationships are the most important protection against pornography addiction:

> The key to militating against these damaging patterns and to protecting against the effects of pornography is to foster relationships of affection and attachment in family. The first and most important relationship is between the father and the mother. The second is engaged parents who love their children. In today's technological society, this means limiting, monitoring, and directing their children's Internet use. This, in turn, provides an invaluable shield against Internet pornography, and allows room for a healthy sexuality to unfold in a natural and socially supported way. In our over-sexualized culture, with a longer pre-marriage period, children need the capacity for abstinence if their sexuality is to be channeled into stable marriage, procreation, and healthy family life for their children. Strong families remain the best defense against the negative effects of pornography, especially when aided by regular religious worship with all the benefits it brings.[22]

Do we still have the strength to pull ourselves out of this morass? If there can be an international campaign against smoking, there could be an international campaign against pornography. Both of them are backed by a powerful industry with billions in revenue. The spiritual deterioration caused by pornography has wider-ranging effects than the

---

22. Patrick F. Fagan, "The Effects of Pornography on Individuals, Marriage, Family and Community," Family Research Council, www.pornharms.com (accessed January 26, 2015).

physical deterioration caused by smoking. The campaign against smoking has succeeded: smoking among teenagers has reduced dramatically. If that can be done, then advertisements and sex education pamphlets for teenagers and adults could have warnings like these:

Pornography is addictive.
Pornography makes you lonely.
Pornography can destroy your family.
Pornography harms your children.
Pornography promotes human trafficking and prostitution.
Pornography leads to sex crime.
It could be your sister.
It could be your brother.
It could be your child.

10

Hetero, Homo, Bi, Trans—Are We All Equal?

Today's decision usurps the constitutional right of the people to decide whether to keep or alter the traditional understanding of marriage. . . . If a bare majority of Justices can invent a new right and impose that right on the rest of the country, the only real limit on what future majorities will be able to do is their own sense of what those with political power and cultural influence are willing to tolerate.

Justice Samuel Alito[1]

To avoid the tyranny of sexual desire, which in the name of freedom and dignity breaks hearts and homes and spawns loneliness, we must commit to witnessing to the truth of human nature.

Ryan T. Anderson[2]

The Homosexual Movement[3]

A SMALL MINORITY of the population (LGBTTI),[4] whose sexual tendencies deviate from those of the vast majority, have succeeded in

1. Dissenting opinion of Justice Samuel Alito to the same-sex-marriage decision *Obergefell v. Hodges* of the U.S. Supreme Court on June 26, 2015.

2. Ryan T. Anderson, "Same-Sex Marriage and Heresy," at *First Things* web-exclusives (July 16, 2015). Cf. *Truth Overruled: The Future of Marriage and Religious Freedom* (Washington, DC: Regnery Publishing, 2015).

3. An excellent book on the subject, elucidating the philosophical underpinnings of the present cultural war, is Robert R. Reilly, *Making Gay Okay: How Rationalizing Homosexual Behavior Is Changing Everything* (San Francisco: Ignatius Press, 2014). Here the reader will find relevant US sources.

4. *Lesbian/gay/bisexual* relates to personal feelings, sexual desire and behavior. Some but far from all people affected choose a homosexual or bisexual identity for themselves.

Transsexuality is a gender identity disorder in a biologically/physically normal person and is listed as a mental illness under this name in the official diagnostic list (ICD-

turning their interests into the dominant issue of the global cultural revolution. This is curious, because fulfillment of these interests does not contribute to solving the existential problems of society as a whole, but worsens them—including the disintegration of families and the demographic crisis.

We live in a secular, liberalized society in which individual freedom is at the top of the value scale. The consensus is that the government should stay out of the bedroom. Decades ago, authorities stopped enforcing laws against homosexuality, and legislatures in Western countries have repealed them, giving homosexual men and women the freedom to live according to their tendencies without official persecution or legal discrimination. In many countries registered civil unions have been introduced, and in some places full marriage equality has been granted to gays and lesbians, as in the U.S. through the decision of the Supreme Court in June 2015. The new sexual ethics treat homosexuality, bisexuality, transsexuality, and transgenderism as equal to heterosexuality, and in many countries this is an established component of preschool pedagogy and school curricula. Where these goals have not been reached, there is a battle over them. At Christopher Street Day parades through Western capitals, the diversity of sexual lifestyles is freely demonstrated. Homosexuals hold political office at the highest levels. In the US, President Obama declared the month of June "Lesbian, Gay, Bisexual and Transgender Pride Month." On May 13, 2012, in the midst of election campaigning, President Obama came out in full favor of equality of registered homosexual civil unions with marriage, prompting *Newsweek* to run the title: "Barack Obama: The First Gay President."

The greatest success of "The First Gay President" of the United States of America is the Supreme Court's historic ruling on June 26, 2015 that made same-sex marriage legal across all 50 states. Until 2013, same-sex

---

10). It defines transsexualism as: "A desire to live and be accepted as a member of the opposite sex, usually accompanied by a sense of discomfort with, or inappropriateness of, one's anatomic sex, and a wish to have surgery and hormonal treatment to make one's body as congruent as possible with one's preferred sex." www.icd-code.de/icd/code/F64.-.html.

Transgender is a new term that describes a lifestyle in which "compulsory heterosexuality" as a man or woman is overcome through free choice of gender. *Intersexuality* is a collective term for certain biological/physical illnesses. The biological characteristics (chromosomes, internal and external sexual characteristics, hormones) are disordered in some way and do not allow clear assignment of male or female gender. The older terms for this are pseudo-hermaphroditism and hermaphroditism. (Definitions from Marion Gebert, "Sexuelle Vielfalt," *Bulletin des Deutschen Instituts für Jugend und Gesellschaft,* no. 20 [Fall 2011].)

marriage was legal only in 12 states. Independent of the will of the people and their political representatives, the Supreme Court voted five-to-four that "the U.S. Constitution contains an inalienable right to same-sex marriage." The four dissenting justices, in their individual statements, see in this ruling a "threat to American democracy" (Antonin Scalia), a usurpation of "the constitutional right of the people whether to keep or alter the traditional understanding of marriage" (Samuel Alito), and argue that "the majority's reasoning would apply with equal force to the claim of a fundamental right to plural marriage" (John Roberts) and that the constitutional protection of liberty "has been understood as freedom from government action, not entitlement to government benefits" (Clarence Thomas). [5]

Justice Anthony Kennedy, who tipped the scales to void marriage of its meaning, used beautiful words to formulate the majority statement: "No union is more profound than marriage, for it embodies the highest ideals of love, fidelity, devotion, sacrifice, and family. In forming a marital union, two people become something greater than once they were." Justice Kennedy wants to fulfill the hope of same-sex partners "not to be condemned to live in loneliness, excluded from one of civilization's oldest institutions. They ask for equal dignity in the eyes of the law. The Constitution grants them that right."

But dignity is innate in every human being, the law cannot bestow it—it has to protect it.

We don't have to go back to the Greeks to study sophistry, the art of deceptive speech—one of the main methods of judicial activism.

On the evening of the Supreme Court decision the White House was lit up in the colors of the rainbow.

The tipping point: APA decision of 1973

The tipping point came in 1973 with a decision by the American Psychiatric Association (APA). Tipping points are inconspicuous at first, but with time they have far-reaching consequences. The APA decided to strike homosexuality from the list of mental illnesses to be treated by therapeutic procedures. This blocked scientific discussion of the long-standing inquiry into the causes of homosexuality. The APA's decision was not the result of scientific discussion, but of political pressure on individuals who could not withstand it. Charles Socarides, a clinical professor of psychiatry and author of several books on homosexuality,

---

5. http://www.supremecourt.gov/opinions/14pdf/14-556_3204.pdf (accessed July 20, 2015).

was present to witness how the APA's decision was brought about by homosexual activists:

> Homosexuals banding together . . . to proclaim their "normality" and attack all opposition to this view. Those who took this view in the past constituted a vocal but very small minority of homosexuals compared to the large number of homosexuals who desired more help, not less, or who remained silent. . . . For the next 18 years, the APA decision was to serve as a Trojan horse, opening the gates to widespread psychological and social change in sexual customs and mores. The decision was to be used on numerous occasions for numerous purposes with the goal of normalizing homosexuality and elevating it to an esteemed status. To some American psychiatrists this action remains a chilling reminder that if scientific principles are not fought for they can be lost—a disillusioning warning that unless we make no exceptions to science, we are subject to the snares of political factionalism and the propagation of untruths to an unsuspecting and uninformed public, to the rest of the medical profession, and to the behavioral sciences. . . . The devastating clinical fallout from this decision was to follow. Those who would wish to retain homosexuality as a valid diagnosis have been practically silenced by lectures, meetings, and publications, both originating within our association and from other sources. Political parties and religious leaders have been utilized to reinforce this silence.[6]

It would be another 17 years (1990) before the World Health Organization (WHO) adopted the APA's decision.

This chapter will critically examine the foundations of the global offensive to topple sexual norms without regard to the prohibitions on thought and speech that have since been established. It will discuss the causes and risks of the homosexual lifestyle, the ability to change one's sexual orientation, the battle for homosexual "marriage" (including adoption), the demands of anti-discrimination legislation, appeals to human rights, and the global political strategies.[7]

---

6. Charles W. Socarides, "Sexual Politics and Scientific Logic: The Issue of Homosexuality," *The Journal of Psychohistory* 19, no. 3 (Winter 1992). Cf. Robert R. Reilly, *Making Gay Okay*, 118 et seq.

7. Scientific research into issues of sexuality and homosexuality can be found here: National Association for Research & Therapy of Homosexuality (NARTH), http://narth.com.

How many people classify themselves as homosexual?[8]

Considering the fact that millions in public money are being spent to push through the LGBTI agenda, and that this issue finds advocates at the highest levels of politics, one would think that this is a phenomenon that affects the masses. It is therefore relevant what percentage of the population self-identify as homosexuals.

The groups involved, even at the very lofty heights of politics and government, use varied and mostly exaggerated figures that do not come from serious sources. Representative surveys in Western societies indicate that 1 percent to 3 percent of the population identifies itself as homosexual.[9] The National Health and Social Life Survey (NHSLS, USA) of 1994 determined that 2.8 percent of men and 1.4 percent of the adult female population of the United States classify themselves as gay, lesbian or bisexual.[10] The same research showed that only 0.6 percent of men and 0.2 percent of women had had nothing but same-sex relationships since puberty. This means that the vast majority of those who classify themselves as "homosexual" have had heterosexual relationships.[11] It raises the question of whether a homosexual identity is really as fixed and unchangeable as it is always claimed to be. The homosexuality figure of 10 percent alleged by Alfred Kinsey is, like many of his results, a matter of propagandistic fraud.

A large-scale government survey, the National Health Interview Survey, released by the Centers for Disease Control and Prevention in July 2014, found that contrary to popular belief, just 1.6% of the population identify as homosexual, while 96.6% say they are heterosexual. This is in sharp contrast to a Gallup survey of 2011. It found that 52% of Americans believed that 25% of the population was either gay or lesbian. Only 4% of people surveyed at the time thought that the homosexual population was less than 5%.[12] The gap between reality and opinion proves how incredibly successful the disinformation and propaganda campaign of the LGBT movement is, with the mainstream media to support it.

---

8. Where homosexuality is discussed below, it is generally intended to include other forms of non-heterosexual orientation (LGBTI).

9. Official figures from the US: www.cdc.gov/nchs/dada/nhsr/nhsr 036.pdf (accessed September 25, 2015).

10. Edward O. Laumann, et al., *The Social Organization of Sexuality: Sexual Practices in the United States* (Chicago: The University of Chicago Press, 1994), 311 et seq.

11. Peter Sprigg (ed.), *Homosexuality Is Not a Civil Right* (Family Research Council), 10. http://downloads.frc.org/EF/EF07K01.pdf (accessed October 3, 2015).

12. CNSNews.com, July 18, 2014.

Views of the Causes of Homosexuality[13]

Interpretation and assessment of homosexuality has changed radically in the past century. Here are the major views:

Under the influence of the great founders of psychology, Sigmund Freud, C.G. Jung, and Alfred Adler, homosexuality was seen as a psychological gender identity disorder. Freud held the view that homosexuality is a "variation of the sexual function produced by a certain arrest of sexual development." In a letter to the mother of a homosexual man, he hinted at the possibility of treatment: "By asking me if I can help, you mean, I suppose, if I can abolish homosexuality and make normal heterosexuality take its place. The answer is, in a general way, we cannot promise to achieve it. In a certain number of cases we succeed in developing the blighted germs of heterosexual tendencies which are present in every homosexual, in the majority of cases it is no more possible. It is a question of the quality and the age of the individual. The result of treatment cannot be predicted."[14]

Anna Freud, the daughter of Sigmund Freud, saw in the homosexual act an unsuccessful attempt in a boy's development to form identification with the masculine. She is the source of the term "reparative drive," upon which so-called "reparative therapy" is based. This view was undisputed for 70 years until the APA decision came in 1973.

C.G. Jung similarly wrote that homosexuality is a repressed, undifferentiated element of masculinity in the man which, instead of being developed from the depths of his own psyche, is sought on a biological plane through "fusion" with another man.[15]

The opinion of the great founders of psychology, that homosexuality was a neurosis that is the expression of subconscious, unresolved childhood conflicts, was undisputed until 1973. In the decades following the decision, homosexuality has come to be considered a "variant of nature" that therefore must be accepted as fully equal by society and those affected. Meanwhile, it has become clear that there is no homosexual gene and that no one is born gay or lesbian. This is shown by research into twins, for example. If homosexuality were inborn, then identical

13. Cf. Christl Ruth Vonholdt, *Homosexualität verstehen,* Bulletin DIJG, special issue, Fall 2006.

14. Quoted in Jakob Cornides, "Natural and Un-natural Law," *Selected Works of Jakob Cornides,* http://works.bepress.com/jakob_cornides/17/ (accessed January 28, 2015).

15. Quoted in Joseph Nicolosi, *Reparative Therapy of Male Homosexuality: A New Clinical Approach* (Lanham, Maryland: The Rowman & Littlefield Publishing Group, 1991), 76.

twins should have the same predisposition. But this is not the case.[16] Peter Tatchell, a prominent homosexual activist, has written on his website:

> There is a major problem with gay gene theory, and with all theories that posit the biological programming of sexual orientation. If heterosexuality and homosexuality are, indeed, genetically predetermined (and therefore mutually exclusive and unchangeable), how do we explain bisexuality or people who, suddenly in mid-life, switch from heterosexuality to homosexuality (or vice versa)? We can't.[17]

Research studies show that identity conflicts in childhood can lead to homosexual tendencies. The National Cohort Study undertaken in Denmark in 2006 surveyed *all* Danes between 18 and 49 years old to find out what influence childhood experiences have on whether a person chooses marriage or a homosexual partnership in adulthood. The result:

> Our prospective analysis based on the entire population indicates: Various childhood experiences in the family have a major influence on whether a person later enters heterosexual or homosexual marriage. . . . Men were more likely to enter a homosexual partnership if they had had one of the following childhood experiences: divorced parents, absent father, older mother, youngest child in the family.[18]

When most psychologically oriented development models are rejected as politically incorrect, despite the results of modern research,[19] then what is left to justify and legitimize the practice of homosexuality?

---

16. M. Bailey, "Genetic and Environmental Influences on Sexual Orientation and Its Correlates in an Australian Twin Sample," *Journal of Personality and Social Psychology* 78, no. 3 (2000), 524 et seq. Also: Peter S. Bearman and Hannah Brückner, "Opposite-Sex Twins and Adolescent Same-Sex Attraction," *American Journal of Sociology* 107, No. 5 (March 2002): 1179–1205.

17. http://www.petertatchell.net/lgbt_rights/gay_gene/homosexualityisntnatural.htm (accessed October 3, 2015). See also Martin Dannecker, *Gutachten für die Bundesregierung*, Protokoll Nr. 15/59 des Rechtsausschusses—Öffentliche Anhörung vom 18.10. 2004, S. 86.

18. Morten Frisch and Anders Hviid, "Childhood Family Correlates of Heterosexual and Homosexual Marriages: A National Cohort Study of Two Million Danes," *Arch Sex Behav* (2006): 533–47. At http://resources.metapress.com/pdf-preview.axd?c ode=al 4574 p6203628w0&size=largest (accessed January 28, 2015).

19. Comprehensive information at National Association for Research and Therapy of Homosexuality (NARTH), www.narth.com.

Only the erroneous idea that human freedom is absolute. The subjective needs of the individual become the only criterion for the exercise of freedom. This entails considerable physical and psychological risks.

Hazards of the Homosexual Lifestyle

Every homosexual man knows that he belongs to a group with greatly increased risk to life and health. The life expectancy of men who have sex with men (MSM) is much shorter than the average for the overall population. A Canadian study published in the *International Journal of Epidemiology* indicates:

> In a major Canadian center, life expectancy at age 20 years for gay and bisexual men is 8 to 20 years less than for all men. If the same pattern of mortality were to continue, we estimate that nearly half of gay and bisexual men currently aged 20 years will not reach their 65th birthday.[20]

What are the reasons for such drastically limited life expectancy?

Physical illnesses

The large shadow looming over any man who has sex with men is infection with the fatal autoimmune disease HIV/AIDS. The US Centers for Disease Control and Prevention (CDC) estimate that homosexual men account for 61 percent of new HIV infections, even though they make up less than 2 percent of the population. Figures for Germany from the Robert-Koch-Institut are even higher: "At 68 percent, MSM are still the largest group."[21] A study at the University of Zurich (1999) comes to this conclusion: "Based on current data, it can be assumed that every fourth man with homosexual contact will be infected with AIDS during his lifetime."[22]

How can that be explained? If one considers that the population is bombarded with posters, TV ads, and AIDS campaigns to use condoms for "safe sex," there are just two possibilities: either condoms are not safe, or homosexual men don't use them much. Based on figures from

20. Robert S. Hogg, et al., "Modelling the Impact of HIV Disease on Mortality in Gay and Bisexual Men," *International Journal of Epidemiology* 26, no. 3 (1977). http://ije.oxfordjournals.org/content/26/3/657.full.pdf (accessed January 28, 2015).

21. Robert-Koch-Institut, *Epidemiologisches Bulletin, Science Blogs*, May 5, 2011. http://www.rki.de/cln_226/nn_2030884/DE/Content/Infekt/EpidBull/Archiv/2011/21__11,templateId=raw,property=publicationFile.pdf/21_11.pdf (accessed January 28, 2015).

22. Ibid.

UN-AIDS, mathematician Michael Horn's calculations indicate that "Despite regular, conscientious use of condoms, the risk of HIV infection is between 10 percent to 18 percent per 500 sexual contacts, for example. For every 10 people in otherwise the same circumstances, one to two people will get infected."[23] That is a considerable risk for an infection that generally leads to early death. The numbers show that major risks even lurk behind "safe sex." Reality contradicts the advertising slogans that extol condoms as reliable protection against HIV/AIDS and other sexually transmitted diseases and that suggest that they are keeping the problem under control.

HIV/AIDS is far from the only risk. The Centers for Disease Control and Prevention state: "Men who have sex with men (MSM) are at elevated risk for certain sexually transmitted diseases (STDs), including Hepatitis A, Hepatitis B, HIV/AIDS, syphilis, gonorrhea, and chlamydia.... Approximately 15%–25% of all new Hepatitis B virus (HBV) infections in the United States are among MSM."[24]

The Gay and Lesbian Medical Association in the US summarizes the risks of sexual illnesses:

> Sexually transmitted diseases (STDs) occur in sexually active gay men at a high rate. This includes STD infections for which effective treatment is available (syphilis, gonorrhea, chlamydia, pubic lice, and others), and for which no cure is available (HIV, Hepatitis A, B, or C virus, Human Papilloma Virus, etc.). [Human Papilloma Virus] infections may play a role in the increased rates of anal cancers in gay men ... the rate at which the infection can be spread between partners is very high.[25]

Lesbians have the highest risk of breast and uterine cancer of any subset of women in the world.[26]

23. Michael Horn, "Kondome: die trügerische Sicherheit," *Medizin und Ideologie* 29, no. 3 (2007): 12. At http://eu-ae.com/images/mui_archiv/29_2007/Medizin_und_Ideo logie_nr3_ 2007_web.pdf (accessed January 28, 2015).

24. http://www.cdc.gov/hepatitis/Populations/MSM.htm (accessed, January 29, 2015).

25. See Victor M. B. Silenzio, *Top 10 Things Gay Men Should Discuss with Their Healthcare Provider* (San Francisco: Gay & Lesbian Medical Association, July 17, 2002). At http://zone.medschool.pitt.edu/sites/lgbt/Shared% 20Documents/10ThingsGay_Doc. pdf (accessed October 3, 2015).

26. Katherine A. O'Hanlan, *Top 10 Things Lesbians Should Discuss with Their Healthcare Provider* (San Francisco: Gay & Lesbian Medical Association). At http://www.lgbt. ucla.edu/documents/TopTenLesbians.pdf (accessed January 2015).

Mental illnesses

Representative studies agree that men who live a homosexual lifestyle have a greater risk of mental illness.[27] J.M. Bailey, an internationally renowned researcher in the field of homosexuality, made this comment on two representative studies: "These studies contain arguably the best published data on the association between homosexuality and psychopathology, and both converge on the same unhappy conclusion: homosexual people are at a substantially higher risk for some forms of emotional problems, including suicidality, major depression, and anxiety disorder." Bailey warns readers not to blame these emotional problems simply on society's negative view of homosexuality.[28]

In 2003, leading American AIDS researchers reported in the *American Journal of Public Health* that homosexual behavior is associated with higher rates of drug abuse, depression, and domestic violence among partners, as well as the experience of sexual abuse in childhood.[29] A Danish study from 2009 showed that homosexual men in registered partnerships committed suicide at eight times the rate of heterosexual married men.[30]

Especially alarming is the higher suicide rate among homosexual youth.[31] In Berlin, a city where homosexuals are supported in every way by the state government, young gays and lesbians attempt suicide about seven times more often than heterosexuals. This was reported by Berlin's gay magazine *Du & Ich* (June/July 2010).

The Remafedi Study of 1991 shows that suicide attempts by homosexual youth are associated with specific risk factors that cannot be explained by public discrimination, as shown in the following chart:[32]

27. DIJG, *Homosexualität und wissenschaftliche Studien*, www.dijg.de.

28. J.M. Bailey, "Homosexuality and Mental Illness," *Arch. Gen. Psychiatry* 56 (Oct. 1999).

29. Ron Stall, et al., "Association of Co-Occurring Psychosocial Health Problems and Increased Vulnerability to HIV/AIDS among Urban Men Who Have Sex with Men," *American Journal of Public Health* 93, no. 6 (June 2003): 941 et seq.

30. Robin M. Mathy, et al., "Association between Relationship Markers of Sexual Orientation and Suicide: Denmark, 1990–2001," *Springer Link* (December 2009) (accessed January 28, 2015). http://link.springer.com/article/10.1007/s00127-009-0177-3.

31. D.M. Fergusson, "Is Sexual Orientation Related to Mental Health Problems and Suicidality in Young People?" *Arch. Gen. Psychiatry* 56 (Oct. 1999). Cf. R. Herrel, "Sexual Orientation and Suicidality," *Arch. Gen. Psychiatry* 5 (Oct. 1999).

32. G. Remafedi, "Risk Factors in Attempted Suicide in Gay and Bisexual Youth," *Pediatrics* 87, no. 6 (1991), 869–75.

Risk Factors in Suicidal Behavior of Homosexual Youth

Sexual abuse	61%
Masculine with "feminine" identity	37%
Experience in sex trade	29%
Illegal drug use	85%
Previously arrested	51%
Without married parents	73%

How are these horrifying facts to be understood? LGBTI interest groups and the parties aligned with them try to blame "homophobic discrimination" for the higher risks of the homosexual lifestyle. This is contradicted by the fact that these figures are similar in all Western countries, regardless of how liberal and tolerant the country is. A recent study from the Netherlands, one of the world's most liberal countries, shows that homosexual women have a higher rate of substance abuse and that homosexual men have a higher rate of anxiety disorders.[33]

Promiscuity

Studies show that the homosexual lifestyle is a promiscuous one, and that fidelity between partners is extremely uncommon.

Udo Rauchfleisch, a clinical psychology professor in Basel, Switzerland, himself an activist in the homosexual movement, claims it is a characteristic of homosexual relationships to have many fleeting, uncommitted, mostly anonymous sexual relationships concurrently with a stable one.[34] Numerous studies confirm this finding.[35] Furthermore, the Zurich Study of homosexual men between 20 and 49 indicated

---

33. Michael King, et al. "A Systematic Review of Mental Disorder, Suicide, and Deliberate Self Harm in Lesbian, Gay and Bisexual People," *BMC Psychiatry* 8, no. 70 (August 8, 2008). At http://www.biomedcentral.com/1471-244X/8/70 (accessed January 28, 2015).

34. Udo Rauchfleisch, *Die stille und die schrille Szene* (Freiburg–Wien: Herder, 1995), 57.

35. Cf. Peter Sprigg, *Homosexuality Is Not a Civil Right*, loc. cit., 143, note 11.

that, on average, those questioned had had 10 to 15 different male sex partners in the 12 months before the survey. Two thirds of all those surveyed had been with at least one stable boyfriend in the previous 12 months, but 90 percent of all men had had one or more casual partners during the same period.[36]

In a 1997 Australian study, 2,583 older men living as homosexuals were asked their lifetime number of sexual contacts. The average number was 251. Only 2.7 percent of those studied had had just one sex partner in their life.[37] Likewise, a study in Amsterdam (May 2003) concluded that partnerships between homosexual men last no longer than an average of 1.5 years. During these partnerships, each partner had had an average of 12 other sex partners.[38] Recent studies on promiscuity show lower figures, but all confirm that sexual exclusivity is the exception even during stable partnerships.[39]

Volker Beck, 2011 parliamentary secretary of Alliance 90/The Greens, confirms this finding. It sounds almost like a joke on the legislature:

> If the legislature hopes to turn gays into faithful marriage partners, they must and will be disappointed by the reality of gay relationships. . . . Obviously, for many couples, living out their sexuality with other partners is an important factor in maintaining the partnership. . . . Positive legal regulation of homosexual unions would accommodate the desire for social integration at the political level, yet politicians cannot be offered a change of behavior in the form of decreased promiscuity.[40]

For this lifestyle, the unambiguous word "fidelity" was combined with an adjective that maintains the appearance of fidelity, but changes the content of the term into its opposite. "Social fidelity" is intended to mean one stable partner and any number of other sex partners in addition.

Why do people whose lifestyle is promiscuous and sterile fight for

---

36. *Zürich Men's Study*, Institut für Sozial- und Präventivmedizin der Universität Zürich, Sumatrastr. 30, CH-8006 Zürich, June 1999.

37. P. Van de Ven, et al., "A Comparative Demographic and Sexual Profile of Older Homosexually Active Men," *Journal of Sex Research* 34, no. 4 (1997): 349–60.

38. Maria Xiridou, et al., "The Contribution of Steady and Casual Partnerships to the Incidence of HIV Infection among Homosexual Men in Amsterdam," *AIDS* 17, no. 7 (2003).

39. Cf. N.W. Whitehead and Briar Whitehead, *My Genes Made Me Do It!—A Scientific Look at Sexual Orientation* (Lafayette: Huntington House Publishers, 1999).

40. Volker Beck, "Legalisierung schwuler und lesbischer Lebensgemeinschaften," *Demokratie und Recht* 4 (1991), 446 et seq.

marriage—a way of life based on lifelong faithfulness between one man and one woman who give life to children?

Sexual abuse

Research shows that homosexual men and women were disproportionately subject to both homosexual and heterosexual abuse in childhood, and that this is a factor that can put young people on the path to homosexuality.

- *Garofalo Study*: Of boys and girls in the 9th to 12th grades who describe themselves as gay or lesbian, 32.5 percent had experienced sexual abuse or molestation. For comparison: Teens of the same age group who did not identify as gay or lesbian had a nine-percent rate of sexual abuse or molestation.[41]
- *Johnson Study*: Considerably more homosexual than heterosexual men have histories of sexual abuse.[42]
- *Krahé Study*: Every fifth man who felt he was homosexual (20.7 percent) reported being a victim of sexual abuse in childhood.[43]
- *Tomeo Study*: This study shows for the first time that homosexual abuse also plays a role in the prior history of homosexual women. Forty-six percent of homosexual men and twenty-two percent of lesbians had been heterosexually abused as children or teenagers, while only 7 percent of heterosexual men and 1 percent of heterosexual women had been. Sixty-eight percent of men and 38 percent of women said they were not homosexual until *after* the abuse.[44]

A reduction or complete abolition of the age of consent, as supported by some homosexual activists, is therefore irresponsible toward children and their parents.[45] Why are there "action plans against homophobia" but no national action plans against sexual abuse?

---

41. R. Garofalo, et al., "The Association Between Health Risk Behaviors and Sexual Orientation Among a School-based Sample of Adolescents," *Pediatrics* 101, no. 5 (1998): 895–902.

42. R. Johnson and D. Shier, "Sexual Victimization of Boys," *Journal of Adolescent Health Care* 6 (1985).

43. Barbara Krahé, et al., "Sexuelle Aggression zwischen Jugendlichen: Eine Prävalenzerhebung mit Ost-West-Vergleich," in *Zeitschrift für Sozialpsychologie*, no.2/3 (1999), 165–78.

44. M. Tomeo, "Comparative data of childhood and adolescence molestation in heterosexual and homosexual persons," *Arch. Sex. Behavior* (May 30, 2001): 535 et seq.

45. The president of the Austrian Homosexual Movement, Helmut Graupner, is an advocate of decriminalizing sexual acts with minors if they are consensual. Cf. Helmut Graupner, "Love versus Abuse, Crossgenerational Sexual Relations of Minors: A Gay Rights Issue?" *Journal of Homosexuality* 37, no. 4, (1999): 203 et seq.

The political consensus that sexual abuse of children and teenagers is reprehensible and should be punished by law was not always present, and even today it is fragile (see chapter 2, 39). In Germany, sexual abuse by priests led to a national outcry in 2010.[46] The chief prosecutor in the cases involving abuse by Catholic priests, Justice Minister Leutheusser-Schnarrenberger, has been on the advisory board of the Humanist Union (HU) since 1997. Until the year 2000, this organization advocated decriminalization of pedophile sex. Not until the autumn of 2000 did the HU decide (with 44 percent of the vote opposing) that "the HU does not approve of or support pedophile sexual contact" and remove links to pedophile groups on its websites.[47]

Examination of the list of past and current members of the Humanist Union shows the majority to be renowned intellectuals of the German left.[48] Considering how many professors, politicians, and journalists are involved in the fight for sexual liberation—even to the point of legalizing sex with children—it is no wonder that this issue is measured with a double standard: charges are brought insofar as they will damage the Catholic Church, but, at the same time, there is less noise made about the outrageous daily rate of sex abuse against minors, and there are even calls for its legalization.

Possibilities of Change?

This is an important question, especially for those who suffer due to their own non-heterosexual tendencies, long for a family and children, and wish to seek therapeutic assistance.[49] Specialists talk about "ego-

---

46. As a Catholic, I am appalled by and ashamed of the sexual abuse by Catholic priests. However, the problem has been distorted. In the Catholic Church in Germany, there were several hundred cases in 60 years. In German society overall, there are 15,000 cases every year, and experts believe the number of unreported cases is 10 to 15 times that number. The numbers are similarly disproportionate in the United States. The Center for Applied Research in the Apostolate (CARA), the independent research organization of Georgetown University, reported that in 2011, the number of *allegations* of priest sex abuse by current minors was 7 "credible," 3 "to be determined," and 3 proven to be false. The U.S. Department of Health and Human Services puts the total of sex abuse cases for the entire United States in the same year at 61,472.

47. http://www.humanistische-union.de/nc/publikationen/mitteilungen/hefte/num mer/nummer_detail/back/mitteilungen-171/article/erklaerung-des-bun-desvorstandes-der-humanistischen-union-zum-sexualstrafrecht/ (accessed August 2012).

48. http://www.humanistische-union.de/wir_ueber_uns/verein/beirat/http://www. humanistische-nion.de/wir_ueber_uns/verein/beirat/historie_bei-rat/ (accessed August 12, 2012).

49. Here are some organizations that offer *open, unbiased counseling* to people who suffer under homosexuality and want help:

dystonic" homosexuality. In a free society, scientific discourse on the topic should be possible. This is no longer the case, even in the humanities.[50] Those who dare to defy the ban are held up for strident persecution by LGBT and pedophile interest groups.

A witness to the ability to change is Robert L. Spitzer, a professor of psychiatry. He played a key role in the APA's 1973 decision to remove homosexuality from the list of mental illnesses. When homosexuals demonstrated at one APA annual conference for their right to therapy, he began a series of studies to examine the success of various therapies in altering homosexuality. In 2003, he published his results. Of the 200 men and women studied, 66 percent of the men and 44 percent of the women had experienced a considerable change and "now lived a good heterosexual life."[51] Two APA presidents, Robert Perloff and Nicholas Cummings, expressed their concern that the APA's 1973 decision had limited therapeutic freedom.[52]

Many scientists and therapists, in fact, attest to successful change

---

- Courage: www.couragerc.net
- Desert Stream: www.desertstream.org
- Deutsches Institut für Jugend und Gesellschaft: www.dijg.de
- Wüstenstrom: www.wuestenstrom.de
- Exodus International: www.exodus-international.org
- Exodus Global Alliance: www.exodusglobalalliance.org
- Homosexuals Anonymous: www.ha-fs.org
- Living Hope Ministries: https://livehope.org
- National Association for Research and Therapy of Homosexuality: www.narth.com
- Jews Offering New Alternatives to Homosexuality: www.jonahweb.org
- PATH Positive Alternatives to Homosexuality: www.pathinfo.org

50. For an analysis of the paralysis of psychology by misguided political correctness, see A. Dean Byrd, *Destructive Trends in Mental Health: The Well-Intentioned Path to Harm* (New York: Routledge, 2005).

51. Robert L. Spitzer, M.D., "Can Some Gay Men and Lesbians Change Their Sexual Orientation? 200 Participants Reporting a Change from Homosexual to Heterosexual Orientation," *Archives of Sexual Behavior* 32 (October 2003): 403–17. Due to his results, Dr. Spitzer suffered the wrath of the homosexual lobby. Since then, he is said to have apologized to homosexuals for supposedly having made unproven claims (*Spiegel online*, May 21, 2012). In addition to many scientists and therapists, even Peter Tatchell, the Greens' representative for gays and lesbians in England, attests that sexual orientation can be changed; see http://www.petertatchell.net/lgbt_rights/queer_theory/not_gla d.htm (accessed October 6, 2015).

52. Joseph Nicolosi, *A Call for the American Psychological Association to Recognize the Client with Unwanted Same-Sex Attractions,* http://static1.1.sqspcdn.com/static/f/362976/ 25576676/1413996439187/callforAPA.pdf?token=EcdEpjDMixBH10AxH81kvbe77N0%3D (accessed October 2015).

from unwanted homosexuality to fulfilling heterosexuality.[53] Anyone who does so, whether a scientist, patient or journalist, is pressured, persecuted, and, if possible, silenced by the LGBTI lobby.

It is obvious that for therapy to help, the patient must undergo it voluntarily and have the will to change. As with any therapeutic or medical intervention, the goal may not be reached and there can be undesirable side effects. However, there is no scientific evidence to show that therapeutic approaches to changing ego-dystonic homosexuality lead to an above-average frequency of undesirable results.[54] The success rates for therapeutic intervention can vary. One important factor seems to be whether the religious dimension is involved.[55]

One of the best-known witnesses for the ability to change is Michael Glatze, founder and former chief editor of the magazine *Young Gay America*. He says:

> In my experience, "coming out" from under the influence of the homosexual mindset was the most liberating, beautiful and astonishing thing I've ever experienced in my entire life. God came to me when I was confused and lost, alone, afraid and upset. He told me— through prayer—that I had nothing at all to be afraid of, and that I was home. I just needed to do a little house cleaning in my mind. Homosexuality took almost 16 years of my life. . . . As a leader in the "gay rights" movement, I was given the opportunity to address the public many times. If I could take back some of the things I said, I would. Now I know that homosexuality is lust and pornography wrapped into one. I'll never let anybody try to convince me otherwise, no matter how slick their tongues or how sad their story. I have seen it. I know the truth.[56]

The LGBTI lobby does everything possible to drive from the public consciousness the message that a homosexual orientation can change to a heterosexual one. With defamation campaigns, they drive organizations providing such help out of existence.

---

53. The website *peoplecanchange.com* shows 23 scientific studies published in the last 40 years that show that homosexuality can change. See http://www.people-can-change.blog spot.com/2009/04/big-lie-no-evidence-of-change.html (accessed October 3, 2015).

54. Joseph Nicolosi, A. Dean Byrd, and Richard W. Potts, "Retrospective Self-reports of Changes in Homosexual Orientation: A Consumer Survey of Conversion Therapy Clients," *Psychological Reports* 86 (2000): 1071–81.

55. Richard Fitzgibbons, "Origin and Healing of Homosexual Attractions and Behaviours," http://www.catholiceducation.org/en/marriage-and-family/sexuality/origin-and -healing-of-homosexual-attractions-and-behaviors.html (accessed October 6, 2015).

56. World Net Daily, July 3, 2007, http://www.wnd.com/2007/07/42385/.

In 2012, the State of California even banned therapy and pastoral care for minors suffering from ego-dystonic homosexuality. There is no scientific basis to justify this, but there is plenty of demand for this type of therapy. Up to now, scientifically qualified professional organizations decided whether therapeutic procedures should be recognized and monitored. The California law puts this decision in the hands of politicians and makes it subject to political power plays. A similar law has been passed in New Jersey. Such a law revokes patients' therapeutic freedom and the right of parents to decide on suitable therapeutic assistance for their minor children.[57]

Christian Spaemann, specialist in psychiatry and psychotherapy and former chief physician of the mental health clinic at St. Joseph Hospital in Braunau, Austria, said in an interview:

> If homosexuality were an inborn trait, like skin color, treatment for those wanting to change sexual orientation would be an unethical therapeutic procedure. However, this is not the case. Even serious representatives of the homosexual movement no longer claim that homosexuality is genetically conditioned. The possibility of permanent change in sexual orientation has been proven many times now. . . . In view of the data, it is fundamentally unacceptable to reject the desire to change sexual orientation or to offer only gay-affirmative therapies. This would be forcing ideology on the psychotherapeutic profession and would be disrespectful of patient autonomy. . . . Dealing with deep emotional conflicts leads to a decrease in homosexual impulses and to a release of heterosexual potential. . . . This is not a matter of "reversing one's polarity" as the homosexual movement repeatedly claims.[58]

It is a glaring contradiction that a movement that fights for abolition of "compulsory heterosexuality" does everything to deny that homosexual tendencies can be changed, to suppress information on therapeutic assistance, to threaten the existence of therapists and organizations offering such help. The homosexual movement marches under the banner of freedom, tolerance and non-discrimination, but it limits freedom of opinion, scientific freedom and therapeutic freedom in particular. The aim is to force the concept of allegedly unchangeable "sexual identity" into constitutional anti-discrimination law.

---

57. http://narth.com/2012/04/narth-statement-on-californis-sb-1172-sexual-orienta-tion-change-efforts/.

58. http://www.kath.net/detail.php?id=20708.

At stake is the view that homosexuality has the same societal value as heterosexuality and thus must be legitimized with the same right to marriage and family.

At stake is the right to portray homosexuality as an equal option to children and teenagers at public educational institutions.

At stake is the ethical responsibility of the individual.

Homosexual "Marriage"

At a time when the marriage of man and woman is disassociated more and more often from the foundation of the family, and more and more children are being raised by single mothers, the fight is raging for full legal equality of same-sex partnership with marriage. The sexual liberators of the late 1960s considered marriage to be stuffy and outdated, a relic of bourgeois possessiveness. This shows an obvious contradiction: the same societal groups that have fought to weaken the institution of marriage are now fighting for marriage to be extended to same-sex relationships. This is proclaimed as a "human right." The cultural battle imposed on the world by Western political powers is raging in all nations and the legislation is changing rapidly.

Media propaganda gives the impression that the alleged "human right" to homosexual "marriage" and all accompanying privileges and bans on discrimination are already the status quo. As of July 2015, reality looked different:

- In the last few years, eleven of 27 EU member states have redefined marriage as a genderless institution: the Netherlands, Belgium, Spain, Sweden, Norway, Portugal, Iceland, Denmark, France, England, Wales and Luxembourg.
- Ten EU member states have introduced the institution of same-sex civil partnerships.
- 13 European countries have codified marriage in their constitutions as the union of one man and one woman: Belarus, Bulgaria, Croatia, Hungary, Latvia, Lithuania, Moldova, Montenegro, Poland, Serbia, Slovakia, Ukraine, and most recently Macedonia.
- Before the Supreme Court forced same-sex marriage on all US states, only 17 states had introduced same-sex marriage.
- Only one African nation has introduced same-sex marriage or civil partnership: South Africa. In 33 African nations homosexual acts are illegal.
- In Asia not a single country has introduced civil partnership or same-sex marriage. In 25 nations homosexual acts are illegal.
- In South America, Argentina, Brazil, Guyana, Columbia and Uru-

guay have introduced same-sex marriage, while Chile and Ecuador
have legalized civil partnerships.

• Australia has introduced civil partnership in some of its states. [59]

More than 50 countries forbid homosexual acts even between consenting adults, and—regrettably—5 countries make them punishable by
death.

These numbers show that redefinition of marriage as a genderless
institution, based on emotional affection and stripped of its procreative
meaning, is a project of Western "cultural imperialism" (Pope Francis).
In respect to the basic values of marriage and family, Europe is no
longer united, but split into West and East, North and South.

Considering that less than one percent of the world population has
any interest in legalizing their relationship with a partner of the same
sex the question arises: could it be that those who have the power to
carry out a global sexual revolution intend to pervert the meaning of
marriage—to destroy marriage and the family?

Marriage and family: An indispensable contribution
to the public good

Equating same-sex partnership with marriage between a man and
woman represents a historic break with the millennia-old worldwide
concept of marriage and family and with the entire history of law up to
now.[60] It substantially hollows out the concepts of the legal institution
of marriage and family.

Marriage is a pre-political institution created by its very nature for
procreation. It does not owe its existence to the state. The Universal
Declaration of Human Rights of 1948 states:

> The family is the natural and fundamental group unit of society and
> is entitled to protection by society and the State. (§16, Art. 3)

The family serves the common good in a unique, irreplaceable manner. To develop criteria for the common good, Pope Benedict XVI gave
a groundbreaking talk in the German parliament on September 22, 2011.
He said:

> There is also an ecology of humanity. Man too has a nature that he
> must respect and that he cannot manipulate at will. Man is not
> merely self-creating freedom. Man does not create himself. He is

---

59. Wikipedia, "Gesetze zur Homosexualität" (accessed July 2015).

60. Cf. Johann Braun, *Ehe und Familie am Scheideweg: Eine Kritik des sogenannten
Lebenspartnerschaftsgesetzes* (Regensburg: Roderer Verlag, 2002).

intellect and will, but he is also nature, and his will is rightly ordered if he respects his nature, listens to it and accepts himself for who he is, as one who did not create himself. In this way, and in no other, is true human freedom fulfilled.[61]

Law professor Robert George of Princeton University and his colleagues Patrick Lee and Gerard V. Bradley define marriage as "a union of a man and a woman, committed to sharing their lives together on the bodily, emotional, and rational-volitional levels of their being, in the kind of community that would be naturally fulfilled by having and rearing children together."[62] That marriage is "naturally fulfilled by having and rearing children together," and same-sex unions are naturally infertile, represents the major distinguishing characteristic between the two realities.

Marriage and family serve society in a way that only they can: "reproduction" and "creation of the human wealth" of a society.[63] These are the terms of economists behind which the human experience of family is concealed: the joy over a newborn child whose laughter renews the world in the eyes of its parents; the long, sacrificial path of the father and mother as they raise their children into adults who contribute to the human, cultural, intellectual, social and economic well-being of society as a whole. When a large number of families are no longer willing to perform this duty, when men and women are no longer willing to bond for life and create descendants and raise them into people capable of bonding and achieving, this threatens a nation's existence—not only its purely physical existence, but also its cultural and political existence. This can be seen in the divorce statistics, the rate of illegitimate births, of single parenthood, of absent fathers—with all the consequences that come with them, including lowered achievement, mental disorders among youth, crime, and the exploding costs of the social welfare system.

61. http://www.vatican.va/holy_father/benedict_xvi/speeches/2011/september/documents/hf_ben-xvi_spe_20110922_reichstag-berlin_en.html). Cf. Wolfgang Waldstein, *Ins Herz geschrieben. Das Naturrecht als Fundament einer menschlichen Gesellschaft* (Augsburg: Sankt Ulrich Verlag, 2010).

62. Patrick Lee, Robert P. George and Gerard V. Bradley, "Marriage and Procreation: Avoiding Bad Arguments," *Public Discourse: Ethics, Law and the Common Good* (March 30, 2011), http://www.thepublicdiscourse.com/2011/03/2637/.

63. Cf. Manfred Spieker, *Generationenblind und lebensfeindlich,* statement on the hearing of the Hessian state parliament on January 13, 2010, regarding the legal status of registered civil unions. http://www.gemeindenetzwerk.org/?p=4380 #more-4380.

Homosexual "marriage" cannot make the necessary contributions to society. Nor can it give life to children without exploiting the genetic material of third parties, and it cannot give children what they need most: a mother and a father. This deficiency remains even if the same-sex couple are loving, caring "parents" (on adoption, see Chapter 10, section 6).

The new financial privileges for homosexual partners must come from the pockets of married couples and singles. Parents who have raised children are put at a great disadvantage by the equal-pension rights of those who remain childless. Why should they also subsidize homosexual partnerships, which make no procreative contribution?

Recourse to registered civil unions

In June 2011, Germany's Federal Statistical Office reported the "Number of the Week": "In 2010, about 23,000 same-sex couples lived together in the same household in registered civil unions. That same year, 63,000 couples indicated that they lived together in same-sex partnerships."[64] With a population of 80 million, of which an estimated 2.5 percent have homosexual tendencies, this means that 0.16 percent of the population lives in same-sex—unregistered—partnerships. Of these, 37 percent have taken advantage of the new legal institution of registered civil unions, i.e., 0.058 percent of the population and 2.3 percent of people with homosexual tendencies. In other countries that have introduced the new legal institution, about 2 percent have actually taken advantage of it.

When one considers that the UN, the EU, the US government, and many other national governments, the global LGBTI NGOs and all institutions promoting gender mainstreaming have pulled out all the stops to legalize this new institution everywhere—often against huge resistance at the grassroots level—one has to ask if this agenda conceals objectives that go beyond the interests of such a small minority.

Is homosexual "marriage" a human right?

Within a few decades, radical homosexual minorities have succeeded in hijacking the terminology of human rights for their own specific interests and to empty them of their actual content. Legal expert Jakob Cornides writes of:

---

64. https://www.destatis.de/DE/PresseService/Presse/Pressemitteilungen/zdw/2011/P D11_025_p002.html (accessed October 6, 2015).

The emergence of "new human rights" which, not being generally recognized as such, in fact stand in radical contradiction to "traditional" ethical and cultural values; and, consequently, are also in conflict with the existing domestic legislation and jurisprudence in most countries. . . . what was once considered a crime is to be transformed into a right, and what was once considered justice, into a human rights violation.[65]

Through this process, human rights lose their universal character. They can only retain it if their foundation is universal in character. This is the nature of the human being, born as man or woman and dependent on complementarity with the opposite sex for procreation.

Even British Prime Minister David Cameron sees the danger of hollowing out human rights, although he otherwise backs LGBTI rights. On January 25, 2012, he spoke before the Parliamentary Assembly of the Council of Europe of the concern of many member states:

The concept of human rights is being distorted. As a result, for too many people, the very concept of rights is in danger of slipping from something noble to something discredited—and that should be of deep concern to us all. And when controversial rulings overshadow the good and patient long-term work that has been done, that not only fails to do justice to the work of the Court, it has a corrosive effect on people's support for human rights. The Court cannot afford to lose the confidence of the people of Europe.[66]

The course was set to give same-sex partnerships equality with marriage when the Charter of Fundamental Rights of the European Union of 2009 no longer mentioned men and women who have the right to marriage and family.[67] This opened the door to implementation of homosexual "marriage." The people of the democratic member states of the

---

65. Jakob Cornides, *Natural and Un-Natural Law*, loc. cit., 144, note 14. The same strategy of calling on human rights to demand the revolutionary overthrow of the value system is also used in the fight for worldwide legalization of the murder of unborn children. http://works. bepress.com/jakob_cornides/.

66. *Speech on the European Court of Human Rights*, https://www.gov.uk/government /speeches/speech-on-the-european-court-of-human-rights (accessed October 6, 2015).

67. The commentaries on the convention of the Charter of Fundamental rights contain the following interpretation: "The wording of the Article has been modernized to cover cases in which national legislation recognizes arrangements other than marriage for founding a family. This Article neither prohibits nor imposes the granting of the status of marriage to unions between people of the same-sex. This right is thus similar to that afforded by the ECHR, but its scope may be wider when national legislation so provides." At http://www.europarl.europa.eu/charter/pdf/ 04473_en.pdf.

European Union hadn't the slightest notion that a switch had been flicked that would allow change to the fundamental social structure of Europe.

Anti-discrimination law

Since 1994, the EU parliament has regularly passed resolutions that demand equal treatment of gays and lesbians in the EU, including homosexual "marriage" and adoption of an unrelated child (see p.142). In EU nomenclature, the term *family* is frowned upon. A new term has been invented that is a bit unwieldy but is free of the weight of tradition: *intergenerational solidarity.*

Step by step, the EU commission expanded the anti-discrimination legislation that the member states implement in national law. The decisive breakthrough came in 1999 with the adoption of "sexual orientation" as an anti-discrimination criterion in the Amsterdam Treaty. This made possible legislation that was invasive to private law.

In Germany, the "General Equal Treatment Act" has been in force since 2006. Any form of "disadvantage for reasons of race, ethnic origin, gender, religion or world view, disability, age or *sexual identity*" is to be prevented or eliminated. The principle of burden of proof was turned on its head: The plaintiff does not have to prove discrimination, but rather the defendant must prove that he *did not* discriminate. "An employer who has to choose between a Muslim, a disabled person and a woman who all have the same qualifications is up a creek without a paddle," says Austrian Michael Prüller in his article *Wenn die Freiheit ganz leise Ade sagt* ("When Freedom Quietly Bids Adieu").[68]

On April 2, 2009, the European Parliament decided to tighten its anti-discrimination directive, or more precisely the "Directive for Using the Principle of Equal Treatment Regardless of Religion or World View, Disability, Age or Sexual Orientation."[69] The only reason it is not in force today is that Germany has refused to approve it so far. Germany's conservative parties (the CSU and FDP) fear an overgrown anti-discrimination bureaucracy, since this is really about a new monitoring system. Not a peep from the populace. Prüller again: "Like any absolute principle, the principle of anti-discrimination is suited to establishment of a society of totalitarian denunciation, especially since it provides the excuse to slander for noble reasons."

---

68. *Die Presse,* June 19, 2010.

69. KOM 2008, 426; http://eur-lex.europa.eu/LexUriServ/LexUriServ.do?uri=COM: 2008:0426:FIN:de:PDF.

Step by step: Equating same-sex partnership with marriage

On November 10, 2000, the German Parliament passed an act on registered civil unions. On July 17, 2002, Germany's Federal Constitutional
Court ruled that this law was constitutional. The court found that "'The
Special Protection of Marriage' in Art. 6 paragraph 1 of the constitution
does not prevent the legislature from granting the rights and obligations
that are the same or similar to those of marriage."[70] With this decision,
the constitutional court opened the door for further demands by LGBTI
interest groups to be implemented in law one by one—giving them an
inch so they would take a mile:

- 2004: The German parliament passes a new version of the civil
  unions act that eliminates many deviations from marriage law (ali-
  mony, inheritance and adoption rights).
- 2009: Germany's Federal Constitutional Court declares as unconstitutional the inequitable treatment of civil unions and marriage in
  regard to survivor pensions.
- June 2010: The German Parliament and Federal Council establish
  identical treatment of civil unions and marriage in regard to estate tax
  law.
- July 2010: The Federal Constitutional Court declares that the instruction on protecting marriage in Article 6 of the constitution does not
  justify disadvantages to other living arrangements.
- November 2010: The German federal government introduces a proposed law to parliament that would align the two institutions in public
  service law.
- November 2010: The justice ministers of the German states advocate
  full adoption rights for registered civil partnerships.

In 2011, Justice Minister Sabine Leutheusser-Schnarrenberger moved
straight ahead with the policies of her predecessor Brigitte Zypries to
bring complete equality with marriage in regard to foreign adoption
and artificial methods of reproduction with the genetic material of
anonymous third parties (anonymous sperm donation for lesbian couples or purchased egg cells and surrogate motherhood for male homosexual couples). In 2012, she and other politicians demanded that tax
privileges for married couples be extended to same-sex couples.

Providing arbitrary privileges

Why should only homosexual couples enjoy the privileges that were
previously reserved for marriage? Why not other people—pairs of sib-

---

70. Judgment of July 17, 2002—Az. 1BvF 1/01, 1 BvF2/01, p. 1.

lings, friends or any people who live under one roof for a certain time or their whole lives? Why shouldn't bisexual, transsexual, polygamous, polyandrous, or polyamorous relationships also be granted similar status to marriage? What makes the homosexual relationship so special that only it is to be equated with marriage?

Actually, there is no convincing reason. Once government recognition of the monogamous union of a man and a woman has been loosened, it is only a question of time before people in other forms of relationships demand equality with homosexual partnership, and therefore with marriage, and force it in court. Anything else would be "discrimination." With that, we will have what Germany's leftists officially advocate: the family will be defined independently of marriage and descent.

Franziska Brychcy, an unsuccessful direct candidate of the Berlin Left Party in 2011, told the public: "I myself live in a long-term polyamorous partnership with two men, with whom I have four children. Our children have one mother and two social fathers who lovingly care for them. And that is the main thing: that children be able to grow up with love, that their parents have the time and space for them and accompany them on their path through life. For this, it is irrelevant whether their parents are their biological parents or foster, adoptive or simply their social parents."[71]

Has anyone asked the children how loving they feel life to be in a polyamorous partnership, where the fabric of relationships is always tearing and being patched? A survey in England of 1,600 children under 10 years old shows how severely children suffer from their parents' divorces. To the question of what they would change if they were king or queen and could enact new laws, the most frequent answer was, "Ban divorce." Can children cry out their suffering and fear any louder than they did here?[72] It remains to be seen what children will say and do after puberty starts and how they will behave toward their "social parents" when they are old and need care.

European Court of Human Rights: Homosexual "marriage"
is not a human right

Late June 2010 marked the end of a case two Austrian men had fought all the way to the European Court of Human Rights (ECHR) to get judi-

---

71. http://www.medrum.de/content/direktkandidatin-der-linkspartei-ich-lebe-einer-polyamoren-partnerschaft (accessed October 3, 2015).

72. http://www.telegraph.co.uk/news/uknews/3759675/What-children-want-most-is-a-ban-on-divorce-says-poll.html (accessed October 3, 2015).

cial recognition of same-sex "marriage" as a human right (*Schalk and Kopf v. Austria*). The ECHR ruled that "The European Convention on Human Rights does not oblige States to guarantee the right to marriage for homosexual couples."[73]

The ruling hung by a hair—just one justice's vote. The rationale for the judgment seemed almost to show regret that "a majority of states do not yet grant legal recognition to same-sex couples." This time the shot barely missed the target. What seemed like a win for the marriage and family movement turned out to be a Pyrrhic victory: the court applied Article Twelve (which guarantees "men and women" the right to marry) to same-sex couples because it "might be interpreted so as not to exclude the marriage between two men or two women."[74] The court itself signaled how to hit the bull's-eye—by fighting to change the law at the level of the member states. There are strategic handbooks for this, such as the *Activist's Guide to The Yogyakarta Principles* and the US State Department's Toolkit (see pp. 64 and 172).

Yet, the people of thirteen East European countries, by defining marriage as the union of one man and one woman in their constitutions, obstructed the "evolutionary interpretation" of the Convention. The court recognized the increasing divergence between European countries, which threatens the stability of the whole European edifice:

> In a landmark case[,] Hämäläinen v. Finland the ECHR, sitting as a Grand Chamber, ruled very clearly in July 2014 that neither Article Eight protecting private and family life, nor Article Twelve guaranteeing the right to marry, can be understood "as imposing an obligation on Contracting States to grant same-sex couples access to marriage." The Court clarified that the right to marry and to found a family "enshrines the traditional concept of marriage as being between a man and a woman." It seems clear that the norms of the Council of Europe do not require member states to grant same-sex couples access to marriage nor prevent them from defining marriage as exclusively the union of one man and one woman.[75]

73. European Court of Human Rights, Application no. 30141/04, Judgment of June 24, 2010.

74. For a detailed analysis see Gregor Puppinck, "Same-sex Union and the European Court of Human Rights," *Public Discourse* (May 4, 2015). http://www.thepublicdiscourse.com/2015/05/14848/ (accessed October 3, 2015).

75. Puppinck, ibid.

Adoption

The right of children to their parents

Another intermediate goal in the battle to make homosexual partnerships fully equal to marriage is the right of same-sex couples to adopt other people's children. Adoption of step-children was already implemented in 2005: For example, if a father discovers that he is homosexual, divorces his wife and "partners" with a man, this new man can adopt the father's biological child.

Imagine: a child grows up with a mother and father. The marriage goes bad and the parents split, which is traumatic for any child. Somehow he can manage with the divorced parents if they aren't battling each other. Because the child is still a dependent, he has to accept the new partner. What does it mean for the child if the archetypes of father and mother start to falter because the father or mother discovers a greater attraction to the same sex? The dependent child must accept a man as her new "mother" or a woman as her new "father" and navigate the change to the gay community with them. What does she call the man who is now to be the new "mom" and has full parental power over her? Mom? Dad 2? How will the boy or girl feel when the new parental units come to school or when inviting friends home? How will the child deal with his feelings of sorrow, depression, forlornness and loss of direction if everyone says, "It's completely normal!" Everything is in order!—even though nothing is normal and nothing is in order. How will the relationships with relatives be formed, to the many grandmothers and grandfathers the child now has? What view of life does the child form— conscious or unconscious? Whom can he trust, and what does he have to build on? Add to that the fact that children from patchwork families statistically show a highly increased risk of sexual abuse by stepfathers.[76]

The ability to adopt stepchildren is not enough for the LGBTI organizations. Every type of adoption is to be possible, and anything else is decried as "discrimination" and a violation of homosexuals' "human rights." Up to now, conditions have been strict for adoption. Generally,

---

76. In his article "Die dunkle Seite der Kindheit" ("The Dark Side of Childhood"), (*Frankfurter Allgemeine Zeitung*, April 4, 2012, 7), Dirk Bange cites a study by Russell: Every sixth girl who has a stepfather is abused by him before she is 14, but "only" every fifteenth girl by her biological father (http://www.inhr. net/book/patchwork-familie-beguenstigt-missbrauch). A study from England and Wales shows that 32 percent of children growing up with at least one stepparent became victims of abuse, versus 3 percent of children who lived with their biological parents. At http://www.sueddeutsche.de/wissen/ frage-der-woche-wie-boese-ist-die-stiefmutter-1.52 8256 (accessed October 3, 2015).

adoptive parents have to be married and able to "emotionally accept the child as their own and offer him or her good conditions for socialization." Does it serve the good of children if they are adopted by homosexual couples whose lifestyle is characterized by promiscuity and who have an above-average incidence of mental and physical illnesses? Catholic adoption agencies in the United Kingdom that answered "no" to this question and therefore refused to procure children for homosexual couples were forced to close on grounds of discrimination. However, enough non-Catholic agencies could meet this demand without any ethical qualms. How humane is a society that awards a "right to a child" to adults, but weakens the child's right to a father and mother who have created and are responsible for the child? Many studies[77] have shown that a child grows up best with his or her parents, as long as they are not extremely negligent in their duties.

When the state legitimizes same-sex outside adoption, it places the alleged rights of an adult minority above the welfare of the child. This contradicts all of Western legal tradition. Even biological parents do not "own" their children but are merely "trustees" with the task of providing the child with the best possible conditions for arriving at his or her unique individuality.

What does social science say about same-sex parenting?[78]

The media keep presenting studies that seem to "prove" that children raised by same-sex couples suffer no ill effects compared to children raised by their natural heterosexual parents. In a world that seems ready to believe anything stamped as "scientific," these so-called studies can serve to advance the interests of people who want children but do not want to engage with a partner of the opposite sex in order to have them.

---

77. "Made for Children: Why the Institution of Marriage Has Special Status," Iona Institute, http://www.ionainstitute.ie/assets/files/MADE%20FOR%20CHILDREN_web.pdf (accessed January 28, 2015). The paper contains further references.

78. Here, in the original German edition, followed an analysis of the *Bamberger Studie* (Marina Rupp [ed.], Pia Bergold and Andrea Dürnberger, *Die Lebenssituation von Kindern in gleichgeschlechtlichen Lebenspartnerschaften* [Cologne: Bundesanzeiger Verlag, 2009]), which intended to show that children cared for by same-sex couples suffered no disadvantages compared to children growing up with their biological parents. The study was commissioned by former Minister of Justice Brigitte Zypries, who was pushing for adoption rights for same-sex couples. At closer look, this study had severe flaws and for methodological reasons could not prove what it pretended to prove. This did not stop the media from using the fabricated results in a public campaign for legalization of same-sex adoption and artificial child-production. The analysis of the German study is replaced with the findings of outstanding American scholars, presented to the Supreme Court in an amicus brief.

In an amicus brief, backed by the American College of Pediatricians and filed with the United States Supreme Court, Professors Loren D. Marks, Mark D. Regnerus, and Donald Paul Sullins state:

> The alleged consensus that children suffer no disadvantage with same-sex parents is a product, not of objective scientific inquiry, but of intense politicization of research agendas in the social science associations. Pervasive methodological flaws undermine the alleged "consensus finding" that children of same-sex parents fare just as well as children of opposite-sex parents.[79]

After scrutinizing all the research there is, this is their shattering conclusion—shattering, because it demonstrates that the West is beginning to let go of the ethics of science essential for the unparalleled flourishing of the European culture—that the West has relinquished the commitment to truth. Before ruling on *Obergefell v. Hodges* the Supreme Court was informed that

> Despite being certified by almost all major social science scholarly associations—indeed, in part because of this—the alleged scientific consensus that having two parents of the same-sex is innocuous for child well-being is almost wholly without basis. . . .
>
> Of the several dozen extant studies on same-sex parenting in the past two decades, only eight have used a random sample large enough to find evidence of lower well-being for children with same-sex parents if it exists. Of these eight, the four most recent studies, by Dr. Mark Regnerus, Dr. Douglas Allen and two by Dr. Paul Sullins, report substantial and pertinent negative outcomes for children with same-sex parents. The four earlier studies, by Dr. Michael Rosenfeld and three by Dr. Jennifer Wainright and colleagues, find no differences for children with same-sex parents because, due to errors in file coding and analysis, a large portion of their samples actually consists of children with heterosexual parents. When the sample used by Wainright's three studies is corrected of this error and re-analyzed, these data also show negative outcomes for children with same-sex parents similar to those reported by Regnerus and Sullins. More importantly, they also show substantially worse outcomes for children who have lived an average of ten years with same-sex parents

who are married than for those who have lived only four years, on average, with unmarried same-sex parents.

[G]iven the mounting evidence of harmful outcomes in children raised in households with same-sex parents, state laws restricting marriage to opposite-sex partners have a rational basis, and it would be imprudent to restrict the states from limiting marriage to opposite-sex partners for the well-being of children.

But the Supreme Court was not impressed. Nor could Justice Anthony Kennedy be reached by the powerful words of a woman who, after the divorce of her parents, was brought up in a lesbian household. In an open letter she implored him not "to let the desires of the adults trump the right of the child."[80] Her open letter is a powerful plea for the right of children to their own natural mother and father who have given them life. As Katy Faust knows from experience, and indeed we all know, "We are made to know, and be known by, both of our parents. When one is absent, that absence leaves a lifelong gaping wound. . . . Making policy that intentionally deprives children of their fundamental rights is something that we should not endorse, incentivize, or promote. . . . It moves us well beyond our 'live and let live' philosophy into the land where our society promotes a family structure where children will *always* suffer loss."

Justice Kennedy and the other four activists on the bench, entrusted to ensure justice in the United States of America, refused to recognize the obvious as obliging truth.

Strategy and Tactics

In a strategy paper by the lobbying group Center for Reproductive Rights (CRR), which is influential in the UN and EU, the tactics for pushing homosexual "marriage" and abortion as "human rights" are described in plain language: the impression is to be given that there is a broad consensus, so that governments adopt the recommended policies (abortion and homosexual "marriage") because they think they have to. The CRR explains the strategy in this way:

There are several advantages to relying primarily on interpretations of hard norms. As interpretations of norms acknowledging reproductive rights are repeated in international bodies, the legitimacy of these rights is reinforced. In addition, the gradual nature of this approach

---

80. Katy Faust, "Dear Justice Kennedy: An Open Letter from the Child of a Loving Gay Parent," *Public Discourse, Ethics, Law and the Common Good* (February 2, 2015), http://www.thepublicdiscourse.com/2015/02/14370/ (accessed September 20, 2015).

ensures that we are never in an "all-or-nothing" situation, where we may risk a major setback. Further, it is a strategy that does not require a major, concentrated investment of resources, but rather it can be achieved over time with regular use of staff, time and funds. Finally, there is a stealth quality to the work: we are achieving incremental recognition of values without a huge amount of scrutiny from the opposition. These lower profile victories will gradually put us in a strong position to assert a broad consensus around our assertions.[81]

This also seems to be the strategy of the Fundamental Rights Agency (FRA), founded in Vienna in 2007, which has the task "to provide the relevant institutions and authorities of the Community and its Member States when implementing Community Law with information, assistance and expertise on fundamental rights in order to support them when they take measures or formulate courses of action within their respective spheres of competence to fully respect fundamental rights."[82] This agency's first large project—with an annual budget of €20 million—was the pan-European investigation *Homophobia and Discrimination on Grounds of Sexual Orientation in the EU Member States.*[83] Apparently, the FRA's 80 or so employees weren't enough to conduct this investigation. The project was handed over to the Fundamental Rights Agency Legal Experts (FRALEX), a network of longstanding activists from the former EU Network of Independent Experts on Fundamental Rights.

If one asks how much discrimination the study has brought to light, in the view of FRA director Morten Kjaerum, it is astonishingly little. "It is remarkable how little official or unofficial data currently exists in the EU regarding discrimination complaints due to sexual orientation."[84] Most of the complaints filed cannot be legally classified as discrimination upon closer examination. Nonetheless, the experts recommend that all member states set up "Equality Bodies" with extensive powers to actively observe even the most meager discrimination. "The suggestions made by FRALEX remind one of a new kind of Holy Inquisition, veh-

81. Congressional Record, Extension of Remarks—E 2534-2547 of December 8, 2003, quoted in Jacob Cornides, "Human Rights Pitted Against Man (II): The Network Is Back," *The International Journal of Human Rights* 14, no. 7 (2010): 1139–64. At http://www.informaworld.com/smpp/content~db=all~content=a930666426~frm=titlelink (accessed October 6, 2015).

82. Council Regulation (EC) No. 168/2007 of February 15, 2007, Article 2.

83. Olivier de Schutter, *Homophobia and Discrimination on Grounds of Sexual Orientation in the EU Member States, Part I: Legal Analysis* (Vienna: EU Agency for Fundamental Rights, 2008).

84. Ibid., 7.

mic court or witch-hunt rather than of a democratic society under the rule of law," writes Jakob Cornides.[85]

The War Against "Homophobia"

The word "homophobia" is a new creation intended to defame people who object to homosexuality and the deregulation of sexual norms (see Chapter 8, p. 184). For this purpose, the European Parliament passed the "European Parliament resolution on homophobia in Europe."[86] It is the template for subsequent "action plans against homophobia" as they were introduced by the leftist parties in Germany.

In reference to "human rights obligations," which despite constant manipulative statements do not exist, the European Parliament defines homophobia as "an aversion to gay, lesbian, bisexual and transsexual (LBGTI) people" and places it at the level of "racism, xenophobia and anti-Semitism." Thus a *feeling* is criminalized, not a clearly defined act.

"Homophobia" is manifested "privately and publicly" "as hate speech and appeals for discrimination" and is "veiled as religious freedom." In a number of EU member states, it has led "to alarming cases" such as "a ban on gay pride parades or equal rights marches" or constitutional amendments "to prevent same-sex marriages or other marriage-like associations."

"At the level of both the EU and the member states, further measures are needed to eradicate homophobia." For these reasons, the European Parliament calls on the member states to:

1. Strengthen the battle against homophobia through *educational measures*—such as information campaigns against homophobia in schools, universities and the media—or through *legal and administrative decrees* and by legislative means.
2. Ensure that homophobia-based *hate speech or incitement to discrimination is avenged with extreme efficiency.*
3. Forbid discrimination based on sexual orientation in all spheres, and by completing anti-discrimination legislation . . . to cover *all types of discrimination in all spheres.*
4. Consider the battle against homophobia in *financial allocations* for 2007 . . . and strictly monitor this process and to *report to the European Parliament on any failure of a member state* to implement these measures.

---

85. Jakob Cornides, "Human Rights Pitted Against Man (II)," loc. cit., 169, note 81.
86. European Parliament Resolution on Homophobia in Europe, B60025/2006.

5. Take any other measures aimed at realizing the principle of equality in their social and legal systems.

Here the spirit of totalitarianism emerges undisguised. The aversion to homosexuality (LGBTI) must be eliminated. Freedom of religion is curtailed, and the people must be trained in a new morality. If that is not enough, laws must be created to classify the "aversion" as "hate speech" and persecute those who engage in it. *All* types of discrimination in *all* spheres of life are to be avenged with *extreme efficiency.* For this, the state must provide funds to *strictly monitor the process* and report *any failure* of a member state in this regard.

Don't be fooled: The totalitarian, cultural revolutionary objectives that the European Parliament presents here *are* being put forth with extreme efficiency. The "educational measures" are being implemented in K–12 schools through sex education. The battle for homosexual "marriage" is being fought in every country. Anti-discrimination laws and new criminal offenses such as "hate speech" are being created. Many forms of speech are being reclassified as "behavior" to facilitate prosecution. The UN, EU and national governments are providing billions in funding for the culture war. The EU is establishing monitoring authorities in every member state. This is all in the name of freedom, tolerance and human rights.

A Socialist delegate to the Council of Europe, Christine McCafferty (United Kingdom), wanted to take freedom of conscience away from doctors and medical personnel who refuse to participate in abortion and euthanasia. However, on October 7, 2010, the resolution was not only rejected by the majority of the Council of Europe, but turned upside down. The Council decided:

> No person, hospital or institution shall be coerced, held liable or discriminated against in any manner because of a refusal to perform, accommodate, assist or submit to an abortion, the performance of a human miscarriage, or euthanasia or any act which could cause the death of a human fetus or embryo, for any reason.[87]

This decision was brought about through deployment of hundreds of European pro-life and pro-family organizations.

---

87. For freedom of conscience: http://www.europeandignitywatch.org/de/day-to-day/detail/article/council-of-europe-for-freedom-of-conscience.html (accessed October 2015).

Hillary Clinton and the "Human Rights of LGBTI People"

In celebration of Human Rights Day on December 6, 2011, US Secretary of State Hillary Clinton gave a talk at the UN Palace of Nations in Geneva to convince the world that "gay rights are human rights, and human rights are gay rights."[88] Those who have an opposing opinion are equated with advocates of slavery, honor killing, burning of widows and genital mutilation. Collective action must be taken to "to reach a global consensus that recognizes the human rights of LGBT citizens everywhere." She further states:

> In Washington, we have created a task force at the State Department to support and coordinate this work. And in the coming months, we will provide every [U.S.] embassy with a toolkit to help improve their efforts. And we have created a program that offers emergency support to defenders of human rights for LGBT people. . . . I am also pleased to announce that we are launching a new Global Equality Fund that will support the work of civil society organizations working on these issues around the world. . . . [Those fighting to expand the definition of human rights are] on the right side of history.

This prompts some questions to Hillary Clinton:

• Which "human rights of LGBTI people" is she talking about? Is it correct to assume that she is talking about the right to same-sex "marriage," adoption of children, artificial reproduction and indoctrination of children and teenagers in school? Does she not refer to these demands by name because she knows that they are not recognized as human rights anywhere?
• Could it be that the US Secretary of State is stirring up hate against people who, out of conscience (Universal Declaration of Human Rights, Art. 1), do not agree with the US government's priorities?
• Does the US government have a mandate from voters to give the LGBTI agenda priority in its foreign policy? Where does she get the right to turn laws into an instrument of the global cultural revolution?

Clinton's speech is a masterpiece of demagoguery. It meets the criteria for demagoguery as put forth by Martin Morlock in his book *Hohe Schule der Verführung* ("University of Seduction"):

> A person is pursuing demagoguery when he uses a favorable opportunity for a political purpose by flattering the masses, appealing to their feelings, instincts and prejudices, is guilty of hustling and lying,

---

88. Hillary Rodham Clinton, Remarks in Recognition of International Human Rights Day, December 6, 2011, http://m.state.gov/md178368.htm (accessed October 6, 2015).

represents the truth in an exaggerated or grossly simplistic manner, puts forth his objective as the objective of all well-meaning people, and presents the manner in which he implements it or suggests it be implemented as the only one possible.[89]

No, opponents of the LGBTI are not for honor killing, because they believe that no one has the right to murder anyone, not even unborn children. They are not for burning widows, because they believe that men and women are equal and that their dignity is sacrosanct. They are not for genital mutilation of women, because they advocate fulfilled sexuality in committed love of man and woman. They are not for slavery, because they believe that no person has the right to own, use or exploit another—not even for satisfaction of his sexual desires. Instead, they advocate for human rights as set forth in the 1948 Universal Declaration of Human Rights:

- For the inviolable dignity of the person.
- For marriage as the lifelong union of a man and a woman.
- For the natural family as the best place for children to grow up.

Opponents of the LGBT agenda are convinced that they are on the right side of history.

A New Anthropology

Unlike an animal, a person can ask, "Who am I?" Is man a creation of God or a higher mammal whose life ends with death? All religions place people in relation to a higher, invisible power and teach people to live in accord with this power in order to have good lives. On this basis, against this horizon, high cultures have arisen. Atheistic belief systems that limit man to his earthly existence have ruptured entire continents and pulled them into the abyss of totalitarian systems of power that have killed hundreds of millions of people to achieve their aims. How a society answers the question "Who is man?" determines the culture and fate of the individual.

No philosophy or religion has a higher image of man than Judaism and Christianity. The first creation story states that "God created mankind in his image; in the image of God he created them; male and female he created them" (Genesis 1:27). On this belief rests all of Western culture, which became the model for the entire world. It could be *true*. It is unlikely that lies or delusions can give rise to such creative force as seen in the Western culture built on Christianity. The fruits of

---

89. Martin Morlock, *Hohe Schule der Verführung: Ein Handbuch der Demagogie* (Wien-Düsseldorf: Econ Verlag, 1977), 24.

the atheistic view of man on the one hand, and the Christian view on the other, for the individual and society as a whole, speak volumes.

Modern and post-modern man have emancipated themselves—from God, from nature, from the family, from tradition—woman from man, children from parents and individuals from themselves as man or woman. They stand naked, restrained by nothing and defined by nothing other than their own wishes, desires and drives. They think they are free to self-actualize, and do not notice that, in their vulnerability and lack of inhibitions, they are more malleable than ever before: the strong can use the weak for their own purposes without the uprooted, manipulated person noticing it *in time*.

A person is born as a man or woman and benefits in life when he unfolds in his natural biological identity and matures. Unfolding and maturing means overcoming the limits of egocentricity to embrace the other. Everyone yearns and everyone fears to step beyond his small self. This happens naturally when devoting one's love to another and when the two devote their love to the child. This gives rise to life, it gives rise to the elemental bond, it gives rise to the basic social unit of human life: the family. It is dependent on the everyday moral decision in favor of the good, on the exercise of virtues. Parents have the task of raising their children to be people who strive toward the good, a task that they can only fulfill if they themselves were raised to do this by their parents. The real source for striving for goodness is religion, which awakens and maintains the transcendent motivation toward eternal salvation.

Equating same-sex couples' relationships with the marriage of a man and a woman is a dagger thrust to the heart of marriage and family. It guts their nature. Loyal devotion in a committed relationship of man and woman and the essential willingness to create children and raise them is the only justification for the special position of this nucleus of society. The capriciousness of the individual who wishes to determine his gender himself, and who wishes to act out his sexual needs without limits, corresponds to the capriciousness of the state in defining as family relationships that do not possess these important characteristics. All types of human relationships are now to be considered family, even though they are merely broken families in which the promise of happiness transforms into bitter sorrow and lifelong trauma for the children.

LGBTI activists love to say that they call for equal rights and not for destruction of the family. Michaelangelo Signorile, journalist and homosexual activist, says it plainly:

> The goal of the homosexual movement is: to fight for same-sex marriage and its benefits, and then, once this is achieved, to completely

redefine the institution of marriage, not to demand the right to marriage as a way to bind ourselves to society's morals, but to debunk a myth and to turn an age-old institution on its head. . . . The subversive act that gays and lesbians are undertaking . . . is the idea of completely changing the family.[90]

The model of marriage and family must have validity in society and be a desirable life goal, so that the moral behavior that marriage and family makes possible is supported by social standards and imparted by family upbringing and state educational institutions. Marriage and family are built on monogamy. While lifelong commitment is the desire of any person who has ever experienced love, it is especially the growing desire of young people, as studies show.[91] However, bringing such longings to fruition makes high demands on people and must be learned. If this model is undermined through constant mass sexualization and a hollowing-out and distorting of the concept of marriage and family, then the foundation on which the culture rests is destroyed. If the foundation crumbles, then sooner or later so does the house built on it. High culture requires high moral standards.

90. Johann Braun, *Ehe und Familie am Scheideweg*, loc. cit., 157, note 60.

91. In the *Shell Jugendstudie 2010* (Shell Youth Study 2010), in Germany, 92 percent said that "leading a good family life" was one of their most important goals. At the author's request, IfD Allensbach, a German polling organization, has confirmed that young people's desire for marriage and family has continuously grown over the past 10 years. http://s05.static-shell.com/co ntent/dam/shell-new/local/country/deu/downloads /pdf/youth-study-2010flyer.pdf (accessed October 6, 2015).

11

Christian Belief and Homosexuality

For the time will come when people will not tolerate sound doctrine but, following their own desires and insatiable curiosity, will accumulate teachers and will stop listening to the truth and will be diverted to myths. But you, be self-possessed in all circumstances; put up with hardship; perform the work of an evangelist; fulfill your ministry.

2 Timothy 4:3–5

Ethical Monotheism

WHEN THERE IS resistance to the deregulation of sexuality in Christian-influenced countries, it comes from the Church. Many denominations have separated from Christ's one Church, but all rely on the Bible and preach the good news of God becoming man in Jesus Christ, who came to put men on the path to God's kingdom. Orientation toward God's commandments has been the mark of Western culture, a culture that has spread to all ends of the earth and has set the standard for human dignity, freedom, art and science for all cultures. This high culture is based on high morals.

If the first commandment—adoration of God—breaks down, then all the other commandments do, too. The name of God is being forgotten. Sunday is no longer recognized as the Lord's Day. Father and mother are losing their place in the social order. Unborn children are legally killed by the millions. All types of extramarital sex are seen as normal. Limitless greed is creating ever more poverty around the world. In the media, truth and lies are becoming increasingly difficult to distinguish. Can anyone show that disregard of the Ten Commandments has been beneficial to humanity?

In the pagan world of ancient times, Judaism's ethical monotheism was something completely new. Before that, sexuality saturated all aspects of life. Even the gods were sexually active, and people believed that they had created the world by sexual acts. There were very few

176

restrictive sexual norms. Homosexuality was not outlawed, but, at most, the passive role was considered inferior.

The revelation of God to his chosen people brought a sexual revolution of unheard-of proportions. Teacher, author, and talk show host Dennis Prager describes this radical change.[1] The sex act was sanctified and sheltered in the marriage of a man and a woman. This laid the foundation of the family, which Jews held in high regard throughout the millennia and which enabled the Jewish people to survive all attempts at extermination.[2] Homosexuality was outlawed (Lev 18:22; 20:13). Prager writes:

> Given the unambiguous nature of the biblical attitude toward homosexuality, however, such a reconciliation [between Judaism, Christianity and homosexual behavior] is not possible. All that is possible is to declare: "I am aware that the Bible condemns homosexuality, and I consider the Bible wrong."

Prager believes that no book has contributed more to civilizing the world than the Hebrew Bible:

> And the bedrock of this civilization, and of Jewish life, of course, has been the centrality and purity of family life. But the family is not a natural unit so much as a value that must be cultivated and protected. The Greeks assaulted the family in the name of beauty and Eros. The Marxists assaulted the family in the name of progress. And, today, gay liberation assaults it in the name of compassion and equality. I understand why gays would do this. Life has been miserable for many of them.... What I have not understood is why Jews or Christians would join the assault. I do now. They do not know what is at stake. At stake is our civilization. [3]

The Biblical Order of Creation

According to Genesis, human beings were created in the image of God as man and woman to be complementary to one another; and they were created to be fruitful. The binding love between man and woman, which culminates in a child, is an analogy of the Trinitarian love of the Father, Son, and Holy Spirit. Because God *is* love, He created people out

---

1. Dennis Prager, "Judaism, Homosexuality and Civilization," *Ultimate Issues* 6, no. 2 (April–June 1990): 9 et seq.

2. Cf. Jonathan Sacks, *Radical Then, Radical Now: The Legacy of the World's Oldest Religion* (London: Bloomsbury, 2001).

3. Denis Prager, "Judaism, Homosexuality and Civilization," 24.

of love and called them to love. He destined them to be co-creators of new human beings. Therefore, the practice of homosexuality contradicts the reality of human creation. To live by it separates one from God and ultimately from one's own destiny. Behavior that separates one from God is called sin in the Bible. Even non-Christian religions share this view. Until now, this view of the human being in relation to God has been predominant in most countries on this earth.

It is not just isolated passages in which homosexual behavior is condemned, but the entire biblical tradition. It reveals an entire order of creation that is given to man that he is to violate at his own risk. This order of creation forbids crossing the set boundaries in sexuality: crossing the boundary of complementary gender through homosexuality, the boundary of blood relationship through incest, and the boundary of species through sexual relations with animals. The pagan people whom the Jews were surrounded by did all of those things (see Gen 18:20).

The analogy of bride and groom for the relationship of God to people extends from the first to the last page of the Bible. God offers people a covenant of love and presents it by analogy with the marital love between man and woman: "And as a bridegroom rejoices in his bride, so shall your God rejoice in you" (Isaiah 62:5). This God is a jealous god and becomes angry when his bride, his chosen people, becomes involved with other gods, particularly Baal and Asherah, the male and female gods of sexual excess that the pagan peoples indulged through temple prostitution and orgiastic sex. Again and again, God's people are untrue to him, and again and again it ends in disaster.

The prophet Elijah fights his greatest battle against the priests of Baal and Asherah, to which Israel fell through the corruption of its king Ahab and his wife Jezebel. (This exciting narrative can be found in 1 Kings 16–19.) The king curses Elijah as the "disturber of Israel," but Elijah counters: "It is not I who disturb Israel, but you and your father's house, by forsaking the commands of the LORD and you by following the Baals" (1 Kings 18:17–18).

Elijah goes all out. He challenges the priests of Baal to a public showdown on Mount Carmel between the God of Israel and the god Baal. He comes out alone against 450 prophets of Baal and stakes his life on the true God of Israel revealing himself. Both are to put a sacrificial animal on a pile of wood and call to their god. "The God who answers with fire is God" (1 Kings 18:24). All of the Baal prophets' fury is for naught. Elijah teases them, asks if their god is sleeping, on a trip, or has just stepped out. The prophets of Baal call louder and even slash themselves in a blood ritual; "but there was no sound, no one answering, no one listening" (2 Samuel 22:42).

Before Elijah called upon his God, he had water poured over the wood pile and then loudly pleaded:

> "Lord, God of Abraham, Isaac, and Israel, let it be known this day that you are God in Israel and that I am your servant and have done all these things at your command. Answer me, LORD! Answer me, that this people may know that you, LORD, are God and that you have turned their hearts back to you." Then the fire of the Lord came forth and consumed the burnt offering, the wood, the stones and the earth. Even the water in the trench was lapped up. The entire people saw it, fell prostrate and cried: "The Lord is God! The Lord is God!" But Elijah ordered them: "Seize the prophets of Baal. Let none of them escape!" The people seized them, and Elijah had them taken to the stream of Kishon, where he slaughtered them. (1 Kings 18:36–40)

Then, after years of drought, rain fell again. King Ahab celebrated, ate, and drank. However, Elijah climbed to the top of Carmel, "crouched down to the earth, and put his head between his knees" (1 Kings 18:42). Now he had to save himself from Jezebel, who had called for his life. Elijah, who has risked everything and won, is afraid.

The Book of Hosea

The dramatic love relationship between God and his people is portrayed in the Book of Hosea. Written more than 500 years before Christ, it reads like a warning to those in the present as much as in the past. God as a passionate, betrayed lover to his people—this is a language, *a relationship,* that we can hardly understand today. But what God is to accuse his people of, and the consequences of their rebelliousness, are at their core no different now from then.

God laments over his people who have broken their bond of love with him. His people pursue foreign gods, they commit sexual offenses and there is "no birth, no pregnancy, no conception" (Hos 4:10; 9:10–12). They do not know their God "for the spirit of prostitution is in them" (Hos 5:4). Even the priests become apostates (Hos 4:6), and the prophets are persecuted (Hos 9:7–8).

The consequences threaten the existence of Israel. Four kings are murdered within 15 years, Israel is conquered by its enemies, all of its fortresses are destroyed, and the people are scattered. "They have not cried to me from their hearts when they wailed upon their beds" (Hos 7:14).

God, who was so angry that he wanted to destroy his disloyal people, makes a surprising turnaround. He is seized by compassion: "How could I give you up, Ephraim, or deliver you up, Israel? . . . My heart is overwhelmed, my pity is stirred" (Hos 11:8).

At the end of the song of the prophet Hosea, God's people are ready to return. They plead to God: "Forgive all iniquity, and take what is good" (Hos 14:3). God, who loves His people as the groom loves his bride, showers them with grace: "I will heal their apostasy, I will love them freely; for my anger is turned away from them" (Hos 14:5–9).

The drama between people and God always remains the same: when God is no longer worshiped as Creator and Lord of his people, then the people's own creative force, sexuality, becomes an idol. "They exchanged the truth of God for a lie and revered and worshiped the creature rather than the creator, who is blessed forever" (Romans 1:25). Idols are empty shadow-images that draw their power over people through the misdirection of worship, which belongs to God alone. They are a portal to demonic powers of which the modern world wishes to know nothing. Time and again, the Bible warns people not to surrender to them, but again and again the people are deaf to this warning until the bad consequences can already be seen.

Jesus Christ

Jesus reestablished the original mandate of creation—loving devotion between man and wife. It has been hard to live by in all eras, and, as we have seen, it was always challenged by the Jews. Jesus demands not only purity of love, but also purity of heart (Matthew 5:8). For him, it is not about externally adhering to legislation, but about the pure, true attitude of the heart. In the conversation with the Pharisees, he points to the *beginning* and declares marriage between a man and a woman to be a sacramental bond instituted by God that men cannot dissolve. Jesus says:

> Have you not read that from the beginning the Creator "made them
> male and female" and said, "For this reason a man shall leave his
> father and mother and be joined to his wife, and the two shall
> become one flesh?" So they are no longer two, but one flesh. There-
> fore, what God has joined together, no human being must separate.
> (Matthew 19:4–6)

This plan of God has been obscured by the *hard-heartedness* of man. "Because of the hardness of your hearts Moses allowed you to divorce your wives, but from the beginning it was not so" (Matthew 19:8). The hard, lustful heart that tends toward exploiting others to satisfy its own desires, this is the hard heart that Jesus wishes to make "soft"—honest and true—so that the Kingdom of God can descend upon this world.

Nowhere does Jesus oppose sexuality. He is concerned about one thing: he calls people to take the high road of love and at the same time gives them the grace that allows them to do so. He does not force anyone into it;

on the contrary, he protects the adulteress from the stones, the cold, hard projections, of her fellow men. Jesus awakens the yearning for self-giving love in the hearts of people and shows the way for this yearning to be fulfilled. Sexuality as a fruitful, life-giving expression of love is the plan created for humanity by God—the God who is Himself love and life.

Jesus does not explicitly condemn homosexuality. But he consecrates marriage and elevates it to a sacrament, because it reflects God's bond with humanity and is therefore the only sphere in which the sexual act is in keeping with the dignity of human beings. Rejection of homosexuality is so deeply anchored in Judaism that Jesus did not have to waste words on it.

The Apostles

The Apostles unfold the teachings of Jesus, who came not to abolish the law, but to fulfill it. They carry the good news of Jesus out into the Greek and Roman world, in which all types of sexual perversion and excess were common. Paul names them in the so-called catalog of vices (1 Corinthians 6:9 and 1 Timothy 1:10) and states very clearly that people engaging in them "will not inherit the kingdom of God." The members of the new community who came from this world were themselves embroiled in this vice; Paul tells them, "but now you have had yourselves washed, you were sanctified, you were justified in the name of the Lord Jesus Christ and in the Spirit of our God" (1 Corinthians 6:11). This is the sanctification of the flesh, which "is not for immorality, but for the Lord, and the Lord is for the body. . . . Do you not know that your body is a temple of the Holy Spirit within you, whom you have from God, and that you are not your own?" (1 Corinthians 6:12–19). The complete affirmation of love is specific to Christianity. There is no separation between spirit and flesh—the entire person is called to sanctification, and as a child of God is empowered to achieve it (see John 1:12).

In the first chapter of the Epistle to the Romans (Romans 1:18–32), Paul explains how people fall away from God: first comes injustice, through which people suppress the truth. Because they have recognized God but have not honored him as God, this is not excusable. Their thought darkens, and they fall prey to the lusts of their heart and degraded passions. Now they exchange the truth of God for a lie and worship the creature instead of the creator. This has consequences for sexual behavior: their women exchange natural intercourse for the unnatural, and men give up natural intercourse with a woman and burn with lust for one another. Adultery becomes common practice. People begin to hate God and use other people as objects.

Especially among women, the Bible shows the hate and mercilessness of those whose sin is exposed: Jezebel wanted to murder the prophet Elijah, and Herodias demanded the head of John the Baptist and had it served on a platter by a weak, drunken king. Why? Why was Jesus' precursor, who had recognized him even in his mother's womb, to die so ignominiously? Because he, who had authority but no power, told Herod, who had power but no authority, that he did not have the right to marry his brother's wife. King David was different: he does not kill Nathan, who confronts him with his crime, but confesses his deed: "I have sinned against the Lord." Nathan immediately grants him forgiveness (cf. 2 Samuel 12).

The center of the Apostle Paul's teaching is not the vice of humanity but the call to holiness, which can be achieved in the marriage of a man and a woman, in which the spouses are "subordinate to one another out of reverence for Christ" (Ephesians 5). He presents the "great mystery" of marriage as an analogy for the mystery of Christ and the Church, which is characterized by spousal love.

John Paul II's Theology of the Body

The seed of God's plan for man was planted by the Holy Spirit in the creation stories of the Bible, slowly unfolded during the millennia before Christ, and blossomed into full light of day with Jesus. Pope John Paul II preaches this same seed in his book *The Theology of the Body* to announce *human love as part of God's plan of salvation.*[4] His life's work, as Karol Wojtyla and as Pope John Paul II, was to interpret the deep dimensions of man and woman, of love and sexuality, of marriage and family, for modern people, because these are the crucial questions at the crossroads between the "culture of life" and the "culture of death."

> "I have set before you life and death, the blessing and the curse.
> Choose life, then, that you and your descendants may live." (Deut.
> 30:19)

John Paul II wanted us to have life in abundance.

In an era marked by materialism at all levels, that idolizes physical health and satisfaction of carnal yearnings, John Paul gives the body back its personal integrity. Theologically, he restores it to its original condition as a temple of the Holy Spirit. Only integrity of body and spirit reflects the dignity of the person. Any separation—be it in favor of the spirit, as with the Manicheans, or in favor of the body, as with the

---

4. John Paul II, *Man and Woman He Created Them: A Theology of the Body* (Pauline Books & Media, 2006). See also Karol Wojtyla, *Love and Responsibility* (San Francisco: Ignatius Press, 1981).

materialists—splits the person and alienates him from himself. Far from seeing the body as inferior to the spirit, John Paul II says that the body and only the body can make the invisible visible: the spiritual and divine. "It was created to bring the mystery eternally hidden in God into the visible reality of the world and thus become a sign of this mystery."[5]

As *man and woman*, the human person is made in the image and likeness of God. Both are complete in and of themselves, and yet each is faced by his opposite, to which he feels attracted and with whom he wishes to and can become one, if he transcends himself. It is exactly this dual nature of the human person that John Paul sees as the image of God's love. This God is love. He is the triune God of Father, Son and Holy Spirit—a union of persons that is mirrored in the human family. As John Paul wrote, "The world contains no better, more perfect image of God than the union of man and woman and the life that issues from it."[6]

Thus the family appears as a human reflection of the Trinity. It is also a community of persons unified by love. The only-begotten Son entered the history of humanity through the family and, through his own example, taught the deep truth of the family, the Church and the Trinity.

However, that can be only a clue to the treasure that the church is called to tend and *uphold* in a world that seems to have lost its orientation and is about to override the compass in people's hearts.

Churches under Pressure from the Global Sexual Revolution

In all eras, the unchangeable truth of the Gospel has challenged the ruling power structures. If that were not so, the "New Jerusalem" would already have arrived. Christ's Church has the task of speaking anew the truth of the Gospel in every era, to expose every ideology and all totalitarianism, and to protect freedom, so that the path to salvation remains open for all who seek it. It can do this only if it is *in the world* but not *of the world.*[7]

---

5. John Paul II, *Theology of the Body* (February 20, 1980).

6. John Paul II, *Homily on the Feast of the Holy Family* (December 30, 1998).

7. At his Freiburg Concert Hall speech, Pope Benedict XVI held this up for the Church in Germany to view. He said: "All the more, then, it is time once again to discover the right form of detachment from the world, to move resolutely away from the Church's worldliness. This does not, of course, mean withdrawing from the world: quite the contrary. . . . Openness to the concerns of the world means, then, for the Church that is detached from worldliness, bearing witness to the primacy of God's love according to the Gospel through word and deed, here and now, a task which at the same time points beyond the present world because this present life is also bound up with eternal life." At http://www.vatican.va/holy_father/benedict_xvi/speeches/2011/september/documents/hf_ben-xvi_spe_20110925_catholics-freiburg_en.html (accessed October 2015).

All through history, the ideology of the time has penetrated the church and corrupted a part of it. *After* the given political power structure has collapsed, this becomes the basis for bitter accusations against the Church—and reason for remorse and penance within the Church. If this happens, the door is opened to a new beginning. One thinks of the German Christians under National Socialism or the pact that portions of the Russian Orthodox Church made with Stalinism.

In each era, however, there were also those who sacrificed their lives for the truth of Christ. The more forcefully the ideology dictates people's thinking and behavior, the more these martyrs become brilliant icons, sources of hope and strength for those who follow.

The ideology of our era's sexual revolution is targeting the very core of Christian belief, the question "What is man?" Because the ideologues of the sexual revolution deny God, human beings are degraded to a pure product of evolution who do not significantly differ from animals and are consequently delivered to manipulation by their own kind. The fact that this can spiral to denial of the binary sexual identity of man and woman would likely have surprised anyone who lived on this earth before Judith Butler.

Today even the churches are caving in to the ideological pressure of the time, although to varying degrees. All Christian denominations combined have more than 2 billion members worldwide. When that is compared to the numbers belonging to sexual activist groups, one is astounded that the resistance is so weak. Even within the church, they are shaking the foundations of Christian anthropology and morals which recognize man as a creation of God, made in the image and likeness of the triune God as man and woman, and called to become one flesh and be fruitful. For Christians, this is one of the *non-negotiable* fundamentals. Nonetheless, everywhere in the church it is being negotiated under pressure from the LGBTI agenda and is leading to division.

In our time, the pope's is the one voice of Christian conscience heard worldwide. Not even the biggest pop stars can attract so many young people to one place as the popes gather at World Youth Days. Isn't it strange that this can be done by old men whom the mainstream media depict as divorced from reality, hostile to sex, hostile to women, and authoritarian dictators? The special status of the Holy See, which allows him to send messages (as papal nuncios) into the world and accredit 180 ambassadors in Rome to act as UN observers and to speak at the annual General Assembly of the UN, gives him insight into and influence on international politics.

Because he is the voice of conscience, he is hated by all who themselves live in "sexual diversity" and want to impose this "human right" on the world. Never does the secular world feel as provoked and as furious—throwing all rationality overboard—as when the subject of sexuality comes up. It would much rather blame the pope for AIDS than address questions such as why men who have sex with men constitute 70 percent of all new AIDS infections. They would rather make all priests scapegoats for sexual abuse than deal with questions such as why hundreds of thousands of children are abused in their everyday environment.

The Anglican Church

Farthest away from biblical revelation are parts of the Anglican Church. The tactic is to cut it away like a salami—slice by slice—and before you know it, there's no more sausage. At the 1930 Lambeth Conference, the Anglican Church broke with the contraception ban then valid for all Christians and allowed contraception "in exceptional cases." Only 40 years later, what was forbidden among Christians for 2000 years had become an assumed aspect of life in the West, resulting in a demographic decline that threatens its very existence.

The Anglican Church also leads in acceptance of homosexuality. This first occurred in the blessing of same-sex couples, because, after all, "God loves everyone." Then followed tolerance in pastoral offices, followed by the "abolition of hypocrisy" through ordinary appointments of homosexuals, and finally in grasping for the bishop's miter, which divorced homosexual Gene Robinson succeeded in getting in New Hampshire in 2003. This resulted in several hundred Anglican bishops boycotting the Lambeth Conference and holding an alternative conference in Jerusalem.

You might think, a couple of homosexual priests and a bishop—so what? But cultural revolutionary change is not a question of numbers but of principle—and both sides know it. The Church has the task of protecting the truth that has been valid through the ages. Open one gate, and the whole Trojan horse is wheeled in. The devastation this brings was described by Dietrich von Hildebrand in his book *Trojan Horse in the City of God*.[8]

The Lutheran Church

In a mere 20 years, the Lutheran Church in Germany (EKD) has drifted with the times from unambiguous biblical rejection of homosexuality to legalizing homosexual concubinage in the rectories.

---

8. Dietrich von Hildebrand, *Das trojanische Pferd in der Stadt Gottes* (Regensburg: Verlag Josef Habbel, 1968).

At Christopher Street Day on June 24, 2011, for example, openly homosexual mayor Klaus Wowereit "preached" at St. Mary's Church in Berlin. He took the opportunity to praise the Lutheran church as a "reliable ally" of gays and lesbians.[9]

The departure from biblical teaching began with a small step that seemed harmless: permission to "bless homophilic people in their partnership" (1993 Fürth Declaration of the regional synod of the Evangelical Lutheran Church in Bavaria). In the time that followed, this small liberal concession was "excessively hashed out and repeatedly overstepped without anyone intervening against it. The practice of church-approved tolerance gradually made people used to ministers with homosexual tendencies increasingly outing themselves . . . as well as services blessing homosexual couples, complete with vestments and pealing bells in the public area of the church."[10]

Misunderstood "tolerance," a mixture of permissiveness and well-meaning open-mindedness, created a reality that was powerfully reinforced by socio-political developments: In 2001, the first step toward homosexual "marriage" came with the enactment of Germany's civil partnership act. Shouldn't the Church then follow suit and offer gays and lesbians liturgical blessing of their partnerships? In 2006, Germany's general equality act was passed. Would the Church still be allowed to "discriminate" by rejecting the practice of homosexuality?

There was temporarily fruitful resistance from the Arbeitskreis Bekennender Christen in Bayern, or ABC (Working Group of Professed Christians). Blessing services were not allowed—but they happened anyway. The EKD published a disoriented guide called *Mit Spannungen leben* ("Living with Tension"). It provided pages of learned reference to biblical teaching on marriage and family, only to conclude: "For those who have not been given the charism of sexual abstinence, same-sex cohabitation that is formed in the commandment to love, and therefore ethically responsible, is advisable" (Point 3.5).

This prompts the question: if the ability to control one's drives is a *charism*, how should the state and church then deal with people who have not been given the gift of sexual restraint and want to direct their sexual desires to several partners or even animals?

---

9. http://www.medrum.de/content/schenkte-gott-dem-menschen-am-achten-tag-d ie-sexuelle-identitaet (accessed October 3, 2015).

10. Martin Pflaumer, "Genese einer Fehlentscheidung. Gleichgeschlechtliche Paare im evangelischen Pfarrhaus," in Andreas Späth (ed.), *Und schuf sie als Mann und Frau. Kirche in der Zerreißprobe zwischen Homosexuellen-Lobby und Heiliger Schrift* (Ansbach: Verlag Logos, 2010), 11–17.

The ground beneath the church was so loosened in two decades that in 2010, the EKD synod passed a new law on pastoral service that accepts gay and lesbian couples, with or without children, in the Lutheran rectory as heads of the parish, as long as they have been legally joined and meet the requirements of "commitment, reliability and mutual responsibility."

Its rationale: "The term *family cohabitation* has deliberately been selected for its broad meaning. It includes not only cross-generational cohabitation, but any type of legally binding organized cohabitation of at least two people that represents a permanently entered union of solidarity."[11]

The Lutheran Church has thereby emptied the term "family" of all its meaning: it requires no parents and no children, but places demands that men living as homosexuals extremely seldom meet, because among homosexual men fidelity is the exception and promiscuity is the rule. Why does the EKD synod demand this behavior specifically from homosexual couples when things have long been extremely lively even among heterosexuals in the Lutheran rectory?

Consider what is at stake. Emptying the terms "marriage" and "family" of their meaning by eliminating opposite sexes and procreation represents a break with biblical teaching and with all of human history— not just Christian history. It leads to uncertainty among the faithful, to their walking away from the church, and to splits within the church itself, and it poses a considerable obstacle to attempts at ecumenism. However, the most serious consequence is that the shepherds are leading their flocks along the wide path that leads to loss of eternal salvation.

And what is left in the plus column when people take risks that so endanger their existence? The chair of the synod of the Evangelical Lutheran Church in Bavaria (ELKB), Dorothea Deneke-Stoll, an advocate of the pastoral rules, expected that the issue would not gain much attention. No more than "a total of five cases" of same-sex partners were known of in the Lutheran Church in Bavaria. But why are only "five cases" enough to throw fundamental principles of Christian belief out the window?

Consider that this involved the needs of a minority of a minority of a minority. Less than 3 percent of the population has homosexual tendencies. Of them, only about 2 percent take advantage of the legal institu-

---

11. Documentation of the conflict around the *Pfarrdienstgesetz der EKD* (Law of Pastoral Service in the Lutheran Church, 2011) is documented here: http://www. medr um. de / content / 126-synodale-beschliessen-einstimmig-epochales-pfarrdienstgesetz (accessed October 2015).

tion of same-sex partnership (the "divorce" numbers are not published), and of these only a tiny percentage are Protestant ministers. Why is the EKD willing to incur all the aforementioned risks and consequences to satisfy this minuscule group?

Today, in the Lutheran rectory—once, and in many cases still today, a blessed place for the family—anything goes: divorce, remarriage of divorcees, cohabitation, and now even homosexual partnerships. How will the parents of the 3.2 percent of families who still go to church explain to their children the wedding rings on the hands of two men or women standing before the congregation who *are* role-models, no matter how they live? How will a pastor in a gay "marriage" explain God's biblical order of creation, which places clear (sexual) ethical requirements on people? If he doesn't want to look like a hypocrite in front of everybody, he has to gut and distort this teaching and must adapt his Bible interpretation to his own rebellion against the Gospel.

What happened to the doctrine of *Sola Scriptura*, which underlies the identity of the Lutheran Church? There was and is resistance to it in the Lutheran Church. Eight senior bishops wrote an open letter of admonishment stating that they see this fundamental principle of Protestant churches as endangered:

> Because it is in effect nothing less than a question of whether Lutheran churches assert that the Holy Scripture remains the sole basis for the belief and life of their members and for the ministry and life of their ordained pastors, or whether one state church after another considers it so important to the ways of life that have become common in society that the orientation toward the Holy Scripture must be abandoned or diluted.[12]

The senior bishops were immediately inundated with torrents of abuse. According to their detractors, they were disrespectful, spouting "defamation"; they did not respect the "freedom of Christians," were "homophobes," "fundamentalists," "biblicists," "sexists," "biologistics," and "naturalists." Can a dispute over the fundamentals of belief, the Bible, sexuality, biology and nature be settled with such epithets?

There is certainly a sorrowful inner conflict for a believer if he is not to be accepted by God due to sexual behavior that may appear to him to be his immutable identity. The conflict can only be resolved by abandoning the faith or by sexual abstinence with or without attempting

---

12. http://www.medrum.de/content/offener-brief-acht-bischoefe-jan-2011 (accessed October 2015).

therapeutic treatment. It is understandable that those affected might wish to resolve the conflict by urging God, the Bible and the church to give up their ethos that is based in the order of creation. But Christians cannot bend to this urging if they wish to remain true to their faith.

The Catholic Church

Throughout history, the magisterium of the Catholic Church has, in keeping with the Holy Scripture, taught that:

> Homosexual acts are intrinsically disordered. . . . They are contrary to the natural law. They close the sexual act to the gift of life. They do not proceed from a genuine affective and sexual complementarity. Under no circumstances can they be approved. (Catechism of the Catholic Church, 2357)

True, the Church judges homosexual behavior as immoral, but at the same time it calls for people who have this objectively disordered tendency "to be treated with respect, sympathy and tact. Every sign of unjust discrimination in their regard should be avoided" (CCC 2358).

From homosexuals, as from all unmarried people, the Church requires sexual abstinence. Homosexuals are called to chastity. Through the virtue of self-control, which leads to inner freedom, they can and should—perhaps with the help of a selfless friendship—come slowly but surely to Christian perfection through prayer and sacrificial grace (CCC 2359).

In view of the cultural landslide toward homosexual "marriage," the Congregation for the Doctrine of the Faith found it necessary in 2003 to reconfirm the stand of the Church by publishing "Considerations Regarding Proposals to Give Legal Recognition to Unions between Homosexual Persons." At the time, the prefect of the Congregation was Joseph Cardinal Ratzinger, who became Pope Benedict XVI. The Church's statement is also intended to provide Catholic politicians with orientation and indicate "the approaches to proposed legislation in this area which would be consistent with Christian conscience." The Church points out the difference between homosexual behavior as a "private phenomenon" and "as a relationship in society, foreseen and approved by the law, to the point where it becomes one of the institutions in the legal structure":

> This second phenomenon is not only more serious, but also assumes a more wide-reaching and profound influence, and would result in changes to the entire organization of society, contrary to the common good. Civil laws are structuring principles of man's life in soci-

ety, for good or for ill. They play a very important and sometimes decisive role in influencing patterns of thought and behaviour. Legal recognition of homosexual unions would obscure certain basic moral values and cause a devaluation of the institution of marriage. . . . By putting homosexual unions on a legal plane analogous to that of marriage and the family, the State acts arbitrarily and in contradiction with its duties.[13]

Canon lawyer Peter Mettler summarizes the reasons why the church *cannot* change or abandon its position:

> The Church cannot change its stand on homosexuality because it knows it to be bound to the authority of Holy Scripture. No attempt to ease or even deny the ban on the practice of homosexuality within a biblical theological perspective can be traced back to biblical foundations. The entire biblical witness holds the practice of homosexuality to violate the order God willed and established for creation. The entire Judeo-Christian tradition has interpreted the relevant biblical texts in this way, and the church therefore cannot abandon the distinction between the norm and the deviating behavior. This is where the Church's limit lies, and anyone pressing to change the teaching on this issue must know that he is promoting the church's division. The situation in which the Protestant churches now find themselves confirms this with the utmost clarity.[14]

The battle to rescind moral standards is also raging in the Catholic Church. The Church's position in the German-speaking countries can hardly be called aggressive or uncompromising. He who dares to be so—as did the late Bishop Johannes Dyba—must expect persecution and blasphemous acts in response. The church is under constant, aggressive pressure from the LGBTI activist groups to abandon its position. Academies, educational institutions and Church congresses are the preferred strategic targets. As tolerant bishops avert their eyes, there are blessing services and Eucharistic celebrations for gays and lesbians. No homosexual is excluded in the Catholic Church from receiving a blessing as a believer. However, it is a completely different matter to give

---

13. Congregation of the Doctrine of the Faith, "Considerations Regarding Proposals to Give Legal Recognition to Unions between Homosexual Persons." At http://www.vatican.va/roman_curia/congregations/cfaith/documents/rc_con_cfaith_doc_20030731_homosexual-unions_en.html (accessed October 6, 2015).

14. Peter Mettler, "Warum die Kirche ihre Haltung zur Homosexualität nicht ändern kann" (Why the church cannot change its teaching on homosexuality), *Theologisches* (Lugano, Switzerland: n.p., May–June 2010): 173–93.

blessings to people *because* they are gay or lesbian. That crosses a line that the Church is not authorized to pass. The attack from inside the Church can always count on support from the media. On the other hand, resistance from the Church prompts media campaigns aimed at eliminating people who dare to oppose dissolution of the Christian concept of humanity. The longer people knuckle under to the undemocratic, unchecked power of the media, the more courage and willingness to suffer are necessary to halt the gradual abolition of religious freedom.

The organized LGBTI associations have chosen Church congresses as their special field of action and have free rein in them. At Catholic Church conferences, they even get the best locations and times for their booths, actions, and events, while the right-to-life groups are often placed as far as possible from the main attendee traffic.

At the 2010 ecumenical Church conference in Munich, there were 30 LGBTI events but not a single one dealing with biblical sexual ethics and its exposition in John Paul II's *Theology of the Body*. The offerings are a direct, undisguised attack on fundamental Christian principles: "Ecumenical Queer Religious Services"; "Vigil for the Victims of Homophobia"; "Church Blessing of Same-sex Couples"; "Children in Same-sex Partnerships"; "So That You Will Have Hope: On the Relationship of Transsexual/Transgender Life and the Church," a lecture by Mari Günther, who was listed as "systematic therapist and *fatheress*"; "Lesbian Spirituality"; "The Epistle to the Romans Read from a Feminist-Lesbian Queer Perspective"; a "coming-out workshop" for teenagers; and much more.[15]

Why does this happen? Who are the people in the ordinariates and Church offices who *want* the Church undermined? Why do the bishops allow it?

It appears that there are homosexual networks inside the Catholic Church that were established mainly in the 1970s. In his shocking book *Goodbye, Good Men: How Liberals Brought Corruption into the Catholic Church,* Michael S. Rose describes the admissions process in many—but certainly not all—US seminaries: Priestly candidates with a normal masculine identity, who held to Church teaching, were sifted out and, if they made it under the radar, were eliminated on the way to ordination. Liberal, homosexually-oriented candidates were given priority acceptance, promoted and ordained. The book was researched and published shortly before the child abuse crisis broke open. It is key to explaining—not only for the United States—why the force of the Catholic Church's

---

15. Lorenz Jäger, *Hoffnung vom Kirchentag* (April 11, 2010), www.faz.net.

pronouncements and its attraction have suffered so much in the past 30 years.[16]

Pope Benedict XVI used the zero-tolerance principle against the scourge of pedophilia and ephebophilia (homosexual attraction to pubescent boys) in the Church.[17] In November 2005, he issued an instruction on the requirements for seminary admissions, which forbade acceptance of active homosexuals to the priesthood. A priest requires "affective maturity" that enables him to have a "correct relationship with men and women," so that he can develop a "true sense of fatherhood toward the church community."[18]

One would expect that all those who deplore sex abuse in the Church would welcome this instruction. Abuse within the Church was primarily perpetrated by men on boys from puberty onward, and overwhelmingly was not a pedophilia problem but a homosexuality problem.[19] Homosexual and leftist organizations vehemently protested this instruction. Apparently, the door should be left open for all who want to destroy the Church from within.

Priests who intentionally forego marriage and family make a great sacrifice *for the sake of the Kingdom of Heaven*. They bear witness to the world of the fulfillment of the love of Christ, through which they can act as shepherds for the salvation of people's souls. By living true to this ideal, they can authentically preach the Church's concept of marriage and family, grounded in the order of creation. And today the majority of priests live up to this high ideal. They deserve gratitude and support.

16. An outstanding explanation of the problem of homosexuality in the church is the essay by Polish moral theologian Dariusz Oko, "With the Pope against the Homoheresy": http://henrymakow.com/upload_docs/vort-2013-02-22.pdf (accessed January 2015).

17. An overview of his action in this regard can be found here: http://en.wikipedia.org/wiki/Pope_Benedict_XVI#Sexual_abuse_in_the_Catholic_Church (accessed October 3, 2015).

18. Cardinal Zenon Grocholewski, Congregation for Education, Instruction Concerning the Criteria for the Discernment of Vocations with regard to Persons with Homosexual Tendencies in view of their Admission to the Seminary and to Holy Orders, Approved by Pontiff Benedict XVI, Rome, August 31, 2005.

19. A rich source of information on this topic is the document of the United States Conference of Catholic Bishops entitled *The Nature and Scope of Sexual Abuse of Minors by Catholic Priests and Deacons in the United States* 1950–2002 (New York, 2004), commonly known as the John Jay Report 2004: http://www.usccb.org/issues-and-action/child-and-youth-protection/upload/The-Nature-and-Scope-of-Sexual-Abuse-of-Minors-by-Catholic-Priests-and-Deacons-in-the-United-States-1950-2002.pdf (accessed October 6, 2105). See also: Gerard van den Aardweg (interview), "Catholic Psychology and Sexual Abuse by Clergy," http://www.zenit.org/en/articles/catholic-psychology-and-sexual-abuse-by-clergy-part-1 http://www.zenit.org/en/articles/catholic-psychology-and-sexual-abuse-by-clergy-part-2.

Theological Sophistry

Sophists are intellectual con artists who appear to advance truthful arguments in order to achieve a self-serving goal. Plato had his problems with them and attacked and exposed them as venal peddlers of sham knowledge. What are the arguments of theologians who come to the aid of the sexual revolutionaries? What are the arguments opposing them? Christian apologetics are urgently needed in this debate to protect believers from confusion and heresy.

Claim: Because the Bible addresses homosexuality in only a few places,[20] the topic is of only minor importance.

Response: The overall message of the Bible is clear, so that clear conclusions can be arrived at for individual issues. Without exception, the statements about non-heterosexual behavior are negative. In the New Testament, any form of sexuality outside of marriage is an offense of adultery and therefore a serious sin. From the first to the last page of the Bible, indissoluble marriage between man and woman is *the* analogy for God's indissoluble bond with man, and therefore it is the way of life that corresponds to God's bond with the human race.

Claim: The Bible also condemns other behaviors that are no longer judged as negative (such as women preaching to the congregation); therefore the biblical rejection of homosexuality must also be seen as relative.

Response: The Apostle Paul's statements on sexual misconduct and on the ban on women preaching differ in their gravity. According to Paul's teaching, sexual offenses cut one off from eternal salvation, whereas women's preaching to the congregation does not.

Claim: Just as the attitude toward slavery has changed today and this is generally seen as positive, so has the attitude toward homosexuality.

Response: The Bible universally judges slavery as negative. God himself freed his chosen people from the slavery of Egypt. One should be neither a slave of man nor a slave of sin, but only a "slave" of the loving God. One should therefore obey only God—not people and not one's own desires.

When Paul says, "Slaves are to be under the control of their masters in all respects, giving them satisfaction, not talking back to them or steal-

---

20. Lev 18:22; Rom 1:24–27; 1 Cor 6:9–10; 1 Tim 1:10.

ing from them, but exhibiting complete good faith, so as to adorn the doctrine of God our savior in every way" (Titus 2:9–10), it is an instruction for missionary holiness in a world where slavery was firmly established. What was revolutionary about the New Covenant is that all people are similar to God: "you have taken off the old self with its practices and have put on the new self. . . . Here there is not Greek and Jew, circumcision and uncircumcision, barbarian, Scythian, slave, free; but Christ is all and in all" (Colossians 3:9–10).

> *Claim:* Only certain types of homosexuality were condemned, such as temple prostitution, intercourse with catamites or the passive role in the sex act. Today's forms of committed same-sex relationships were not known in biblical times.

> *Response:* Homosexuality is always condemned without limitation. The Bible makes no distinction between acceptable and unacceptable homosexual behavior.

Martin Luther emphasized the principle of *sola scriptura*. Five hundred years later not much remains of it.

The Trivialization of Love

Again and again, "love" is cited to justify committed homosexual relationships. Many theologians use the hoary old question found in a 1930s German chanson, "Can love be a sin?" and immediately answer along with the lyrics, "Love cannot be a sin. Even if it were, I wouldn't care. I'd rather sin than have no love at all."[21]

But what is love? Pope Benedict XVI devoted his first encyclical, *Deus Caritas Est*, to the topic to lead us out of the great confusion that clouds the word "love." Among the Greek words for love are *philia, eros,* and *agape. Philia* is the love found in platonic friendship, which is apparently unknown to those who wish to read a homosexual relationship into the friendship of King David and Jonathan or even Naomi and her daughter-in-law Ruth. *Eros* is the love of desire, which requires elevation and purification to become self-giving love. *Agape* is the term for "love grounded in and shaped by faith."

> [Agape] expresses the experience of a love which involves a real discovery of the other, moving beyond the selfish character that prevailed earlier. Love now becomes concern and care for the other. No longer is it self-seeking, a sinking in the intoxication of happiness;

---

21. http://www.youtube.com/watch?v=0zDL4j9haQo (accessed October 6, 2015).

instead it seeks the good of the beloved: it becomes renunciation and it is ready, and even willing, for sacrifice.[22]

If love in the full sense of the word means mutual deep recognition of the uniqueness of the other person and therefore requires exclusivity and finality, this places great demands on us. That is expressed in the sixth commandment, "Thou shalt not commit adultery," and the ninth, "Thou shalt not covet thy neighbor's wife," handed down on stone tablets by God to Moses.

The legalism of the Jews is overcome or "fulfilled" by Jesus by showing adherence to the commandments as the interior result of love for him. Three times in succession, he repeats this mutual conditionality as he bids farewell to the Apostles: If you love me, you will keep my commandments. Whoever has my commandments and observes them is the one who loves me. Whoever loves me will keep my word (John 14:15–24).

Jesus describes the communion between God and man. Whoever loves Jesus *wants* to obey his commandments. This is no external demand or burden, but describes the righteous life that makes it possible for this exhilarating love relationship to grow. Those who have not found this living contact with Jesus Christ are constantly searching for human love. In so doing, they can become so entangled in satisfaction of carnal desires that what they are seeking, and the real meaning of love, sink beyond the horizon.

However, God makes entry to this realm possible through his own love of his creation. God's desire for every person to be saved means that he shows everyone the way to salvation. The guideposts are revealed as moral standards. The Bible is an invitation and exhortation to turn away from behavior that separates one from God—and toward conversion. "Preaching that God is unconditional love [love without commandments] destroys the foundation of Christian morality. . . . This preaching has emptied the confessionals," writes Uwe Lay regarding "the triumph of indifference."[23] Only self-knowledge and repentance open the door to the merciful God, who forgives the contrite person *every* sin.

We most often hear from the pulpit: God loves you, God loves you, God loves you just as you are. No need to change, no need to convert, no need to regret, no need for confession, no penance at all, but you can feast at the Lord's Table. Just one problem: no one who is at odds with

---

22. Pope Benedict XVI, *Deus Caritas Est* (Rome: Libreria Editrice Vaticana, 2005). At http://www.vatican.va/holy_father/benedict_xvi/encyclicals/documents/hf_ben-xvi_enc_20051225_deus-caritas-est_en.html (accessed October 6, 2015).

23. Uwe C. Lay, "Liebt Gott unbedingt? Anmerkungen über den Triumph des Indifferentismus," *Theologisches* (Sept./Oct. 2010): 383–88.

himself or others, or has ever actually experienced mercy, believes this message. It sounds like snake oil. Dietrich Bonhoeffer called this kind of "cheap grace" the "deadly enemy of our Church":

> Today we are fighting for costly grace. Cheap grace is bargain-basement mercy, squandered forgiveness, squandered consolation, squandered sacraments. Grace inexhaustibly slopped out from the church soup kitchen, carelessly, thoughtlessly and limitlessly. Grace that costs nothing and is worth nothing. . . . Costly grace is the Gospel, which must be sought again and again, the gift that must be asked for, the door one has to knock at. It is costly because it calls us to follow; it is grace because it calls us to follow Jesus Christ. It is costly because it costs one his life; it is grace because it gives one his only true life. It is costly because it condemns sin, and grace because it justifies the sinner. . . . Costly grace is the incarnation of God.[24]

The Church's dilemma is that it wants to and must be close to the people to preach the good news of the Gospel. However, if it reduces the high standards placed on believers to mere background noise that no longer reaches their ears and hearts, the message loses its transformational power and thereby its attraction.

Excursus: Humanae Vitae

Crucial resistance to the deregulation of sexuality came from the Catholic Church, for which the life of every person is holy and must be protected. John D. Rockefeller III tried everything to dissuade the pope from this policy—a battle for which he even found allies *within* the Catholic Church. His personal visit to the Holy Father in 1965 did not achieve the success he had hoped for. On October 4, 1965, Pope Paul VI gave a speech to the United Nations leaving no doubt that the sanctity of life rules out artificial birth control. He said:

> It is in your Assembly, even where the matter of the great problem of birth rates is concerned, that respect for life ought to find its loftiest profession and its most reasonable defense. Your task is so to act that there will be enough bread at the table of mankind and not to support an artificial birth control that would be irrational, with the aim of reducing the number of those sharing in the banquet of life.[25]

---

24. Dietrich Bonhoeffer, *Discipleship*, Dietrich Bonhoeffer Works, vol. 4 (Minneapolis, MN: Fortress Press, 1937), 1037.

25. http://w2.vatican.va/content/paul-vi/en/speeches/1965/documents/hf_p-vi_spe_19651004_united-nations.html (accessed October 6, 2015).

Pope Paul VI was working on an encyclical on birth control. On July 25, 1968, despite immense resistance—even from within the Church—the pope released his encyclical *Humanae Vitae [On Human Life]: On the Regulation of Birth*. It reminds the reader that the Church urges people to observe the precepts of natural law and that, by necessity, every marital act must "retain its intrinsic relationship to the procreation of human life" (Article 11). "This particular doctrine, often expounded by the magisterium of the Church, is based on the inseparable connection, established by God, which man on his own initiative may not break, between the unitive significance and the procreative significance which are both inherent to the marriage act" (Article 12). This view leaves room for "responsible parenthood," which means that "with regard to physical, economic, psychological and social conditions," parents can "for serious reasons and with due respect to moral precepts, decide not to have additional children for either a certain or an indefinite period of time"—but by natural means, that is founded on respect for the natural fertility-cycle of the woman (Art. 10).

The pope foresaw the grave consequences that would ensue if the sexual act were systematically disassociated from fertility, which "the pill" had made possible for every woman since the early 1960s. In the encyclical, he calls on responsible men and women to "consider how easily this course of action could open wide the way for marital infidelity and a general lowering of moral standards." He further argues that "A man who grows accustomed to the use of contraceptive methods may forget the reverence due to a woman, and, disregarding her physical and emotional equilibrium, reduce her to being a mere instrument for the satisfaction of his own desires, no longer considering her as his partner whom he should surround with care and affection." The pope was also aware of the dangerous power this could give to authorities. "Who will prevent public authorities from favoring those contraceptive methods which they consider more effective? Should they regard this as necessary, they may even impose their use on everyone" (Art. 17).

Half a century later, it is clear to everyone that the Holy Father's fears were prophetic. Contraception has become an assumed part of sexual behavior, and children are taught about it as early as elementary school. The "natural law" that was still supported by custom, legislation and society in the middle of the last century was torn from its moorings in the hearts and minds of people. But, despite his prescience, the pope did not foresee the demographic change and its threat to the survival of European, Christian and Western culture.

At Castel Gandolfo, a few days after the encyclical was released, the pope told the public about his struggle with this position:

Never before have We felt so heavily, as in this situation, the burden of Our office. . . . How many times have We trembled before the alternatives of an easy condescension to current opinions, or of a decision that modern society would find difficult to accept, or that might be arbitrarily too burdensome for married life! . . . after imploring the light of the Holy Spirit, We placed Our conscience at the free and full disposal of the voice of truth. We pondered over the consequences of one or other decision; and we had no doubt about Our duty to give Our decision in the terms expressed in the present Encyclical.[26]

At the end of the encyclical, Pope Paul VI candidly pleads with the bishops to follow him in this difficult decision: "For We invite all of you, We implore you, to give a lead to your priests who assist you in the sacred ministry, and to the faithful of your dioceses, and to devote yourselves with all zeal and without delay to safeguarding the holiness of marriage, in order to guide married life to its full human and Christian perfection. Consider this mission as one of your most urgent responsibilities at the present time."[27]

But the bishops' conferences in many countries refused to follow the Holy Father in crucial points of the encyclical. They issued statements releasing married Catholics from obedience to the teaching authority of the Catholic Church regarding birth control *methods*, leaving that up to their subjective conscience (in Germany the *Königsteiner Erklärung*, in Austria the *Maria Troster Erklärung*, in Switzerland the *Solothurner Erklärung*, in Canada the *Winnipeg Statement*). While this was not meant to release couples from accountability to God for their *motivation* for contraception, it nonetheless left them free to use artificial contraception.[28]

Evidently, the bishops' conferences didn't foresee one of the consequences of these statements: allowing Catholic couples to use the pill could be generalized in the mind of society. It could be separated from the Christian conscience of married couples and applied to all sexual relationships, including those before and outside of marriage. In the early 1960s, the pill triumphed not only because it gave women control over their fertility, seemingly without complications, but also because spreading worries about the "population bomb" made contraception seem like the right thing to do for humanity.

---

26. Pope Paul VI, Address at General Audience, Castel Gandolfo, July 31, 1968, published in *L'Osservatore Romano*, English edition, August 8, 1968.

27. Pope Paul VI and Marc Caligari, *Humanae Vitae: Encyclical Letter of His Holiness Pope Paul VI, on the Regulation of Births* (San Francisco: Ignatius Press, 1983), 30.

28. Cf. Vincent Twomey, SVD, *Moral Theology after Humanae Vitae: Fundamental Issues in Moral Theory and Sexual Ethics* (Dublin: Four Courts Press, 2010).

In the meantime, in almost every country in Europe the pill led to a catastrophic drop in birth rates. On March 27, 2008, at holy Mass in the Upper Room in Jerusalem, Cardinal Christoph Schönborn told 150 bishops from around the world that "The future of Europe is at stake. Over the past 40 years, Europe has said 'no' to its future three times. In 1968 it said 'no' to Paul VI's encyclical *Humanae Vitae*, a few years later through abortion regulations in most European countries, and finally with homosexual 'marriage.'" He asked, "Did it weaken the Church's resistance to the advancing sexual revolution when the bishops allowed the faithful to rely on subjective conscience in choosing a birth control method that violates the doctrinal instruction of the pope?"[29]

Irish moral theologian Vincent Twomey, SVD, who earned his doctorate under Joseph Ratzinger, sees this as a decisive turning point. He says: "I think that the debate over *Humanae Vitae* brought the entire crisis within Western cultural history to a climax. I am convinced that the Church in Europe, not least in Germany, will not recover until it accepts *Humanae Vitae*."[30]

29. Christoph Kardinal Schönborn, "Jerusalem homilie," March 27, 2008, http://kath.net/news/21357 (accessed October 6, 2015).

30. C.f. Vincent Twomey SVD, *Der Papst: die Pille und die Krise der Moral* (Augsburg: Sankt Ulrich Verlag, 2008) and interview in *Die Tagespost*, August 4, 2007.

12

Sex Education from K through 12

Without a well-developed idea of shame, childhood cannot exist.
Neil Postman[1]

The Sexualization of Youth by the State

WHOEVER controls the youth owns the future. This will decide who wins the culture war we find ourselves in. Christian Western culture is based on the family and the sexual norms that make family possible, specifically monogamy. Until a few decades ago, customs, mores and laws helped the individual civilize his sex drive so that he was capable of fidelity and responsibility within the family. That is all over.

Let's be clear. If orientation toward Christian values is not passed on from *one* generation to the *next* generation, the tradition is over. As the proverb says, "God has no grandchildren." Tradition comes from the Latin word *tradere*—to pass on, to forward. If one generation does not receive what is good, true, and just, then they have nothing to pass on to subsequent generations. This is a breakdown in culture. It takes a long time to build a house, but just a couple of hours to burn it down.

Since mandatory sex education was introduced in German schools in the 1970s, it has progressed from information to education to indoctrination—a journey toward complete demoralization of sexuality. According to leading "sex educators," "sexual formation" begins at birth. Children are incited to masturbate and are provided snuggle corners for playing doctor in kindergarten. All kinds of broken families are now depicted in picture books as equal, and homosexuality is offered as a "normal" option. Ever more aggressive techniques are used to irreversibly mold children and teenagers. This involves destruction of their sense of shame, activation of sexual urges starting in early childhood,

---

1. Neil Postman, *The Disappearance of Childhood* (New York: Vintage Books, 1982), 9.

and obstruction of the conscience. Only one standard remains: don't do anything your sex partner doesn't like. This is squaring the circle, because these limits can only hold if a person has learned self-control. The rampant sexual abuse of children by adults, and increasingly also sexual abuse of children by other children, shows that this standard cannot be adhered to in a hypersexualized society.

Obligatory sex education in schools and preschools undermines the parents' right to raise their children as they see fit. Parents have given their children life. In contrast to clients of sperm banks and surrogate mothers, parents know that their child is a gift of God, and that they do not own the child, but are only trustees called to the task of raising the child to become a person on the giving side of society. At the same time, this obligation is their natural right. It is not imparted by the state, and the state cannot take it away.[2] The Universal Declaration of Human Rights (Art. 16.3), the European Convention on Human Rights, and countless nations' constitutions place the authority for child-rearing in the hands of parents, because it is understood that, as a rule, parents love, care for, are responsible for, and sacrifice for the well-being of their children. Article 2 of the first additional protocol of the European Convention on Human Rights (ECHR) states:

> No person shall be denied the right to education. In the exercise of any functions which it assumes in relation to education and to teaching, the State shall respect the right of parents to ensure such education and teaching in conformity with their own religious and philosophical convictions.

This is the fulfillment of the principle of subsidiarity as specified in Article 5, paragraph 3 of the EU's Lisbon Treaty, a core element of Catholic social teaching. The principle of subsidiarity says that the state is only to assume tasks that cannot be autonomously carried out at a lower level.

Human rights treaties place the utmost authority and obligation on parents to rear their own children. Nonetheless, these treaties have not stopped the state from seizing the authority to initiate schoolchildren in hedonistic, lust-oriented sexuality from an early age. The right of parents to teach their children moral standards for sexuality is thus subverted.

Even from a democratic point of view, comprehensive sex education cannot be justified. More than 50 percent of marriages do *not* end in

---

2. Cf. Wolfgang Waldstein, *Ins Herz geschrieben*, loc. cit., 158, note 61.

divorce. On average, in the European Union, 75 percent of children live with their biological, married parents[3]—an astounding number, because TV screens overwhelmingly show broken homes. Even those who have suffered through the breakup of a marriage want their children to be happy in a stable marriage and establish a family. Where are there fathers or mothers who want their sons or daughters to get divorced and raise children alone, or to enter a homosexual partnership? The vast majority of young people want families.[4] But the state, the entire educational system, and nearly all organizations that have anything to do with youth have stopped teaching children the ability to love and bond.

The instruction in chastity and self-control, as preparation for marriage and as a basic prerequisite for fidelity (which was a main component of youth work before 1968), is now rare in Western Europe, even in Catholic schools and youth organizations. Even the terms *chastity* and *self-control* are barely understood anymore. We are seeing a huge failure not only of the state, but even of the Church. Theology and pastoral care have barely tapped the treasure of John Paul II's *Theology of the Body* and the wealth of outstanding directives (see Ch. 13), but the vast majority of people and organizations responsible for formal instruction of the faithful have fallen down on the job. Abandonment of Christian sexual morality is the core of the Church's self-secularization.

Introduction of Mandatory Sex Education in Schools

School sex education in Germany is a product of the student revolts of 1968. Its core objective was "sexual liberation" through destruction of Christian values. Resistance could have been expected from the Christian churches, but it largely did not materialize. The leftist protagonists soon took their "march through the institutions" right to the levers of power, where they have used legislation and government-financed programs to implement their revolutionary goals.

This happened in all Western countries. In just a few decades, international organizations like the UN and the EU became centers of power for global overthrow of the traditional system of values. They have the material resources and the cultural-revolutionary know-how to bury the social, cultural, legal, and moral preconditions for marriage

---

3. Eurostat, search: *Living arrangements in the EU27*, press release 156/2011—October 27, 2011. http://www.europarl.europa.eu/RegData/etudes/note/join/ 2014/474407/IPOL-F EMM_NT(2014)474407_EN.pdf (accessed October 3, 2015).

4. Cf. *Shell Jugendstudie 2010* (Shell Youth Study 2010), loc. cit., 175, note 91.

and family. This is all possible because the mainstream Western media supports this agenda and have themselves largely served as manipulators of public opinion in the service of cultural revolutionary goals. In the overthrow of Judeo-Christian values in regard to sexuality, a central role has been played by the criminal sadomasochist Alfred Kinsey (see Ch. 2). He is still treated as a serious "sexologist" in sex education textbooks. In her excellent book *You're Teaching My Child What?* Dr. Miriam Grossman explains the lies and dangers of sex education and describes Alfred Kinsey's key role in this way: "Dr. Kinsey was to sex education what Henry Ford was to the automobile. He was the master architect of a new model of human sexuality—a model based on his conviction that in modern society traditional morality is irrelevant and destructive."[5]

After Kinsey's death in 1956, his successor Paul Gebhard led the Kinsey Institute at Indiana University and joined Kinsey intimate Wardell Pomeroy in founding the Advanced Institute of Human Sexuality in San Francisco, the first major instructional institution for "sexology" and sex education. Soon thereafter, Mary Calderone, former director of Planned Parenthood, founded the Information and Education Council of the United States (SIECUS). At her side was Lester Kirkendall, who wrote "a bill of sexual rights" in 1976. It still influences the sexual revolutionary agenda of the IPPF and UNESCO and can be seen as a forerunner of the 1990 UN Convention on the Rights of the Child. The claim is that children have a "right" to sexual information and activity from birth, regardless of their parents' values—and a right to *every* form of sexuality, as long as it is voluntary and consensual. What just decades ago was seen as unnatural, perverse, abnormal and abhorrent—sexual practices that belonged in the red light district and that children certainly should know nothing about—have become obligatory instructional material today.

In Germany, it is *Bundeszentrale für gesundheilitche Aufklärung* (BZgA), which is the German branch of International Planned Parenthood; the Federal Centre for Health Education; and the *Institut für Sexualpädagogik* (Institute for Sex Education) that are driving the sexualization in schools and preschools with budgets in the millions. Their main figures include professors Uwe Sielert, Rüdiger Lautmann, Elisabeth Tuider, Karlheinz Valtl, and, formerly, Helmut Kentler.

---

5. Miriam Grossman, *You're Teaching My Child What? A Physician Exposes the Lies of Sex Education and How They Harm Your Child* (Washington DC: Regnery Publishing, 2009), 20.

Attempts through the legal process to protect parents' rights in child-rearing, as guaranteed in the German Constitution, have been fruitless so far. The situation is all the more grave because school attendance is obligatory in Germany and homeschooling is forbidden. Parents have no legal right to keep their children away from sexual indoctrination in school. There are some cases where parents have been imprisoned and their children made wards of the state. A constitutional appeal by affected parents to the European Court of Human Rights was rejected.

One key to legitimizing sex education was the emergence of autoimmune deficiency syndrome (AIDS) in the 1980s. German politicians had a simple opportunity to carry out their oath of office, to "promote [the people's] welfare and protect them from harm." They could have used the power of the state to make the population understand that abstinence outside of marriage, and fidelity to one's spouse, is 100-percent effective in preventing AIDS and all other sexually transmitted diseases, and that heterosexuality in particular decreases the likelihood of catching AIDS. Instead, the AIDS alarm was used to legitimize forming school children of ever-younger ages into contraception experts and to feed them the lie of "safe sex" through condom use—despite the explosive spread of sexual diseases. Sex "educators" began visiting schools with contraception kits and practicing condom use on plastic penises. Now they had their foot in the door. With graphic and three-dimensional materials, with movies, role-plays and forced verbal articulation of sex acts, they could disable traditional standards, break children's sense of shame, and initiate children into sexual practices of all types, particularly masturbation.

The largest global player in abortion and deregulation of sexuality is the International Planned Parenthood Federation (IPPF), with subsidiary organizations in 180 countries. In its 2010 annual report,[6] the IPPF boasts of:

- 22 million pregnancies averted
- 131 million contraceptive services provided
- 25 million HIV-related services provided
- 38 million couple years of protection provided
- 621 million condoms distributed
- 80 million services provided to young people

IPPF not only performs millions of abortions around the globe, but also sells intact fetal body parts, obtained through the illegal partial-birth

---

6. IPPF's 2010 *Five-Year Performance Report*. http://www.ippf.org/resource/Five-Year-Performance-Report-2010 (accessed October 3, 2015).

abortion procedure. This was brought to light through a series of undercover videos, beginning in July 2015.[7]

The IPPF misleadingly claims in its Annual Performance Report 2007–2008 that access to safe legal abortion is a public health and human rights imperative. This is a crass falsehood. No internationally binding document from the UN or EU acknowledges abortion as part of sexual and reproductive health (SRH), let alone as a human right. The IPPF's 2010 annual report says that the European Union as a whole is the largest donor to international development and has historically championed sexual and reproductive health and rights. The IPPF European Network leads efforts to ensure sexual and reproductive health remains at the heart of EU development policy.

As a March 2012 report from European Dignity Watch reveals, abortion programs that the IPPF and Marie Stopes International conduct in developing countries are financed by the EU even though there is no legal basis for this.[8] The IPPF's main target group is teenagers: "Over the last five years, IPPF has transformed itself from an organization that works with youth to one that is focused on youth, where youth participation is a principle in our delivery of quality sexual and reproductive health services."[9]

For IPPF, the sexual rights of youth should be limited neither by law nor by social or religious norms. The five-year report proudly says that the IPPF has made 238 legal modifications in 119 countries in favor of reproductive and sexual rights, of which 52 involve liberalization of abortion. The IPPF provided 3.9 million abortion-related services, 41.7 percent of them for young people, an increase of 22 percent.

Pro Familia, the German arm of the International Planned Parenthood Federation (IPPF), implements its strategy on the national and local level. Planned Parenthood was founded in 1942 by Margaret Sanger in the United States, and Pro Familia in 1952 by Hans Ludwig Friedrich Harmsen. As mentioned above, Sanger and Harmsen saw themselves as eugenicists who wanted to reduce the "inferior gene pool in the population" to promote a "worthy" state-supporting gene pool.

7. https://www.lifesitenews.com/news/undercover-video-planned-parenthood-uses-illegal-partial-birth-abortions-to; https://www.lifesitenews.com/static/new-video-planned-parenthood-official-haggles-over-baby-body-part-prices-jo.html (accessed October 6, 2015).

8. European Dignity Watch, "The Funding of Abortion through EU Development Aid—An Analysis of EU's Sexual and Reproductive Health Policy," http://europeandignitywatch.org/fileadmin/user_upload/PDF/Day_to_Day_diverse/Funding_of_Abortion_Through_EU_Development_Aid_full_version.pdf (accessed October 7, 2015).

9. IPPF, Five-Year Performance Report 2010.

Harmsen was founder and president of Pro Familia until 1962 and its president emeritus until 1984. He never distanced himself from his stance on eugenics. From 1973 to 1983, the Marxist Jürgen Heinrichs was president of the association. The name Pro Familia suggests the opposite of what the state-sponsored organization actually promotes.

In Germany, Pro Familia runs about 200 counseling locations, as well as countless websites and advice services. It is the government's main partner in sexualizing children and teenagers. In so doing, Pro Familia continuously creates new customers for its in-house abortion company. Their own statistics state that 77 percent of all pregnancy terminations in Germany were performed in one of Pro Familia's six abortion centers. Nevertheless, Pro Familia is a "charitable organization," exempt from taxes.

Content and Methods of Comprehensive Sex Education

Let's take a closer look at the content of "comprehensive sex education." Nearly all national and international organizations that have anything to do with children or youth put their power and resources behind sexualizing children from birth and removing moral limits to sexual activity. Youth organizations of Christian movements are an exception, but, unfortunately, many of them are being swept into the mainstream. The message is that sexuality is for pleasure only. Undesirable side effects, such as creation of new human life, are to be prevented by contraception or eliminated by abortion. The psychological injuries of broken relationships and the danger of STDs are trivialized and taken in stride.

Globally operating US organizations that promote the sexualization of children and teenagers include:[10]

- Advocates for Youth
- Guttmacher Institute
- International Planned Parenthood Federation
- National Education Association
- Population Council
- Sex Education Forum
- SIECUS
- UNESCO
- UNFPA
- World Association for Sexual Health
- Youth Peer Education Network

10. Other international organizations and resources for comprehensive sexual education can be found at the end of *Standards for Sexuality Education in Europe*, published by WHO and BZgA.

All of the above are agents of the global sexual revolution and use deregulation of sexual moral standards to subvert the social basis of society, that is, the family based on the marriage of a man and a woman.

On November 11, 2014, South African cardinal Wilfrid Fox Napier went on Twitter to accuse the West of spreading a "moral Ebola": "As I observe moral depravity spreading its pall of evil over society I'm reminded of the devastation visited upon West Africa by Ebola."[11] Is the cardinal exaggerating? Let's look more closely at three of the global sex promoters' documents, paying special attention to the wording, because the terms are usually a Pandora's box containing hidden information.

IPPF Framework for Comprehensive Sexuality Education (CSE)[12]

Here are a few excerpts (direct wording is in quotation marks, deletions are not indicated, and italics have been added):

> IPPF "works towards a world" in which "the needs of young people" are fulfilled, namely that "women, men and young people everywhere have control over their own bodies . . . and are free to *choose parenthood or not*; free to pursue healthy sexual lives without fear of unwanted pregnancies and sexually transmitted infections including HIV."

Another statement reads:

> IPPF is committed to promoting, protecting and upholding the sexual and reproductive health rights of *all young people*. This includes the right to information and education on sexuality, and a *right to pleasure* and confidence in relationships and all aspects of their sexuality. *Information should be available to children and young people of all ages*. Broad-based strategies are needed to address young people both *in and out of school.*

The framework contains "Seven Essential Components of CSE":

1. Gender: difference between gender and sex, manifestations and consequences of gender bias, stereotypes and inequality.
2. Sexual and reproductive health and HIV: how to use condoms; other forms of contraception (including emergency contraception); legal and safe abortion.
3. Sexual rights and *sexual citizenship*: rights-based approach to sexual and reproductive health (SRH); available services and resources

11. Radio Vatican, November 8, 2014.

12. http://www.ippf.org/sites/default/files/ippf_framework_for_comprehensive_sex uality_education.pdf (accessed October 7, 2015).

and how to access them; different sexual identities; advocacy; choice; protection; the right to freely express and explore one's sexuality in a safe, healthy and pleasurable way.

4. Pleasure: being positive about young people's sexuality; gender and pleasure; *masturbation; love, lust and relationships; the diversity of sexuality; the first sexual experience;* addressing stigma associated with pleasure.

5. Exploring the various types of violence towards men and women: men/boys as both perpetrators and allies in violence prevention.

6. A positive view of diversity: recognizing discrimination, *supporting young people to move beyond just tolerance.*

7. Different relationships (e.g., family, friends, sexual, romantic etc.).

This brings up some questions.

First of all, is it really the greatest wish of the world's young people to decide for or against parenthood? No! Polls say something much different: most young people want their own stable family.

Second, do *all young people of all ages* really have sexual and reproductive health rights, specifically the "right" to be instructed by adults to discover the body as a lust organ through masturbation?[13] Do they have the right to satisfy this lust in any way they wish, regardless of male and female stereotypes? No! This is how parental rights and religious freedom are being undermined. *All* religions teach sexual moral values which are passed on to the younger generation.

Third, do CSE and the message of "safe sex" provide protection from HIV and other sexually transmitted diseases? No! The sexualization has led to an explosive spread of STDs, including the return of syphilis and gonorrhea, venereal diseases that make many young women sterile forever.

Fourth, can sexualized children really protect themselves against sexual attack better than those whose sense of shame has not been shattered? No, because they can no longer tell the difference between tenderness and sexual advances, especially emotionally needy children.

And finally, should the world's young people be raised and "empow-

---

13. In the book *Lisa & Jan*, Prof. Uwe Sielert, a key figure in comprehensive Sexuality Education, promotes masturbation for children. In the accompanying booklet for parents, he clearly states that children must be guided into it: "Naturally, children discover this pleasure on their own if they are positively caressed ahead of time by their parents. If they don't know at all what lust is, there will also be no sex play." This is a clear call for pedophile behavior. Frank Herrath and Uwe Sielert, *Elterninformation, Lisa & Jan, Ein Aufklärungsbuch für Kinder und ihre Eltern* (Weinheim: Beltz Verlag, 1991), 21.

ered" to murder their own unborn children? No! They should be raised to honor life and respect the dignity of every individual.

Healthy, Happy and Hot: A Young Person's Guide to their Rights, Sexuality and Living with HIV (IPPF 2010)

This guide was distributed by the World Association of Girl Scouts and Girl Guides who took part in the annual meeting of UN's Commission on the Status of Women (CSW).[14] Scouting was originally a Christian youth organization based on character-building values such as duty to God and country, loyalty, and helpfulness.

The IPPF gives young people a different message: "Sexual and reproductive rights are recognized around the world as human rights. Every person living with HIV is entitled to these rights and they are necessary for the development and well-being of all people and the societies in which they live." This opening statement is full of lies. There is no international treaty that recognizes "sexual and reproductive rights" as a "human right." The sexual activities to which IPPF guides young people are certainly not "necessary for the development and well-being of all people and the societies in which they live." The truth is that they could not be more destructive for the well-being of the person and the society.

IPPF directs this guide to "all young people living with HIV who are interested in dating and having sex with people of the same sex or opposite sex, as well as those who are exploring and questioning their 'sexual orientation.'" IPPF further (mis)informs young people that they have the "right to decide if, when and how to disclose their HIV status." There are, according to IPPF, valid reasons not to do so: "People will find out something else they have kept secret, like they are using injecting drugs, having sex outside of a marriage or having sex with people of the same gender." That this could be troublesome to a partner is irrelevant. Being in a relationship with someone who has HIV "is just as fulfilling and satisfying as with anyone else." IPPF provides absolution: "You have done nothing wrong." In addition, IPPF considers it a "violation of your rights" that some countries mandate by law that HIV infection be disclosed to sexual "partner(s)"—for IPPF, this constitutes a reason for young people to get involved in changing these laws.

IPPF encourages a wide variety of sexual practices:

Many people think sex is just about vaginal or anal intercourse . . . but, there are lots of different ways to have sex and lots of different types of sex. . . . There is no right or wrong way to have sex. . . .

14. Sharon Slater, *Stand for the Family* (Mesa, AZ: Inglestone Publishing, 2012), 141.

> Masturbation is a great way to find out more about your body and what you find sexually stimulating. Mix things up by using different kinds of touch from very soft to hard. Talk about or act out your fantasies. Talk dirty to them.

IPPF also sees having sex while drinking alcohol and using drugs as a matter of choice: "Just plan ahead and have your condoms and lube close by."

IPPF is not coy about the increased risks of attracting STIs, especially when one is already infected with HIV:

> STIs can affect the genitals, anus, mouth and throat. STIs can be passed to babies during pregnancy and delivery. Having an STI can increase the chances that your partner will get infected with HIV. Untreated STIs can lead to health problems like infertility, cervical cancer, and anal cancer. HIV can make you prone to vaginal infections—yeast, bacterial vaginosis, and pelvic inflammatory disease (PID)—and abnormal growth of cells on your cervix that can turn into cancer if left untreated. HIV can reduce your resistance to infections that cause open sores or warts on your penis and even discharge. Many young people living with HIV also have Hepatitis C . . . which can also be transmitted sexually. Make sure your healthcare professionals know about your co-infection.

But there is no need, according to the IPPF, to tell your sexual partner(s).

IPPF gives "tips for making sex safer" just in case the condoms didn't do the job: "Keep your vagina healthy by getting an annual gynecological exam and getting any sores, bumps, or irritations on your genitals treated as soon as possible. Keep your penis healthy by checking regularly for sores and discharge (remember to check under the foreskin) and getting a penile examination from your doctor."

Nevertheless, the IPPF is silent about the chances of a cure for the serious consequences of the sexual behavior it promotes.

The IPPF sees it as a matter of choice "not to have safer sex" and advises on methods to "somewhat reduce the risks of HIV, other STIs, and unintended pregnancies without using condoms. You can limit the amount of body fluids like semen and vaginal secretions that you and your partner(s) share."

The IPPF proclaims it as a "right of young people living with HIV to choose if, when, how many, and with whom to have children," even though there is a 25 percent to 30 percent risk of vertical transmission of HIV to the child—which, of course, can be aborted through a "safe abortion" carried out by the "reproductive health services" of the IPPF "without needing the permission of your parents or guardians." If there were an organization whose purpose it was to promote the spread of HIV/AIDS and other venereal diseases, to seduce teenagers into risky, personally destructive sexual behavior, and to encourage them to knowingly endanger others, wouldn't it be banned?

This organization exists, and it is called the International Planned Parenthood Federation. It is not forbidden, but subsidized with hundreds of millions of dollars. However, the tables are turning in the United States. The US Congress has started looking into Planned Parenthood. Seventy-two Congressmen asked the Government Accountability Office to investigate Planned Parenthood. In their letter, dated February 2014, they said:

> It is deeply troubling that despite the fact that Planned Parenthood claims direct responsibility for killing over 6 million unborn babies, including a record 333,964 abortions in 2011 alone, they still receive taxpayer money—since Obama's election U.S. subsidies to the abortion industry at home and abroad have significantly increased.[15]

This is a new form of cultural imperialism that can bring about more destruction than any plundering of resources of other nations or continents.

Anyone can see that *Healthy, Happy and Hot* leads to an inferno of sexual dependency, addiction, disease, and the destruction of relationships. It is an extremely thin cloak that covers the diabolical seduction: pleasure and well-being! Can IPPF prove that young people who follow this advice will experience pleasure and well-being in their lives? Their "healthcare provider" will not give them back their health, and the medical and social welfare system will be decreasingly able to bear the costs.

There is a completely simple way to deal with the gift of sexuality so that it will be an expression of true love from which new human life can be created—and it poses *absolutely* no health risk: *Sex with just one person.* It is the ideal of monogamy that makes family possible. Why are the political and business elites working to systematically destroy this ideal, and the family with it? Because they focus so much on the 2 percent who are not attracted to the opposite sex—or are they using this small minority to destroy marriage and family?

---

15. https://www.lifesitenews.com/news/planned-parenthood-now-under-nationwide-investigation-by-gao-congressmen-an.

Standards for Sexuality Education in Europe
(*WHO and BZgA 2010*)

A third document pursues the same goals, but through more moderate wording: *Standards for Sexuality Education in Europe*, published by the World Health Organization (WHO) and the German Federal Centre for Health Education (BZgA) in 2010.[16]

As in all sex education, the WHO functions on the anthropological premise that humans have a need for sexual activity from birth on, and that they have a "right" to it. Adults allegedly should stimulate this need right from the beginning, speak to the child in detail at every age level about sexual acts, and give them the opportunity to live out their sexual needs free of "gender stereotypes." A chart presents "age-appropriate" sex education:

- Age 0–4: The child has "the right to explore nakedness and the body and gender identities." The child should learn "to differentiate between 'good' and 'bad' secrets and learn: 'My body belongs to me.'"
- Age 4–6: The child learns to name each body part, and caregivers are to "wash every part of the body" and "talk about sexual matters in sexual language." The child should be "given information" about "enjoyment and pleasure when touching one's own body in early childhood masturbation," "friendship and love towards people of same sex," "secret love and first love," and "an awareness of rights."
- Age 6–9: The child should be informed about "menstruation and ejaculation, choices about pregnancy, different methods of contraception, sex in the media, including the Internet, enjoyment and pleasure when touching one's own body (masturbation/self-stimulation), difference between friendship, love and lust, friendship and love towards people of same sex, diseases related to sexuality." They should "examine their body, use sexual language and accept diversity."
- Age 9–12: First sexual experience, variability of sexual behavior, contraceptives and their use, pleasure, masturbation, orgasm, differences between gender identity and biological sex, learn about STDs and HIV and sexual rights. The child is to acquire media competence using the Internet and mobile phones and deal with pornography. The child is to talk about sex and make conscious decisions to have sexual experiences or not.

16. http://www.bzga.de/infomaterialien/einzelpublikationen/who-regional-office-fo r-europe-and-bzga-standards-for-sexuality-education-in-europe/ (accessed October 7, 2015).

• Age 12–15: The child learns the skill to obtain and use condoms; and obtains communication skills to have safe and enjoyable sex, and to deal with shame, fear, jealousy and disappointments. Child learns more modern media competence and deals with pornography.
• Age 15 and up: Time to learn about genital mutilation, circumcision, anorexia, bulimia, hymen and hymen repair, pregnancy in same-sex relationships, contraception services, designer babies, transactional sex [a euphemism for prostitution]—and acquire a critical view of different cultural/religious norms related to pregnancy and parenthood.

All right then, parents, teach your babies about masturbation, talk about sex to your children, push them into sexual activity, and let the school teach them about contraception, abortion and same-sex lust, love and parenthood before puberty. Teach them how to use condoms, immerse them in pornography, get them addicted to sex, let them know that all this is their "right"—drown their childhood in the abyss of sexual obsession, together with the dignity of man and the hope of your children for a happy family.

What school principal, teacher, father or mother can stand up to this international authoritarian pressure? When an organization responsible for the health of the world (the World Health Organization), together with a German government institution, draws up "Standards for Sexuality Education" and creates the impression that they are derived through scientific objectivity, then obviously this serves the welfare of the world population—or does it?

The document's appendix contains comprehensive lists of literature, curricula, organizations, centers, foundations and youth organizations that drive "sex education" of children and teenagers in the United States.

HOW IS IT POSSIBLE that a whole generation has fallen into the hands of a cultural revolutionary mafia that appears bent on turning future generations into amorphous, rootless masses of sex-addicted consumers?

Sexual Abuse of Children and Teenagers and Its "Prevention"

Sexual abuse of children and teenagers is omnipresent in our society. The National Center for Victims of Crime (U.S.) publishes research and statistics concerning child sexual abuse.[17] The figures are alarming:

---

17. http://www.victimsofcrime.org/media/reporting-on-child-sexual-abuse/child-sexual-abuse-statistics (accessed October 7, 2015).

• 1 in 5 girls and 1 in 20 boys are victims of child sexual abuse.
• Self-report studies show that 20 percent of adult females and 5 percent to 10 percent of adult males recall a childhood sexual assault or
sexual abuse incident.
• Over the course of their lifetime, 28 percent of U.S. youth ages 14 to
17 have been sexually victimized.
• Children are most vulnerable to child sexual abuse between the
ages of 7 and 13.

According to a 2003 U.S. National Institute of Justice report, 3 out of
4 adolescents who have been sexually assaulted were victimized by
someone they knew well.

The figures show that a hypersexualized society, a society in which
films, pornography, advertising, magazines, and literature constantly
trigger sexual desire, will use the most defenseless, the most vulnerable,
to satisfy that desire: children.

There is no doubt that the deep wounds of sexual abuse traumatize
the victims and distort their lives. Why is the pervasive sexual abuse of
children not a national topic? Why is it not recognized as a cancerous
disease that society must combat? The answer is obvious: because it is
pervasive; because sexual addiction is a mass phenomenon; because our
culture does not teach control of the sex drive—quite the opposite: it
proclaims a "right to sexual pleasure" from cradle to grave. Only one
group of society will suffer public rage and persecution if they trans-
gress the remaining laws against child sexual abuse: Catholic priests.
When they are ordained as priests, they vow celibacy. From the very first
moment they considered their vocation to the moment of their ordination, they have known that this is part of their calling.

The secularized, sexualized world hates celibacy, attacks it wherever
possible, and rejoices when priests fall. It is a most useful weapon in the
battle against the Catholic Church. For a Catholic, it is a terrible crime
and a bleeding wound on the body of Christ. Not only is the child traumatized, but his relationship to God may be destroyed forever. Thanks
be to God that this festering evil has been exposed.

But there is a glaring contradiction. Why is there no outrage, public
attention or political action against the everyday sexual abuse of hundreds and thousands of children right among us?

Now sexual abuse is not just a problem between adults and children,
but it is also a problem for children and teenagers among themselves. It
is no wonder, then, when the media and schools constantly preoccupy
children with sex. Anita Heiliger, an abuse researcher at the German
Youth Institute, shows that more and more minors are sexually abusing
each other. It is those "14-to-16-year-olds who are at greatest risk for sex-

ually abusing children! . . . In the 14-to-16-year age group, [violent sex crimes] have more than doubled in the past 15 years."[18]

The German association Zartbitter e.V., a contact and information center fighting against sexual abuse of boys and girls, says that more and more parents report their preschool- and elementary-age children as having experienced sexual attacks by children of the same age and older:

> Older children who already have unmonitored media access consider such violations to be normal. Some children consume pornographic material in their parents' home, in the neighborhood or on their classmates' cellphones and reenact the incriminating images during play. Ten years ago, it was an exception when kindergarten boys and girls played out the oral practices of adults. Nowadays, a week doesn't go by when several unsure mothers and fathers phone Zartbitter and ask whether oral touching of genitals is age-appropriate for preschool children.[19]

Electronic communication is playing an ever-greater role in this. Cyberbullying is harassment and coercion through the Internet or a cellular phone, and it very often has a sexual component. A representative study in 2011 by the University of Münster and a health insurance company showed that more than 36 percent of teenagers and young adults have been victims of cyberbullying.[20]

Everyone agrees that children and teenagers must be protected from this. But how? Healthy common sense would say that the sexualization of children by the media and schools must end. Kids have a right to a sheltered environment where they can be children. This shelter must be recreated.

But the professional child sex hucksters who present themselves as "scientific experts" have other strategies. Their idea is to stimulate the children to sexual activity, to remove all limitations on them, to give them room to play doctor and masturbate, to teach them early on about the "diversity" of sexual practices, and then to develop in them the con-

---

18. Anita Heiliger, *Sexuelle Übergriffe unter Jugendlichen, Hintergründe, Risikofaktoren und Ansatzpunkte für Prävention* (Sexual Abuse Amongst Youngsters. Background, Risk Factors and Starting Points for Prevention) (Hanover, Landesjugendamt, July 4, 2006). http://www.jugend schutz-niedersachsen.de/Importe/pdf/Heiliger-Sexuelle-Ueb ergriffe.pdf.

19. http://www.zartbitter.de /content/e158/e66/e6485/index_ger.html (accessed August 16, 2012). Cf. Bernd Siggelkow and Wolfgang Büscher, *Deutschlands sexuelle Tragödie: Wenn Kinder nicht mehr lernen, was Liebe ist* (Germany's Sexual Tragedy: When Children No Longer Learn What Love Is) (Asslar: Gerth Medien, 2008).

20. http://de.wikipedia.org/wiki/Cyber-Mobbing (accessed October 7, 2015).

fidence and self-esteem to protect themselves against sex abuse. Dr. Günther Deegener, a practitioner of child and youth psychology, appears as an expert witness in abuse trials and is chairman of the *Deutscher Kinderschutzbund* (German Children's Protection Association) in the German state of Saarland. In his book *Kindesmißbrauch: erkennen, helfen, vorbeugen* (Child Abuse: Recognizing It, Curing it, Preventing It) he calls for prevention of sexual abuse of children.[21] Yet he also pleads for the "right of children to physical and sexual self-determination." He quotes approvingly that "children must be instructed in school on feelings of lust, fun, erection and orgasm, masturbation, petting and sexual intercourse. The child's natural lustful behavior with his own body must be allowed, even as part of playing doctor with other children."[22]

In a word, sexualization of children is recommended as abuse prevention. It is no wonder that abuse programs have the results they do: "To this day it has not been proven that such prevention programs reduce the frequency of sexual abuse." Deegener confirms Anita Heiliger's figures. Internationally it is assumed "that about 20 percent to 25 percent of rapes and 30 percent to 40 percent of other acts of sexual abuse are committed by children, teenagers or young adults."[23] Thus, even abuse prevention becomes an instrument of the state to sexualize children.

Methods and Risks of Manipulative Sexualization of Children and Teenagers

It is a masterpiece of the cultural revolutionaries to remove society's value system from school sex education without arousing any noteworthy resistance. This requires sophisticated manipulation techniques. These include:

- Presenting themselves to the adult world as "scientific experts."
- Presenting themselves to the young as competent, understanding friends and advocates against strict, unsympathetic parents.
- Adapting the language to youth jargon and the graphics to kids' comics.
- Representing permissive sexuality as mainstream: "That's normal!"
- Simulating peer pressure: "Everybody does it!"
- Not mentioning marriage or family.

21. Günther Deegener, *Kindsmißbrauch: erkennen, helfen, vorbeugen*, 4th ed. (Weinheim, Basel: Beltz Verlag, 1998), 4.

22. Ibid., 197. Cf. Christa Wanzeck-Sielert on sexual assertiveness training in kindergarten and elementary school, http://forum.sexualaufklaerung.de/index.php?docid=13 53 (accessed October 7, 2015).

23. Anita Heiliger, *Sexuelle Übergriffe unter Jugendlichen*, loc. cit., 215, note 18.

- Representing deficient forms of the family—single-parent families, patchwork families, LGBT families—as equal to traditional (mother-father-children) families.
- Destroying the sense of shame by:
  - Fiddling with plastic penises, plush vaginas, and condoms.
  - Detailed representation of sexual behavior in words, images, movies and videos.
  - Forced verbalization of sex acts in the classroom.
  - Sexually-oriented role plays and physical exercises.
  - Peer education: training and use of teenagers for sex education of other teenagers.[24]
  - Tying teenagers' sex drive to the cultural-revolutionary goals of the adult sex educators by constantly stimulating children's and teenagers' sex drive.

The great risks of early sexual activity are widely known, even to the public authorities who promote early sexualization of children and teenagers. These risks include:

- Teen pregnancy and abortion.
- Health damage from contraceptives.
- Infection with sexual diseases.
- Psychological injury that can lead to depression and suicide.
- Lower achievement.
- Weakened ability to bond.

Teen pregnancy and abortion

Nature wants to sustain life and cannot be completely controlled. The expectation that widespread use of the pill would reduce abortions never panned out. In fact, the opposite has occurred: despite the pill—actually, parallel with the spread of its use—abortion numbers skyrocketed after liberalization. Professor Manfred Spieker, a renowned expert in this field, estimates the actual number of children killed in the womb since 1976 in Germany to be more than 8 million.[25] In the United States, the number of legal abortions between 1973 and 2011 was 5 million. It is

---

24. Pro Familia trains students as young as 15 years old as "peer educators" or "sexperts," who then hold sex education classes in school on their own. Bundeszentrale für gesundheitliche Aufklärung: *Peer Education—A Manual for Practitioners*, Order No. 13300721. International Network: Youth Peer Education Network (Y-Peer): www.youth-peer.org/ (accessed October 7, 2015).

25. Manfred Spieker, *Kirche und Abtreibung in Deutschland* (Paderborn: Schöningh Verlag, 2001).

estimated that a fifth of all U.S. pregnancies end in abortion. Among black Americans, the rate is five times higher.[26] Alarmingly, 18 percent of all U.S. abortions are obtained by teenagers (ages 15 to 19).[27] Yet the tide may be turning: a new report from the Guttmacher Institute finds an overall 13 percent decline in abortion numbers from 2008 to 2011 in the U.S.[28]

There was also a major decline—64 percent—in teen pregnancy in the U.S. between 1990 and 2010, and subsequently in the teen abortion rate. As of 2010, the U.S. government estimated 15 abortions per 1,000 teenage girls between 15 and 19 years of age. This is considered a "success" for comprehensive sex education, but it may also be due to postponing sex to a later age.[29] Even if comprehensive sex education is conducive to the drop in teen abortions, the project has other consequences for the young:

- It trains them to be experts on contraception, years before they even reach puberty.
- It presents the killing of a human being in the womb as a "choice" without consequences.
- It guides the girl to the clinic to have an abortion without her parents' knowledge (and where the clinic may even conceal that she is a victim of statutory rape).

Is it really necessary to have 8-, 9-, and 10-year-old children practice pulling a condom over a plastic penis in class? One would think that a teenager who can work a cellphone could handle a condom without academic guidance, if the need arose, but this is about something much different.

What does a girl or boy actually *learn* in the process? A child who is not sexualized early has a natural sense of shame that protects him or her from sexual intrusions and activities. The limits set by this natural sense of shame are normally exceeded only in an intimate, loving relationship where the partner's dignity is respected. Intimacy means no one but the lover is present. Manipulating plastic sex organs and condoms in a

26. For US abortion statistics, see http://www.abort73.com/abortion_facts/us_abor tion_statistics/ (accessed October 7, 2015).

27. http://www.childtrends.org/wp-content/uploads/2012/07/27_Teen_Abortions.p df (accessed July 20, 2015).

28. http://www.guttmacher.org/media/nr/2014/02/03/ (accessed October 7, 2015).

29. Valerie Huber, "Is 'Safe Sex' Education the Reason behind the Drop in Abortion?" *Public Discourse*, June 15, 2015, http://www.thepublicdiscourse.com/2015/06/15174/ (accessed October 7, 2015).

mixed class, coercion to talk about sex acts, and exposure to graphic material damage the sense of shame. A teacher's abuse of authority and peer pressure from the class are hard for a child to evade. Children assume that teachers are role models who are imparting necessary information to them. So they conclude: school is getting me ready for sexual intercourse, so it is normal to have it at the first opportunity. "Everybody does it."

The risks of contraceptives

Hormonal contraceptives, such as birth control pills or syringes, have serious side effects that school sex education is silent about. The World Health Organization (WHO) classifies them as *carcinogenic*. Besides the increased risk of cancer, the pill has other side effects: depression, loss of menstruation, reduced libido, migraines, weight gain, and greatly increased risk of blood clotting, especially in combination with smoking. The pill doubles the risk of stroke. Even ecologists should have reservations, because, after excretion, the hormones get into groundwater, causing genetic changes and deformities in animals and people. Decreased quality of male sperm cells and increased female infertility occur in correlation with this. Nonetheless, young women are prescribed the pill as a matter of course on their first visit to the gynecologist.

Condoms are *the* fetish of the "safe sex" ideology. The illusion of "safe sex" with a condom is spread nationwide through poster campaigns and other media. Condoms may have some effect in preventing disease transmission and pregnancy, but they are not *safe*! If it is a question of life (pregnancy) and death (HIV/AIDS) people should know which risks they take.[30]

Fast spread of sexually transmitted diseases (STDs)

Venereal diseases that were once thought to have been eliminated, such as syphilis and gonorrhea,[31] are back with a vengeance, and new sexual diseases are reaching epidemic proportions. Especially virulent are chlamydia, trichomoniasis, and high-risk human papillomavirus (HPV), which is known to cause uterine cancer. Pediatrician and psy-

30. Michael Horn, "Kondome: die trügerische Sicherheit," loc. cit., 147, note 23. *Medizin und Ideologie* 29, no. 3, (2007): 12. http://eu-ae.com/images/mui_archiv/29_2007/Medizin_und_Ideolo gie_nr3_2007_web.pdf (accessed October 7, 2015).
31. In Germany's large cities, syphilis and gonorrhea are spreading fastest among homosexual men between the ages of 25 and 39 (https://de.wikipedia.org/wiki/Sexu ell_übertragbare_Erkrankung, accessed October 7, 2105).

chiatrist Miriam Grossman exposes the risks of early sexual activity, especially for girls.[32]

In the United States, every year there are up to 19 million new STD infections, and half of those affected are between 15 and 24 years old. Sexually active teenagers are the group at greatest risk. The Centers for Disease Control and Prevention indicate that 25 percent of teenage girls have an STD. STD infections "cost the U.S. healthcare system $16.4 billion annually and cost individuals even more in terms of acute and long-term health consequences."[33] Every year, 24,000 women in the United States become infertile due to STDs. Chlamydia infections are the most common cause. They also increase the risk of infection with other sexual diseases, such as HIV and syphilis.

Recently, doctors in Canada and the US have been alarmed about the increase in throat and mouth cancer. Studies show that the most common cause is human papillomavirus (HPV), even more common than cancer caused by smoking. How does it get into the mouth and throat? Through oral sex. "Younger people that are healthy, that are non-smokers and non-drinkers are developing cancers of the tonsil and the back of the tongue," said Dr. Anthony Nichols of the London Health Sciences Center in Ontario. "Teens really have no idea that oral sex is related to any outcome like STIs (sexually transmitted infections), HPV, chlamydia, and so on," said Dr. Bonnie Halpern-Felsher of the University of California San Francisco.[34]

Depression and suicide

Scientific studies show that teenage boys and girls who are sexually active have a higher risk of depression and suicide than those who are not sexually active. This is the result of data analysis of the National Longitudinal Survey of Adolescent Health (1994–2001).[35]

A quarter (25.3 percent) of sexually active girls say that they are always, usually, or often depressed, compared to 7.7 percent of girls who are not sexually active. For boys the number is 8.3 percent compared to 3.4 percent. Put another way: 60.2 percent of girls who are not sexually

32. Grossman, *You are Teaching My Child What?*, loc. cit., 203, note 5, 35 et seq.

33. http://www.cdc.gov/std/stats/sti-estimates-fact-sheet-feb-2013.pdf (accessed October 7, 2015).

34. Rebecca Millette, "Oral sex causing oral cancer rates to rise: studies," LifeSite, March 4, 2011, https://www.lifesitenews.com/news/oral-sex-causing-oral-cancer-rates-to-rise-studies (accessed January 29, 2015).

35. http://www.heritage.org/research/reports/2003/06/sexually-active-teenagers-are-more-likely-to-be-depressed (accessed October 7, 2015). The data have been carefully analyzed and checked for social background factors.

active are seldom or never depressed, but only 36.8 percent of those who are sexually active. It applies to both sexes: young people who are not sexually active are considerably happier than those who are.

Of girls who are sexually active, 14.3 percent have attempted suicide, but for those who are sexually abstinent, the figure is 5.1 percent. For boys, the number is 6 percent for those who are sexually active but only 0.7 for those who are not.

Further studies, reported in the *Journal of Sex Research*, report that frequent changing of partners causes depression. The majority of young people have had sex before they have finished high school. In college, *hooking up* is the common sexual practice, i.e., impersonal sex for a night or two. It is also common for students to talk of "friends with benefits," meaning otherwise platonic friends with whom one has intercourse:

> Studies have shown that 70 percent of college students report having had sexual intercourse with individuals they did not consider to be their romantic partner. . . . These "relationships" are mainly based on sexual desires or physical attraction alone and commonly involve drugs or alcohol. The study found that . . . for females, as the number of sexual partners increased, symptoms of depression also increased. Female partners who had the greatest number of partners had the highest symptoms of depressive pathology.[36]

Lower achievement

The National Longitudinal Survey of Adolescent Health (Add Health) shows that there is a negative correlation between early sexual activity and subsequent academic achievement. The results prove what one would expect:

> Teens who abstain from sex during high school years are substantially less likely to be expelled from school; less likely to drop out of high school; and more likely to attend and graduate from college. When compared to sexually active teens, those who abstain from sexual activity during high school years (e.g., at least until age 18) are:

> - 60 percent less likely to be expelled from school.
> - 50 percent less likely to drop out of high school.
> - Almost twice as likely to graduate from college.

---

36. Catherine M. Grello, Deborah P. Welsh and Melinda S. Harper, "No Strings Attached: The Nature of Casual Sex in College Students," *The Journal of Sex Research* 43, no. 3 (August 2006), 255 et seq. http://web.utk.edu/~welsh/Documents/Publications/Grel lo,%20Welsh%20&%20Harper,%202006.pdf (accessed January 2015).

The differences cannot be attributed to different social-economic background. The inclusion of social background factors such as race, parental education, family income, and family structure had little impact on the findings. Even after inclusion of background factors, teen virginity was found to be a significant and independent predictor of academic success. [37]

This is not surprising. The teenage years are a time for learning, building friendships, discovering the world, and living a joyful, energetic, creative life, provided that the teen has the support of a stable, loving family and is not ensnared in the turmoil of early sexual relationships.

Weakened ability to bond

Everyone desires true, committed, unconditional love. Demographic studies of youth show that more than 80 percent of young people express this inclination for a faithful relationship and look forward to having a family (see note 4). Fulfilling this desire requires a certain maturity. Early sexual contact impedes maturity and leads to deep disappointments and psychological injury. Every disappointment in love tears away at the ability to bond. Someone who is so deeply affected by love that he or she feels ready for deep devotion, and is then abandoned, may never take the risk again.

Every sexual relationship leads to a bond between the sexual partners, whether they want it or not. There are hormonal reasons for this. Oxytocin, sometimes called a "happiness hormone," greatly influences the emotional bond between two people. It is especially secreted during birth, breast-feeding, orgasm, and loving physical proximity. Oxytocin strengthens trust and reduces anxiety. The stronger the love, the greater the oxytocin secretion and the stronger the bond—a mutually reinforcing process. Women's greater ability and willingness to bond reflects the female hormone estrogen's positive support for oxytocin secretion. If this bond is torn again and again, secretion of oxytocin reduces.[38]

If sex is promiscuous right from the beginning, the yearning for a

37. Robert Rector and Kirk A. Johnson, "Teenage Sexual Abstinence and Academic Achievement" (October 27, 2015). http://www.heritage.org/Research/Reports/2005/10/Teenage-Sexual-Abstinence-and-Academic-Achievement (accessed January 2015).

38. Eric Keroack and John R. Diggs, "Bonding Imperative," http://www.physiciansforlife. org/index2.php?option=com_content&do_pdf=1&id=1492 (accessed August 16, 2015); Physicians for Life, "The Two Become One: The Role of Oxyztocinand Vasopression," http://www.physiciansforlife.org/the-two-become-one-the-role-of-oxytocin-and-vasopression on/ (accessed October 7, 2015).

deep, faithful love relationship weakens, as does the belief that such a thing is even possible. Eventually there is a separation of body and mind, and sex becomes mere physical gratification.

Twelve Good Reasons to Stop the Sexualization of Children by the State

The premise of all present-day sex education and so-called abuse prevention is the assumption that children want and need sexual stimulation and activity right from infancy. Without any scientific justification, this is presented as an anthropological law of nature. It contradicts natural hormonal development, which shows a long latent stage until puberty (see point 5 below). It conceals the fact that how people deal with sex is a basic moral decision. Wilhelm Reich knew that sexualization of children would collapse the foundation of "bourgeois society." And this is exactly what he wanted. Disguised as modern science, modern sex education does just that and achieves the same goal. Sexually stimulating education, a sexualized (media) environment, and spiritual deprivation are the preconditions for children developing sexual needs. In the interest of the child and the future of society, state and media sexualization of children and youth must come to an end. A government oriented toward the public welfare, and responsible parents, owe it to the next generation to prepare them for marriage and family. There are 12 good reasons for this.

1. *Deregulation of sexuality leads to cultural decay*

Because human beings have a free will, they need a compass for good and evil. When it comes to sexuality, people experience a tension between the biological drive and a call to love that is open to the creation of new life. Moral deregulation is a symptom of cultural decay.[39] It damages the individual and creates social chaos. Breakdown of the family, decay in achievement, widespread psychological disorders, the spread of sexually transmitted diseases, and the killing of unborn children by the millions are alarms signaling that society is in decline. Separation of sexuality from procreation through contraception and abortion has caused a demographic catastrophe. It will cause the social welfare state to falter, making it unable to pacify uprooted, impoverished people.

---

39. http://www.dijg.de/sexualitaet/joseph-unwin-sex-culture/?sword_list[0]=unwin, https://archive.org/details/b20442580 (accessed October 7, 2015).

2. *Deregulation of sexuality destroys the family as the best environment for children*[40]

The family is grounded in the lifelong monogamous marriage of a man and a woman who are willing to have children. Divorce destroys the marital community. Children must be taught virtues if they are to be capable of fulfilling their own desire for family. The family, as "the natural and fundamental group unit of society" (Universal Declaration of Human Rights), integrates society at its anthropological break points: the relationship between man and woman, and the relationship between generations. Scientific studies confirm what everyone knows: children thrive most in a stable family with their biological parents in a low-conflict marriage. Only the family can produce a self-confident, independent citizenry. People from destroyed families, without strong ties and without the ability to bond, are rootless, prone to limitless manipulation, and a hazard to democracy.

3. *Sexualization robs children of their childhood*

When we describe an "innocent child," among other things we mean freedom from sexual thoughts, images, desires, and activities. This innocence is virtually the definition of childhood and, until the sexual revolution began in the late 1960s, was actively protected by adults. Children need room for creative play, discovery and learning, where their sense of shame is respected and where they need not fear sexual incursion. They need adults who will respond to their curiosity about the creation of human life responsibly, sensitively and in an age-appropriate manner.

Neil Postman names three factors that lead to the disappearance of childhood, that tear at the limits between adults and children:

- Literacy disappears.
- Education disappears.
- The sense of shame disappears.[41]

All three factors are rapidly increasing in our society.

In 1982, even before the triumph of the internet, Postman blamed the electronic media, "an open-admission technology," for tearing at the boundary between childhood and adulthood. As the lead witnesses for the necessity of shame, Postman calls upon G.K. Chesterton, Norbert Elias, and Sigmund Freud, summarizing their insights thus:

40. Allan C. Carlson and Paul T. Mero, *The Natural Family: A Manifesto* (Dallas: n.p., 2007).

41. Neil Postman, *The Disappearance of Childhood*, loc. cit., 200, note 1.

Civilization cannot exist without control of impulses, particularly the impulse toward aggression and immediate gratification. We are constantly in danger of being possessed by barbarism, of being overrun by violence, promiscuity, instinct, egoism. Shame is the mechanism by which barbarism is held at bay. . . . Therefore, inculcation of feelings of shame has constituted a rich and delicate part of a child's formal and informal education.[42]

4. *Sexualization of children and teenagers undermines parental authority*

Parents are bound to their own children by love and assume permanent responsibility for them. They are therefore obligated to the moral upbringing of their children, which is established as an inalienable human right. In the UN and the EU, there is a battle to establish "children's rights" in the Constitution. The goal is dissolution of parental authority and sexualization of children. Sigmund Freud believed that early sexual activity in children hindered their upbringing: "We have seen from experience that seductive external influences can cause premature breach of the latent stage or its extinction . . . and that any such premature sexual activity impairs the educability of the child."[43] For childrearing to work, children must be allowed to have a childhood. Sexualized children slip from their parents' embrace and threaten not only good parent-child relations but also successful family life.

5. *Sexualization of children and teenagers goes against their hormonal development*

Boys' and girls' hormonal development displays a long latency period, lasting from shortly after birth to puberty. Levels of the male sex hormone testosterone and the female sex hormone estrogen increase in the first one-to-two months after birth and then fall to a constant low level until puberty. Not until puberty does the hormone level rapidly increase again, and it does not reach a relatively constant adult level until several years later.[44] Therefore, at the physical level, young people grow only gradually into sexual maturity. Attainment of *psychological maturity* is a still longer process.

---

42. Ibid.

43. Sigmund Freud, "Gesammelte Werke" (Frankfurt am Main: S. Fischer Verlag), Vol. V, 136.

44. Lise Eliot, *Wie verschieden sind sie? Die Gehirnentwicklung bei Mädchen und Jungen* (Berlin: Berlin Verlag 2010), 141. English Original: *Pink Brain, Blue Brain: How Small Differences Grow Into Troublesome Gaps—And What We Can Do About It* (New York: Houghton Mifflin Harcourt, 2009).

6. Habitual masturbation causes fixation on narcissistic sexuality

Leading children into habitual masturbation initiates them into narcissistic sexual gratification, which then impedes their ability to engage in mature sexual behavior as part of love for another person. A person who is masturbating is egocentrically fixated on himself and is isolated. This blocks the maturity necessary for self-giving love.

Masturbation can quickly become a habit, and a habit can become an addiction. Behind habitual masturbation lie psychological problems, such as the absence of love and fulfilling relationships, which are only exacerbated by masturbation. This results in impaired self-esteem.

Masturbation is accompanied by sexual fantasies, which can often lead to pornography, which itself evokes a desire for further masturbation—a vicious circle in which millions of men are ensnared.

7. Uncertainty about masculine and feminine sexual identity due to gender mainstreaming leads to personality disorders

A person is strong when he knows who he is and positively identifies with it—this is called identity. Identity is what I am, and what I am is good. If a person does not know who he is, he is weak. Inner conflict can become pathological and manifest itself as neurosis, schizophrenia or borderline personality disorder. Bonds that support identity are growing ever weaker today: religion, nation, family, homeland, cultural traditions, and identification with a profession. But one thing has been certain throughout human history: people are born as men or women and find their identity by becoming what they are as man or woman. The desire to rob people of this last certainty is a modern madness that threatens the foundation of human existence.

A recent study by Harvard University shows that uncertain gender identity in children under age 11 increases the probability of sexual, physical, and psychological abuse and lifelong traumatic stress disorders.[45] Deconstruction of gender identity through "diversity education" and dissolution of "gender stereotypes" is an irresponsible experiment on defenseless children.

8. Encouraging "coming out" in adolescence is an attack on the natural development of heterosexual gender identity

Public sex education is encouraging pubescent children to "come out."

---

45. Andrea L. Roberts, et al., "Childhood Gender Nonconformity: A Risk Indicator for Childhood Abuse and Posttraumatic Stress in Youth," *Pediatrics* (February 20, 2012). http://pediatrics.aappublications.org/content/early/ 2012/02/15/peds.2011-1804.

It makes it attractive to children who are in a changeable pubescent phase of identity formation to declare homosexual orientation, even though the vast majority of children naturally overcome this phase and establish a stable heterosexual identity.

In 2007, a large-scale American study on changeability of sexual orientation in youth between 16 and 22 found that the probability of a homosexual or bisexual orientation changing toward heterosexuality within one year is at least 25 times higher than vice versa. In most teenagers homosexual feelings subside. Among 16-year-olds, 98 percent experience a change from homosexuality or bisexuality to heterosexuality. About 70 percent of 17-year-old boys who indicated exclusively homosexual attractions indicated an exclusively heterosexual orientation at age 22.[46]

A study by openly homosexual researcher Gary Remafedi indicates that the earlier a person "comes out," the greater is the risk of attempted suicide. Each year the "coming out" is delayed decreases the risk of suicide.[47] Promoting early "coming out," therefore, poses a severe hazard to a young person's psychological development and identity formation.

9. *Concealing the risks of practicing homosexuality endangers young people*

Scientific studies indicate increased physical and mental risks from homosexual behavior. As already stated, these include higher rates of depression, anxiety disorders, alcohol, drug, and medication abuse, the risk of suicide, and infection with HIV and other STDs. Dr. Christl Vonholdt, an expert on social factors of homosexuality, astutely observes that "Homosexuality lobbying groups often claim that these problems are caused by society's rejection of homosexuality. So far, there is no proof of this claim."[48]

It is the duty of responsible politicians and caregivers to explain to youth the dangers of homosexual behavior. This is no more "discrimi-

---

46. R. C. Savin-Williams and G. L. Ream, "Prevalence and Stability of Sexual Orientation Components during Adolescence and Young Adulthood," *Arch Sex Behavior* 36 (2007): 385 et seq. Cited in Neil and Briar Whitehead, "Adoleszenz und sexuelle Orientierung," *Bulletin des Deutschen Instituts für Jugend und Gesellschaft*, no. 20 (Herbst 2011), http://www.dijg.de/homosexualitaet/jugendliche/adoleszenz-sexuelle-orientierung/?sword_list[o]=whitehead (accessed October 7, 2015).

47. Gary Remafedi, loc. cit., 148, note 2. "Risk factors in attempted suicide in gay and bisexual youth," *Pediatrics* 87, no. 6 (1991): 896 et seq.

48. Dr. Christl Ruth Vonholdt, "Anmerkungen zur Homosexualität," *Bulletin* no. 20 (2011). At http://www.dijg.de/homosexualitaet/fakten-hinweise-wenig-oeffentlichke it/ (accessed October 7, 2015).

nation" against young people with homosexual feelings than explaining the dangers of smoking is discrimination against smokers.

10. *Representing broken family structures as "normal" prevents children from overcoming the painful psychological results*

The reality is that broken families lead to the inability to bond and foster infidelity, adultery, domination, and irresponsibility toward children. Children rely on the unity between father and mother for their existence. Shattering that bond creates deep and often traumatic mental suffering in the children.[49]

The psychological pain, which is often accompanied by drastic material and social consequences, must be acknowledged as real for the children to overcome it. If this does not happen, the unconscious, unhealed damage remains virulent and leads to neuroses and behavioral disorders. The child has no way to emerge from this vicious circle, because adults demand that he consider the signs of social decline to be proper and normal. The Bella study at the Robert Koch Institute indicated that 21.9 percent of all children and youth ages 7 to 17 show evidence of psychological abnormalities. Among those 14 to 17 years old, about 40 percent have behavioral disorders. The greatest risk factors are an unfavorable family environment and low socio-economic status.[50]

11. *Destruction of the family leads to state control of childrearing*

What isn't taught in the family probably will not be learned in adulthood. This includes basic trust, commitment, good manners, willingness to learn, productivity, self-confidence and more. The less this personal formation occurs in the family, the more it has to be taken over by publicly financed youth services, youth homes, psychiatrists, prisons, social workers, therapists, doctors, and the police. School dropouts, the emotionally disturbed, institutionalized children, gang members, anarchists, terrorists, delinquents, drug addicts, and violent felons seldom come from intact families with a father figure present. Social problems for which the government must provide assistance are becoming a justification for increasing state intrusion in parents' right to raise their children.

---

49. Cf. Melanie Mühl, *Die Patchowrk: Eine Streitschrift* (München: Hanser Literaturverlag, 2011).

50. Robert Koch Institut, Berlin, *Psychische Gesundheit von Kindern und Jugendlichen in Deutschland* 2007, http://edoc.rki.de/oa/articles/re4NfvndKi14M/PDF/29327RsS KUczI.pdf (accessed October 7, 2015).

12. *The demographic crisis is a result of separating sexuality
from fertility*

Germany's birthrate is one of the lowest in Europe. In 2009, it was 1.36
per couple—the lowest ever recorded in the country. The working population is shrinking, and increasing life expectancy is swelling the elderly population—a trend sure to collapse the social welfare system.
Considering this development, why is the government educating children and teenagers to become contraception experts and clearing the
path for abortion and homosexuality?

In the summer of 2011, when rampaging youth set entire streets on
fire, Prime Minister David Cameron said:

> If we want to have any hope of mending our broken society, family
> and parenting is where we've got to start. . . . So: from here on I want
> a family test applied to all domestic policy. If it hurts families, if it
> undermines commitment, if it tramples over the values that keep
> people together, or stops families from being together, then we
> shouldn't do it. [51]

Gender mainstreaming is opening the way to family mainstreaming.

The Sexual Revolutionaries' Inconsistencies

All of the negative consequences of early, uncommitted, promiscuous
sexuality can be documented by scientific studies. They are obvious to
anyone whose perceptions have not been clouded by such behavior.[52]
Where are the arguments and scientific research showing that early,
uncommitted, promiscuous, same-sex sexuality makes people healthy,
competent, capable of commitment, willing to procreate, and happy?
Young people need to be informed truthfully of the risks of contraception, the spread of sexually transmitted diseases, the risk of long-term
negative consequences from abortion, the psychological injuries caused
by broken relationships, and the special risks of homosexuality. Why are
homosexual couples sent to classes and not heterosexual married couples—married couples who can give hope, even to the children of broken
homes, that gratifying family life is possible? The sexual revolutionaries
get tangled in the contradictions that are whitewashed by the ideology of
children's alleged sexual needs and of the pluralism offered in "diversity
education."

---

51. David Cameron, Riot statement: http://www.theguardian.com/uk/ 2011/aug/09/
david-cameron-full-statement-uk-riots (accessed October 7, 2015).

52. Comprehensive scientific documentation can be found at Human Life International, www.hli.org.

Sexual revolutionaries talk of love, but they seduce people into limitless gratification of drives, which destroys love. And they do even more damage:

- They promise freedom but deliver sex addiction.
- They speak of responsibility but herd people into behavior that degrades others as sex objects.
- They stump for free choice of gender, sexual orientation, and identity, but they deny the possibility of changing from homosexual to heterosexual.
- They say they want to protect people from HIV, but they encourage withholding knowledge of an infection and promote anal sex with multiple partners.
- They propagandize for "safe sex" with condoms, but cannot hold back the explosion of sexually transmitted diseases—nor can they reduce the number of new HIV infections in men who have sex with men.
- They claim they want to protect children from abuse, but they destroy their sense of shame, leaving them defenseless against sexual attacks.
- They want to strengthen children's self-esteem through experiences of sexual pleasure but destroy their innocence and their childhood.
- They promote "children's rights" but make children defenseless by destroying their family bond to their parents.

Who Gains?

The negative consequences of sexualizing children and teenagers are not "side effects" to be taken for granted while achieving positive goals. On the plus side for sexualization, there is nothing but the false promise of gratification and pleasure. From that, one might conclude that these effects are the real objective. So who benefits from sexualization of children and teenagers and from their "diversity" education? Several players come to mind:

- Those who want to produce rootless people who can be manipulated for global strategic purposes.
- Those who have an interest in reducing global population growth without changing global distribution of wealth.
- Those who have an interest in seeing the Western nations sink into a "demographic winter."
- Those who have an interest in eliminating religion, especially Christianity.
- Those who suffer under "heterosexual normativity" and wish to gain recognition through its dissolution.

Everything described in this chapter has happened because it was concealed by a cloak of silence. It is as if an alligator crawled into a child's bedroom and nobody wants to look at it. Looking away is the easy way. However, people will no longer look away from the sufferings of ruined families once the state can no longer buffer the unpleasant consequences. Accordingly, here is a series of unpleasant questions for all parents and for all those who hope to become parents:

- Do you want your kindergarten children encouraged to masturbate and engage in sex play?
- Do you want your children, in all grades from elementary school on, to be familiarized with contraception methods and all types of sexual practices? Do you want their sense of shame destroyed?
- Do you want your children to consider every "sexual orientation" equal?
- Do you want your son or daughter to be encouraged toward homosexuality in school—and for the risks to be concealed?
- Do you want your children to have their own "rights" that strip your parental authority?
- Do you want your children to grow up without ethical standards or belief in God?

Normative deregulation of sexuality through sexualization and destabilization of children's and teenagers' gender identity undermines the family as the basic unit of society, injures children and teens, and contributes to further reduction of the birth rate. They serve the interests of tiny minorities and not the public good.

Media and political propaganda create the impression that families made up of married parents and their children are a worn-out social structure of earlier eras. If that is so, then 2008 Eurostat figures on lifestyles in the EU (already cited above) are a surprise. According to Eurostat, in 2008, throughout the EU 74 percent of all children under 18 lived with married parents, 11.5 percent with two parents in a common-law relationship, and only 13.6 percent with just one parent. These figures show how robust the family is as the natural foundation of human society.[53] Despite decades of policies destructive to the family, three quarters of children in Europe still live with married parents.

Young people yearn for true love and fidelity. More than three quar-

---

53. As Frank Schirrmacher has shown, in life-threatening crises, the family's chances of survival are greater than those of individuals, even those of vital young men. See Frank Schirrmacher, *Minimum* (Munich: Karl Blessing Verlag, 2006).

ters of teenagers believe "one needs a family to be truly happy."[54] Adults should help them fulfill this yearning.[55]

With a three-quarter majority of "traditional families" in a democratic society, one would expect policy to be aimed at their best interests. Apparently, there has been damage to democracy's basic mechanism for translating the interests of the vast majority of the population into political decision-making by the parties. In the great existential issues of society, those that affect the lives of the individual, the majority of the people are no longer represented by parliament or government: not in financial policy, not in migration policy, and not in family policy.

It is high time to end the sexual politics that work against the welfare of the general public and the next generation, and it is high time for schools to teach children and teenagers the values and skills that will help them fulfill their desire for marriage and family.

54. Shell Jugendstudie 2010.
55. Cf. Gabriele Kuby, *Ausbruch zur Liebe* (Kisslegg, fe-medien Verlag, 2003); *only you: gib der Liebe eine Chance* (Kisslegg: fe-medien Verlag 2007).

13

Comprehensive Sex Education and the Catholic Church: What Is and What Should Be

When we assume that people's actual behavior should be the standard for rescinding the positive laws of the Church, we run right back into the great secular error of our time: the idea that religion should be adapted to people, and not people to religion.

Dietrich von Hildebrand[1]

Catholic Organizations Gone Wrong

THE CATHOLIC CHURCH is still the last bastion for defending Christian sexual morality as an indispensable precondition for marriage and the family. Parents—and not just Catholic parents—who wish to provide their children with a values-oriented education send them to Catholic school. They think that the label "Catholic" means that children will be taught the beauty of love, marriage, sexuality and family, and guided on the path to attaining them. They are usually disappointed. Comprehensive sex education has soaked deeply into the Catholic Church, its youth organizations and schools, and the organizations that conduct sex education, and "abuse prevention."

Since bishops mounted opposition to the encyclical *Humanae Vitae* (1968), as in the 1968 Königstein Declaration (see chapter 11, 196), an ecclesiastical vacuum has arisen in the proclamation and teaching of Catholic sexual morality. It has been filled by the missionaries of hedonistic sexuality. This has given the Church a split personality. Because of its teachings on sexual morality, the Catholic Church has been under

---

1. Dietrich von Hildebrand, *Das trojanische Pferd in der Stadt Gottes* (Regensburg: Verlag Joseph Habbel, 1968), 258.

constant fire from the media, even though these teachings are hardly ever preached, taught or lived in the local parishes anymore. Nonetheless, despite enormous opposition, the Magisterium guards it as a deposit of faith that the Church is not entitled to abandon. Now it is almost exclusively new spiritual communities that follow the high road of love that the Bible obliges everyone to take.

Many German associations that fly the Catholic flag have long conducted "sexual formation" of the type discussed in the previous chapter. These include the Sozialdienst katholischer Frauen or SkF (Social Services for Catholic Women), Caritas, and the Katholische Junge Gemeinde or KJG (Catholic Youth Community). Their speakers are trained by the Institut für Sozialpädagogik or ISP (Institute for Social Education).

On the ISP's references page, the federal headquarters of SkF thanks them for their excellent collaboration in the following words: "The Sozialdienst katholischer Frauen has had years of good cooperation with the ISP and its competent speakers for continuing education."[2] Lela Lähnemann, coauthor of Berlin's *Handreichung* (Helping Hand), recommends the ISP in this way: "If you are lesbian, gay, bisexual or transgender and want to work in sex education, I recommend training from ISP" (see p.325).

In their sex education work, the Catholic organizations are acting on the authority of the "Bishops' Guidelines for Catholic Pregnancy Counseling Centers" enacted in 2000. These call for "preventative work in cooperation with other persons and institutions." Because no content criteria are given for Catholic sex education, this leaves the floodgates open for the sexual-political mainstream. There is a simple reason for this omission: while there are a plethora of clarifications and announcements from the Catholic Church on teaching about love, chastity, marriage and family, there is no practically applied Catholic pedagogy integrating the topic of sexuality in the context of Christian anthropology. There is no ecclesiastical education institute where parents and teachers can learn to equip children and teenagers for the Christian path of love.

Youth projects run by SkF and Caritas have names like *Hautnah* (literally "skin-close"), *Herzklopfen* ("Heartbeats"), *Love Tours* and *Love Talks* (names in English). They work with materials from Germany's Bundeszentrale für gesundheitliche Aufklärung or BZgA (Federal Centre for Health Education), with briefcases of contraceptives and artificial genitalia—now not only with penises in various sizes and condoms to fit them, but also with model vaginas made of soft material with a

---

2. http://www.isp-dortmund.de/institut-sexualpaedagogik/referenzen.html (accessed October 17, 2011).

matching hymen ring for insertion. If teens have problems with implementation, the SkF offers *flirt coaching*.[3]

Donum Vitae, which is involved in sex education throughout Germany, is not a formal Catholic association. However, it benefits from the halo of its prominent Catholic cofounders and patrons at the highest levels of government and support by members of the Zentralkomitee der deutschen Katholiken or ZdK (Central Committee of German Catholics). Donum Vitae is completely in line with the bundeszebntrale gesundheitlicher Aufklärung or BZgA (Federal Center for Health Education) and Institut für Sexualpädagogik or ISP, whose literature is distributed in its counseling centers.

The vacuum in sex education in the Catholic Church leads to a situation where even the website of the German Conference of Catholic Bishops recommends materials that actively sexualize children and teenagers and undermine the moral foundations of a life oriented toward marriage and family. The "prevention boxes" for kindergarten and elementary school contain the book *Lisa and Jan* ("Lisa and John") by Uwe Sielert, *Mein Körper gehört mir* ("My Body Belongs to Me") from Pro Familia (the German division of Planned Parenthood), *Schön & blöd* ("Beautiful and Stupid") by Ursula Enders and Dorothee Wolters, and their guide for parents *Doktorspiele oder sexuelle Übergriffe* ("Playing Doctor or Sexual Assault?"). The message: "Playing doctor is just a kids' game." As part of the game, the authors include masturbation, imitating sexual intercourse, stripping nude, and "affectionate" touching of the genitalia. According to the book, kids should not do anything the other doesn't want, should insert no objects into body orifices, and not imitate any oral practices, because these are not age-appropriate. They say that parents should react positively to children playing doctor, and if they fail to do so, there can be serious consequences, such as "anxiety, screaming fits at night, temper tantrums, nightmares, joylessness, physical reactions, infantile behavior and baby talk . . . after a few weeks they will generally be better again."[4]

Education for Love: Catholic Principles

Those who have been in love know what love invokes in the heart: you and only you forever. When the miracle of love occurs between two peo-

---

3. www.herzklopfen-muenster.de (accessed October 7, 2015).
4. Ursula Enders and Dorothee Wolters, *Doktorspiele oder sexuelle Übergriffe* (Zartbitter e.V.), 19. http://www.praevention-bildung.dbk.de/fileadmin/redaktion/praeventio n/microsite/Downloads/Zart-bitter_Doktorspiele_druckgesperrt.pdf (accessed August 19, 2015).

ple, the ego bursts open and the person in love is prepared to make a gift of him or herself to the other. To love and be loved is a person's greatest yearning and at the same time the greatest risk, because the chance of being hurt is as great as the promise of happiness.

If God exists, and if the Trinity—Father, Son and Holy Spirit—*is* love, and if this God became man in Jesus Christ so that people would share divine life with him forever, then people have the chance to learn to love—in fact, they are called to it. To teach this to people, and to open up the sources of grace and mercy to them, is the Church's main task. If the Church does not fulfill this task, it loses its appeal and the purpose of its existence.

The sex act is the most complete expression of love possible between a man and a woman. The two become one flesh and thus co-creators of new life. It is therefore one of the Church's core tasks to teach people to handle the power of sexuality in true freedom, so that it becomes an expression of freely given love, and to protect them from losing their freedom, dignity and happiness by giving in to domination by their urges.

This is the sole sense of the commandments of Catholic sexual morality. If they are not supported by religious practice and informed by faith experience, they seem to become an excessively heavy yoke of oppression. However, if people are lovingly raised from an early age to live in a vital relationship with God, they discover that it is a light load (Matthew 11:30) that allows them to fulfill their own yearning for lasting love. As Jesus said, "If you love me, you will keep my commandments" (John 14:15). Observation of the commandments arises from a love of God and of one's brothers and sisters. However, if it is the result of fear of punishment, the person is cheated out of the real meaning of the teaching and runs the risk of hypocrisy and of falling sooner or later.

Taking this high road to love requires education in chastity. The word *chastity* comes from the Latin word *castus*, meaning *pure* (Merriam-Webster). It is part of the cardinal virtue of temperance, a virtue being "a habitual and firm disposition to do good" (CCC 1833). Chastity is defined as "the successful integration of sexuality within the person and thus the inner unity of man in his bodily and spiritual being" (CCC 2337).

The Catholic Church has expressed the principles of education in chastity, which truly is education in love, in countless documents that were published during the pontificate of John Paul II and draw from his work *Theology of the Body*. The most important are *Familiaris Consortio* of 1981 (FC), the "Charter of the Rights of the Family" of 1983 (Charter), *Preparation for the Sacrament of Marriage* (1995), and *The Truth and Meaning of Human Sexuality* (HS) (1995). The last of the documents constitutes "Guidelines for Education within the Family." It responds to the plight of Christian parents who see their rights to rear their own children being torpedoed by mandatory sex education in the schools. (In the following quotations from this document, the numbers in parentheses indicate the section, and the omissions are not marked.)

The Christian View of Man

The starting point is the Christian view of man. Because man was made in the image and likeness of God, he possesses a sacrosanct dignity that prohibits his being used as an object.

> Human life is a gift received in order then to be given as a gift (HS 12). One cannot give what one does not possess. If the person is not master of self—through the virtues and, in a concrete way, through chastity—he or she lacks that self-possession which makes self-giving possible. Chastity is the spiritual power which frees love from selfishness and aggression. To the degree that a person weakens chastity, his or her love becomes more and more selfish, that is, satisfying a desire for pleasure and no longer self-giving (HS 16). Chastity includes an apprenticeship in self-mastery which is a training in human freedom. The alternative is clear: either man governs his passions and finds peace, or he lets himself be dominated by them and becomes unhappy. (HS 18)

Parents' rights to raise their children

The right and obligation to raise children lies with the parents.

> As a gift and a commitment, children are their most important task, although seemingly not always a very profitable one. Children are more important than work, entertainment and social position (HS 51). Since they have conferred life on their children, parents have the original, primary and inalienable right to educate them; hence they must be acknowledged as the first and foremost educators of their children. Parents have the right to educate their children in conformity with their moral and religious convictions, taking into account the cultural traditions of the family which favor the good and the dignity of the child. Parents have the right to freely choose schools or other means necessary to educate their children in keeping with their convictions. In particular, sex education is a basic right of the parents and must always be carried out under their close supervision, whether at home or in educational centers chosen and controlled by them (Charter Art. 5). The Church is firmly opposed to an often widespread form of imparting sex information dissociated from moral principles.

> That would merely be an introduction to the experience of pleasure and a stimulus leading to the loss of serenity—while still in the years of innocence—by opening the way to vice. (FC 37)

Educating children in chastity within the family is required "to help them understand and discover their own vocation to marriage or to consecrated virginity for the sake of the Kingdom of Heaven in harmony with and respecting their attitudes and inclinations and the gifts of the Spirit" (HS 22). If this does not happen, the inevitable result is disintegration of the family. "A lack of vocations follows from the breakdown of the family" (HS 34).

Deriving from the human right of parents to raise their own children, the Pontifical Council specifies:

> As we have recalled, this primary task of the family includes the parents' right that their children should not be obliged to attend courses in school on this subject which are not in harmony with their religious and moral convictions. The school's task is not to substitute for the family, rather it is "assisting and completing the work of parents, furnishing children and adolescents with an evaluation of sexuality as value and task of the whole person, created male and female in the image of God." (HS 64)

> Therefore, it must be stressed that education for chastity is inseparable from efforts to cultivate all the other virtues and, in a particular way, Christian love, characterized by respect, altruism and service, which after all is called charity. Sexuality is such an important good that it must be protected by following the order of reason enlightened by faith: From this it follows that in order to educate in chastity, self-control is necessary, which presupposes such virtues as modesty, temperance, respect for self and for others, openness to one's neighbor. (HS 55)

These noble objectives can only be imparted if the parents themselves live by them, the children are strengthened by an active faith life and receipt of the sacraments, and the purpose of sexuality is imparted in thoughtful, age-appropriate conversation.

> Formation in chastity and timely information regarding sexuality must be provided in the broadest context of education for love. It is not sufficient, therefore, to provide information about sex together with objective moral principles. Constant help is also required for the growth of children's spiritual life, so that the biological development and impulses they begin to experience will always be accompanied by

a growing love of God, the Creator and Redeemer, and an ever greater awareness of the dignity of each human person and his or her body. (HS 70)

Parents know that children develop very differently and are therefore in a position to "provide this information with great delicacy, but clearly and at the appropriate time" (HS 75). The first explanations given to a child upon the birth of a sibling should be given "always in the deepest context of wonder at the creative work of God, who wants the new life he has given to be cared for in the mother's body, near her heart" (HS 76). Sex education must be adapted to the major stages of the child's development.

> From about the age of 5 until puberty, the child is in a stage Pope John Paul II called "the years of innocence." This period of tranquility and happiness must never be clouded by unnecessary sexual information. At this age, boys and girls are not particularly interested in sexual topics and prefer the company of children of their own gender.
> Premature sexual information threatens to damage their emotional life and formation and to destroy the unselfconsciousness of this stage of life. This is because children are not yet able to understand the emotional side of sexuality in its full significance. They cannot understand the image of sexuality or place it within a framework of moral standards. In other words, they cannot incorporate premature sex education with the necessary sense of moral responsibility. (HS 83)

Education in love through an education in chastity lays the child's foundation for giving and protecting life later on:

> Awareness of the positive significance of sexuality for personal harmony and development, as well as the person's vocation in the family, society and the Church, always represents the educational horizon to be presented during the stages of adolescent growth. It must never be forgotten that the disordered use of sex tends progressively to destroy the person's capacity to love by making pleasure, instead of sincere self-giving, the end of sexuality and by reducing other persons to objects of one's own gratification. In this way the meaning of true love between a man and a woman (love always open to life) is weakened as well as the family itself. Moreover, this subsequently leads to disdain for the human life which could be conceived, which, in some situations, is then regarded as an evil that threatens personal pleasure. The trivialization of sexuality is among the principal factors which have led to contempt for new life. Only a true love is able to protect life. (HS 105)

Because so much is at stake, parents are called to resistance. At stake are individual happiness, the family, procreation of life and propagation of faith to the next generation, and therefore the future of the entire society.

> It is recommended that parents associate with other parents, not only in order to protect, maintain or fill out their own role as the primary educators of their children, especially in the area of education for love, but also to fight against damaging forms of sex education and to ensure that their children will be educated according to Christian principles and in a way that is consonant with their personal development (HS 114). No one can bind children or young people to secrecy about the content and method of instruction provided outside the family (HS 115). It is recommended that parents attentively follow every form of sex education that is given to their children outside the home, removing their children whenever this education does not correspond to their own principles. (HS 117)

> In fulfilling a ministry of love to their own children, parents should enjoy the support and cooperation of the other members of the Church. The rights of parents must be recognized, protected and maintained, not only to ensure solid formation of children and young people, but also to guarantee the right order of cooperation and collaboration between parents and those who can help them in their task. Likewise, in parishes or apostolates, clergy and religious should support and encourage parents in striving to form their own children. (HS 148)

Smoke and mirrors or a turnaround?

It's one thing to write these principles down, and another to implement them. The right of parents to raise their children, especially in the formative area of sexual morality, has been usurped by the state and filled with content that opposes not only Christian values, but even sound human understanding. Parents no longer have much chance to teach their children chastity, which places moral demands on the child, if the child is being seduced into pleasure-oriented self-gratification beginning in kindergarten.

Children are alienated and withdraw from parental and family influence through headphones, text messaging, the Internet or their peer groups. It recalls the words of Sigmund Freud on premature sexual activity, that it "impairs the educability of the child."[5]

---

5. Sigmund Freud, *Gesammelte Werke*, vol. V, 136.

Even if it looks like time has run out for society, for the Church and those who bear responsibility for others, it is never too late. We need concepts that will resurrect the treasure of Catholic teaching on love, marriage, sexuality and family and will implement them in concrete educational programs. Such programs are a necessary response to young people's yearning for true love and family. The Church has the obligation to open the challenging path to love for the young generation, and not to leave them defenseless against aggressive seduction by hedonistic sexuality. Only those who have developed a mature, responsible personality can deal responsibly with the power of sexuality. Educational programs that strive for this require development and implementation. They will lend Catholic schools integrity, appeal and luster as a future model for society as a whole.

14

Intolerance and Discrimination

The consequences of man's self-belief are hidden from his eyes and destined for calamity. He will declare victories and award crowns. He will call darkness light, he will call the utter depths the heights. He will gain nothing and call it everything. He will lose everything and call it nothing. He will worship. He will worship as all created things must worship, yet as he strains to worship himself alone he will, in the end, value no human being and will come, without knowing it, to worship the father of lies.[1]

Michael O'Brien

Attack on Basic Freedoms

WE HAVE described the goals, strategies, networks, and methods of the global sexual revolution. Their ideological premises are as follows: there is no such thing as man and woman; killing is a human right; and moral standards are discrimination. Strategic implementation is going on behind the scenes, hidden from the eyes of the *demos*, the very people who are supposed to legitimate the power in a democracy. People's values are being numbed by the constant flood of sex and crime in the media. They no longer notice ideological sleight of hand, and, increasingly depressed and uneasy, they let the nanny state's bulging inner tube float them downstream, toward destruction of the family and demographic decline, mucked up by the silt of eroded democratic freedoms. This brings up a number of questions:

- Who worries about freedom of religion, if he doesn't believe?
- Who worries about freedom of conscience, if he keeps a lid on his own?
- Who worries about freedom of opinion, when his opinion is politically correct?

---

1. Michael O'Brien, *Elijah in Jerusalem* (San Francisco: Ignatius Press, 2015).

- Who worries about freedom of speech, if he howls with the rest of the pack?
- Who worries about scientific freedom, when he seeks profit instead of truth?
- Who worries about therapeutic freedom, if the goal of his therapy is approved?

In the descending dusk of blindness to values, a small, active minority can set the spiral of silence in motion. They become spokespeople to confuse and disorient the majority, make their own ideology mainstream, and ultimately start peddling what used to be bad as something good. The price the individual has to pay for objecting and opposing increases the longer he keeps quiet and the more social and political power the minority gains. This can ultimately result in open suppression of opponents. The higher the price, the fewer people are willing to pay it. But the triumphant minority can never get enough. The slippery slope to a new totalitarianism is greased with the fraudulent promise of limitless individual freedom. But because this type of freedom turns people into slaves to their urges, it can lead only to bondage. A society can be free only to the degree that the people who make it up are themselves free to do good. No state can be founded on lust or greed.

Those who hold to Christian values at the start of the third millennium—who live and acknowledge them—collide with growing limitations on the freedoms that are (or were) the marks of European culture. Endangered freedoms include:

- Freedom of religion
- Freedom of conscience
- Freedom of expression
- Freedom of speech
- Freedom of assembly
- Freedom of judiciary
- Scientific freedom
- Therapeutic freedom
- Economic freedom
- Freedom of contract
- Freedom of parents

Questionable legal bases have been created to limit the freedom of those who refuse to obey the cultural pressure of political correctness: anti-discrimination laws, laws on equality or equal treatment, laws against "hate speech," and bans on "homophobia." Countries and institutions come under pressure to legalize abortion and the LGBTI agenda. Submissive judges interpret and apply valid laws in light of this agenda.

Individuals are shunned, defamed, condemned, and threatened, their careers and economic existence ruined.

Those who have had the good fortune to spend most of their lives enjoying a free, democratic order know what freedom of expression really is. In Germany that meant that as long as you didn't glorify the crimes of the Nazis, you said and wrote what you wanted without the threat of government sanctions or social ostracism. Under the protection of this freedom, the student revolts of 1968 got started. This freedom was so wide open that the possibility of violence to people and property was discussed, all authority was questioned, and valid moral standards were subjected to frontal assault. The students of 1968 rebelled and basked in the heroism of a minority that revolted against the "establishment" and were courted by the left-wing media. The left-wing media acted as freedom fighters against the conservative publisher Axel Springer. Then they were still watchdogs against those in power. Today they are part of the political class. The socialist student groups that rebelled against the "establishment" in 1968 were internally organized on Stalinist authoritarian principles. Forty years later they have become the "establishment" and implement their social and political goals by tearing away more and more freedoms.

Additionally, today the entire media landscape has moved to the left. The mainstream media no longer ensure freedom of expression, but actively get behind the culture war. Behind the scenes, the talking points are established, the rules of speech devised, new laws created, global and national action plans forged, and networks are created between powerful politicians, NGOs, the media, and the judicial system. Huge streams of money flow to the activists from billionaires, foundations, and global corporations. Uppity countries and institutions are blackmailed through power politics. This all grabs and squashes anyone who is true to his conscience and dares to oppose a mainstream created in this way. This is done through:

- Social ostracism of those who violate political correctness.
- Character assassination through accusations of being fundamentalist, bigoted, radical right-wing, racist, anti-Semitic, sexist, biologistic or homophobic.
- Exclusion from public discourse.
- Reprimands by superiors and the threat of sanctions.
- New criminal laws: anti-discrimination, hate speech, homophobia.
- Job dismissal.
- Denial of employment and career.
- Heavy fines.

- Obligatory training in gender ideology.
- Imprisonment.
- Prohibition of homeschooling, revocation of custody.
- Telephone and e-mail harassment, hate mail, death threats.
- Media campaigns.
- Social media campaigns.
- Disruption of events.
- Vandalism.
- Physical attack.

This all happens when people dare to resist enslavement through sexualization—not through discrimination, hate, violence, or any of the methods named above, but just because they state their opinion, make use of their civic freedoms, and refuse to behave in ways forbidden by their conscience. The homosexual movement is the spearhead of the movement to curtail democratic freedoms. It is supported by the UN, the EU, most Western governments, the mainstream media and big business (like Google, Facebook, Twitter, and Apple) that have the power to change public opinion.

Countries whose identities are especially associated with the fight for freedom and democracy—Great Britain, the United States and Canada—are leaders in implementing the LGBTI agenda. The war is taken to every nation, every party, every government department, every university, every judicial court, every church community, to the military, the scouts, families—creating schisms wherever it enters. Individual cases show what this means in concrete terms.

The Observatory on Intolerance and Discrimination against Christians,[2] an Austrian charitable organization, observes and publishes cases of intolerance and discrimination against Christians in Europe. From 2005 to the end of 2014, more than 1,400 cases have been documented and published in a yearly Shadow Report. Dr. Gudrun Kugler, director of the Observatory, explains that "Studies show that in Europe 85% of crimes committed on the basis of religious intolerance were directed against Christians. It is time for an open public debate on this issue!" Especially noteworthy is the Canadian website *LifeSiteNews*, which reports comprehensively on the intensifying global culture war over the family, the right to life and the LGBTI agenda. The British Coalition for Marriage published a flyer listing 30 cases of people being punished for

---

2. *Observatory on Intolerance and Discrimination against Christians in Europe*, abbreviated as IAC. The keyword can be used to find the case using the search function at www.intoleranceagainstchristians.eu.

believing in traditional marriage.[3] These cases clearly demonstrate that same-sex "marriage" is not about freedom for a minority of a minority. Only around two percent of the homosexual minority, constituting around two percent of the population, make use of the legalization of same-sex unions. It is about a new sexual totalitarianism that seeks to destroy the meaning and reality of marriage and family. New cases arise daily in which freedoms are curtailed. A few will be given here as examples.

Concrete Discrimination

Attack on: Religious freedom, freedom of conscience, freedom of speech, freedom of assembly.

Methods: Boycott of the State of Indiana, travel bans, ban of organizations, public mobbing, financial ruin, charges of discrimination, fines, telephone and e-mail harassment, vandalism, violent attacks.

Cases: Indiana Religious Freedom Restoration Act of March 26, 2015; InterVarsity Christian Fellowship; Army Chaplain Wes Molder; Navy Chaplain Joseph Lawhorn; Pastor Åke Green; Bishop Anthony Priddis; Catholic adoption agencies; Christian retreat house; Church of San Vicenç; Archbishop André-Joseph Leonard; Pope Benedict XVI; Catholic University of Milan.

The Religious Freedom Restoration Act (RFRA) of Indiana is nearly identical with the RFRA signed into law by President Clinton in 1993. The law prohibits substantial government burdens on religious exercise unless the government can show that 1) it has a compelling interest in burdening religious liberty and 2) is doing so through the least restrictive means possible. An unprecedented, nationwide, hysterical campaign for the protection of "sexual orientation" and "gender identity" ensued, including urging state governments to proclaim travel-bans on Indiana, closing down of businesses, and threats to individuals. Indiana had to amend the law. The rights of the non-heterosexual minority were given preference over the personal moral conscience of citizens.

Donald and Evelyn Knapp, both ordained ministers of an evangelical church in Coeur D'Alene, Idaho, declined to marry a same-sex couple in October 2014. On the grounds of a non-discrimination statute that

---

3. http://www.c4m.org.uk/downloads/30cases.pdf (Accessed May 2015).

includes sexual orientation and gender identity, the ministers were informed that they had to officiate same-sex marriages in their own chapel. Idaho's constitutional amendment defining marriage as the union of a man and a woman had been previously struck down by the 9th U.S. Circuit Court of Appeals. The Knapps now face a 180-day jail term and a $1,000 fine *for each day* they decline to celebrate the same-sex wedding.[4]

InterVarsity Christian Fellowship, a well-established Christian college group, founded in 1947 with 860 chapters in the United States, was "de-recognized" by California State University, with 23 campuses; as well as by Vanderbilt University, Rollins College, and Tufts University. This means defunding as well as no access to on-campus meetings rooms, student fairs, or official school functions. The reason is that InterVarsity refused to sign a general nondiscrimination policy, which demands that leadership positions be open to all (i.e. *all* "sexual orientations"). InterVarsity spokesman Greg Jao said that changing InterVarsity leadership policy would undermine its Christian foundation.

Lieutenant Commander Wes Modder, a highly respected Navy chaplain, was removed from his position because his gay assistant officer filed a complaint against him. Having been on the job just for a month, his assistant accused him of telling a student that homosexuality was wrong. The chaplain was accused of being unable to "function in the diverse and pluralistic environment of the Naval Nuclear Power Training Command." Franklin Graham, President and CEO of the Billy Graham Evangelistic Association, said, "It's a sad day in America when military chaplains have to choose between being true to their faith and keeping their jobs."[5]

Army Chaplain Joseph Lawhorn, who conducted a suicide prevention training session with the 5th Ranger Training Battalion, received a Letter of Concern that accused him of advocating for Christianity and "using Christian scripture and solutions." The offense: the chaplain had provided a two-sided handout that listed Army resources on one side and a

4. https://www.lifesitenews.com/news/idaho-ministers-face-fines-jail-time-for-refusing-to-perform-same-sex-marri (accessed October 7, 2015). Keyword: *Donald and Evelyn Knapp*.

5. http://www.foxnews.com/opinion/2015/03/12/more-than-40000-rally-for-navy-chaplain-accused-being-anti-gay.html (accessed May 15, 2015).

biblical approach to handling depression on the other side. Because one person complained, the chaplain was warned to be "careful to avoid any perception you are advocating one system of beliefs over another." All the chaplain did was to give his personal testimony of how he himself had dealt with depression.[6]

A Christian retreat house in New Jersey was ordered by the court to provide spaces for same-sex wedding receptions with the justification that the Constitution allows "some intrusion into religious freedom to balance other important societal goals."[7]

Anthony Priddis, Anglican bishop of Hereford, United Kingdom, was fined £47,345 in 2008 and ordered to participate in "equal opportunity training" because he was not willing to hire active homosexuals for youth work. Additionally, the bishop had to pay the rejected applicants £7,000 for "psychiatric injury" and £6,000 for "injury to feelings."[8]

All Catholic adoption agencies in the United Kingdom have been forced to close, because of their policy of only placing children with married heterosexual couples.

Archbishop André-Joseph Leonard of Brussels was attacked by having pies thrown at him during Holy Mass and at a lecture at the Catholic University of Louvain. One of the attackers said, "He deserves it for all the homosexuals who don't dare come out to their families, and all the girls who want an abortion."[9] In April 2013 again he was attacked by four topless, "femen" activists, who interrupted the Archbishop's speech at a conference at the University of Brussels, screaming loudly and holding up a poster labeled "Stop Homophobia."[10]

Pope Benedict XVI was formally condemned by the Belgian parliament for saying on his trip to Africa that condom distribution could not pre-

6. http://www.foxnews.com/opinion/2014/12/09/chaplain-punished-for-sharing-his-faith-in-suicide-prevention-class.html (accessed May 15, 2015).

7. https://www.lifesitenews.com/news/judge-rules-christian-facility-cannot-ban-same-sex-civil-union-ceremony-on (accessed October 7, 2015).

8. http://www.intoleranceagainstchristians.eu/case/anglican-bishop-fined-47-345-and-sent-to-re-education-in-gay-employment-case.html. Keyword: *Priddis*.

9. http://www.intoleranceagainstchristians.eu /case/belgian-archbishop-hit-in-face-with-cream-pies.html. Keyword: *Leonard*.

10. http://www.intoleranceagainstchristians.eu /case/archbishop-of-brussels-andre-leonard-attacked.html.

vent the spread of HIV/AIDS. Edward C. Green, director of the AIDS Prevention Research Project at the Harvard Center for Population and Development Studies, says, "The best evidence we have supports the pope's comments."[11]

The Catholic University of Milan was forced by a 2009 ruling of the European Court of Human Rights (ECHR) to extend the contract of Prof. Luigi Lombardi Vallauri. The university had wanted to dismiss the professor because he agitated against Christianity with statements such as "Jesus was through and through a bad human being." The ECHR felt this came under the right to free expression of opinion at a Catholic university.[12]

Vladimír Spidla, EU commissioner for Employment, Social Affairs and Equal Opportunities, declared in November 2009 that there could be no exceptions to anti-discrimination laws in regard to "sexual orientation," even based on religious conscience.[13]

Attack on: Freedom of expression, freedom of speech, freedom of assembly, scientific freedom.

Methods: Defamation, character assassination, exclusion from public discourse, pressure through politics and the media, disruption of events, vandalism, exclusion from party, incarceration, fines, demonstrations, disciplinary measures.

Cases: Marburg Conference, politically incorrect journalists.

Marburg Conference

At the *Fachkongress der Akademie für Psychotherapie und Seelsorge* (Professional Conference of the Academy of Psychotherapy and Pastoral Care) in Marburg, Germany, May 20–24, 2009, the Lesbian and Gay Association in Germany (LSVD) fought by every means the public appearance of two invited speakers: Dr. Christl Vonholdt, publisher of the bulletin of the German Institute for Youth and Society, which pub-

---

11. http://www.intoleranceagainstchristians.eu/case/parliament-issues-formal-protest-against-popes-statement-on-condoms.html (accessed October 7, 2015).

12. http://www.intoleranceagainstchristians.eu/case/italy-european-court-of-human-rights-violates-freedom-of-religion.html. Keyword: *Vallauri.*

13. http://www.intoleranceagainstchristians.eu/case/eu-commission-demands-uk-abolish-religious-freedom-rights.html. Keyword: *Spidla.*

lishes scientific research on homosexuality; and Markus Hoffmann, director of the organization Wüstenstrom, which offers help to people with ego-dystonic same-sex attraction—i.e., helps people who suffer due to their homosexuality. An "action coalition of queer, feminist, anti-sexist, anti-fascist groups, critical scientists and individuals" intended to bring down the entire conference.

In a public statement 370 well-known figures, including philosophy professor Robert Spaemann, constitutional judge Martin Kriele and constitutional expert Ernst-Wolfgang Böckenförde, published a *Declaration for Freedom and Self-Determination*. It says:

> We protest the LSVD's acting on unproven claims and by slanderous means against *Wüstenstrom e.V.* and the *Deutsches Institut für Jugend und Gesellschaft* and discrediting them in the media. Intimidation is being used to create a climate of fear to silence politicians, journalists, scientists and therapists.[14]

This time, the LSVD campaign did not succeed. The conference took place. A thousand police officers had to be deployed to protect a thousand conference participants against a thousand demonstrators. The protesters carried picket signs reading:

> We're here to offend your religious feelings!
> God is a lesbian!
> Fuck your neighbor as yourself!
> Freedom to all perverts!
> Better to gang bang than to pray!
> If Mary had aborted you wouldn't be here!

That same year, Germany celebrated the 60th anniversary of its constitution. Public institutions and party-affiliated foundations are contributing to curtailment of the freedoms this magnificent constitution gave the German people in the wake of the Nazi terror. They regularly stigmatize politically incorrect journalists as the "radical right" who come out against gender mainstreaming, the LGBTI agenda and abortion.

Prof. Edith Düsing. In December 2012, the Autonomous Lesbian and Gay student organization of the University of Cologne (LuSK) demanded a ban on a lecture by philosophy professor Edith Düsing on the occasion of the 250th anniversary of Friedrich Schiller's birth. The

---

14. http://www.medrum.de/content/initiative-fuer-freiheit-und-selbstbestimmung (accessed October 7, 2015).

sole reason for the attack: Prof. Edith Düsing had signed the *Declaration for Freedom and Self-Determination* in support of the Marburg Conference. The lecture was disrupted by a half-hour same-sex "kiss in."[15]

Melanie Phillips, a prominent British columnist, received death threats after her criticism in *The Daily Mail* of positive treatment of homosexuality in all school subjects. "The response, however, exceeded even my expectations.... I have been subjected to an extraordinarily vicious outpouring of hate and incitement to violence [through e-mail, the Internet and the mainstream media]."[16]

Phillip Lardner, a Scottish Tory candidate, was thrown out of the party in April 2010 because on his website, he spoke out against treating the homosexual lifestyle as equivalent to marriage and supporting it with state subsidies.[17]

A street preacher in Scotland called homosexuality a sin. He was arrested by the police and levied a fine of £1,000 for his "homophobic statements."[18]

The Spanish government under Prime Minister José Luis Rodríguez Zapatero fined a Christian TV broadcaster €100,000 Euros for broadcasting a series of ads promoting the family and opposing the homosexual lifestyle.[19]

Attack on: Therapeutic freedom.

Methods: Defamation, character assassination, exclusion from public discourse, pressure through politics and the media, disruption of events, threats, spying, employment ban.

15. http://www.medrum.de/content/vorlesungsverbot-fuer-die-philosphin-edith-duesing (accessed October 7, 2015).

16. https://www.lifesitenews.com/news/death-threats-against-uk-columnist-for-opposing-homosexualist-agenda (accessed October 7, 2015). Cf. Melanie Phillips, *The World Turned Upside Down* (New York: Encounter Books, 2011).

17. https://www.lifesitenews.com/news/i-stand-by-my-statement-absolutely-scottish-candidate-sacked-by-conservativ (accessed October 7, 2015).

18. https://www.lifesitenews.com/news/street-preach er-arrested-in-scotland-for-condemning-homosexuality (accessed October 7, 2015).

19. http://www.intoleranceagainstchristians.eu/case/100-000-euro-fine-for-christian-broadcaster.html. Keyword: 100,000 Euro Fine.

Cases: Wüstenstrom e.V., Weißes Kreuz ("White Cross"), Lesley Pilkington, Dr. Hans-Christian Raabe.

Stefan Schmidt, an employee of Wüstenstrom, reported on attacks against Wüstenstrom's work at an OECD conference in Vienna on freedom of religion on December 9, 2009:

- Defamation as right-wing radical and Holocaust denier.
- Public pressure on the event organizer to deny Wüstenstrom employees a forum.
- Rioting and violent attacks at events.
- Pressure on newspapers and publishers not to publish information on the organization and its work.
- Pressure on service providers, insurance companies and professional organizations to forbid and penalize therapy for ego-dystonic homosexuality.[20]

Lesley Pilkington, a psychotherapist in the United Kingdom, was asked by journalist Patrick Strudwick for therapeutic assistance because he allegedly suffered due to his homosexual orientation. He secretly recorded two sessions and published a report on them in *The Independent*. After that, the therapist was threatened with expulsion from the professional association because she was said to work "recklessly, disrespectfully, dogmatically and unprofessionally." The journalist was designated as "Journalist of the Year" by the homosexual organization Stonewall.[21]

Dr. Hans-Christian Raabe, a Christian physician, was fired in February 2011 from Britain's Advisory Council on the Misuse of Drugs under pressure from homosexual organizations, because he pointed out a relationship between the homosexual lifestyle, drug abuse and sexual abuse of children. In an expert report, he said: "While the majority of homosexuals are not involved in pedophilia . . . an above-average portion of pedophiles are homosexuals, and there is overlap between the homosexual movement and the movement for acceptance of pedophilia." This statement was in accord with a document from the British Home Office, his employer, which had determined that 20 percent to 33 percent of child abuse is homosexual in nature.[22]

20. http://www.intoleranceagainstchristians.eu/case/list-of-attacks-against-christian-sexual-orientation-group.html. Keyword: *Stefan Schmidt*.

21. https://www.lifesitenews.com/news/christian-psychotherapist-found-guilty-of-professional-misconduct-for-repar/. Keyword: *Pilkington*.

22. http://www.intoleranceagainstchristians.eu/case/christian-drug-expert-sacked-from-government-advisory-panel-over-gay-dispute.html. Keyword: *Raabe*.

Attack on: Freedom of conscience.

Methods: Dismissal, telephone and e-mail harassment, prosecution.

Cases: Christian relationship counselor, midwives, registrar, county clerk.

Gary McFarlane, of the United Kingdom, was dismissed from the counseling organization Relate because he refused to counsel same-sex couples on improving their sexual relations. Because he considered himself to have been discriminated against based on conscience, he brought his case before the Employment Appeal Tribunal, which decided that the firing was legal. The European Court of Human Rights dismissed his appeal, in January 2013, saying that it was up to national authorities to decide on the balance of rights between sexual orientation and freedom of religion.[23]

Two Catholic midwives at Southern Hospital in Glasgow sued Scotland's largest healthcare organization because the hospital wanted to force them to participate in performing abortions, even though their option to refuse based on conscience is explicitly protected by the Abortion Act of 1967.[24]

Lillian Ladele, a registrar in the UK, had requested, for reasons of conscience, to be excused from presiding at same-sex marriage ceremonies. For this, she was threatened with dismissal. Because she felt "intimidated and humiliated," she brought an employment suit, which she won. The opposing side brought the case before the ECHR, where Ladele lost.[25]

County Clerk Kim Davis from Kentucky refused to issue marriage licenses for homosexual couples because this was against her faith and conscience. U.S. District Judge David Bunning sent her to jail because fining her "would not bring about the desired result of compliance." The case of Kim Davis divided the American nation. Hilary Clinton tweeted her support, saying all elected officials "should be held to their duty to uphold the law—end of story." The jailing of Kim Davis was also

---

23. http://www.intoleranceagainstchristians.eu/case/no-conscientious-objection-with-regard-to-affirming-homosexuality-in-the-workplace.html. Keyword: *McFarlane.*

24. http://www.intoleranceagainstchristians.eu/case/scotland-no-right-to-conscientious-objection-for-midwives.html. Keyword: *Mary Doogan.*

25. http://www.intoleranceagainstchristians.eu/case/registrars-wish-not-to-register-homosexual-unions-rejected.html. Keyword: *Lilian Ladele.*

supported by the Obama administration. On the other hand, two Republican presidential contenders, Mike Huckabee and Senator Ted Cruz, sided with Kim Davis. Ted Cruz said the arrest constituted "judicial tyranny."

Attack on: Freedom of conscience, freedom of judiciary, economic freedom.

Methods: Defamation campaign ("shit storm"), expulsion, dismissal, juridical persecution, forced closing down of business, death-threats, defamation on social media, financial ruin.

Cases: Rocco Buttiglione, Eunice and Owen Johns, Peter and Hazelmary Bull, Karolina Vidovic-Kristo, Barronelle Stutzman, Kevin O'Connor, Brendan Eich.

Rocco Buttiglione, appointed as an EU commissioner for Justice, Freedom and Security, was brought down by a single vote in the home-affairs select committee of the European Parliament because, as a Catholic and a philosopher, he spoke out against homosexuality.

Eunice and Owen Johns, married couple in the United Kingdom, lost their right to take in foster children because, as Christians, they did not want to represent the homosexual lifestyle positively and insisted on taking the children with them to church services on Sunday. The court decided that protection from discrimination based on sexual orientation trumped protection from discrimination on religious grounds. Their appeal to the British High Court was unsuccessful.[26]

Peter and Hazelmary Bull, of the United Kingdom, refused a double room to two men in their guest house. In February 2012, they were ordered to pay a £3,600 fine for this. The appellate court upheld the judgment, because they had violated the Equality Act Regulations.[27]

Karolina Vidovic-Kristo, a well-respected journalist with the Croatian TV channel HRT, was the editor and host of a popular program, *Slika Hrvatske*, produced specifically for Croatians living overseas. In January,

26. http://www.intoleranceagainstchristians.eu/case/government-requires-foster-parents-to-affirm-homosexuality-rules-uk-high-court.html. Keyword: *Owen John.*

27. http://www.intoleranceagainstchristians.eu/case/guesthouse-owners-fined-for-married-couples-only-policy.html. Keyword: *Peter Bull.*

2013, she was suspended after editing and hosting a show which criticized the government's sex-ed program. Vidovic-Kristo was suspended from her duties and the show taken off the program.[28] On January 8, 2015, her employment was terminated completely.

Barronelle Stutzman, 70, a florist in Washington, refused to provide flowers for the gay marriage of a regular customer and friend, "because of my relationship with Jesus." For the attorney general of Washington State this was a violation of the state's anti-discrimination law and reason to sue Stutzman. She was also sued by the two homosexual partners, represented by the ACLU. On February 19, 2015, a Washington State judge ruled that she must provide full support for same-sex wedding ceremonies. The state and the same sex-couple are entitled to collect damages and attorneys' fees not only from her business, but also from Stutzman personally. Stutzmann may lose her business, her home and her savings.[29]

Kevin O'Connor, owner of Memories Pizza, who made no secret of his Christian faith and support of the Indiana Religious Freedom Restoration Act, had stated in response to the question of a journalist that anyone was welcome in his restaurant, but that he would not cater a homosexual "wedding." Public mobbing forced the family to close down their pizza shop and hide from the public.

Brendan Eich, Mozilla co-founder, was appointed as CEO on March 24, 2014. A week later he resigned because of a public campaign of gay rights activists against him who called for a boycott of the company. The reason: In 2008 Eich had made a donation of $1,000 to the campaign for California Proposition 8, which defined marriage as the union of one man and one woman.

Attack on: Rights of parents.

Methods: Mandatory sex education, school courses in gender ideology, supervision of children by school authorities, fines and prison sentences, deprivation of parental custody.

---

28. Intoleranceagainstchristians.eu/case/tv-host-suspended-for-critical-show-on-governments-sex-ed-programme.html. Keyword: *Karolina Vidovic-Kristo*.

29. http://edition.cnn.com/2015/02/20/living/stutzman-florist-gay/?inf_contact_key =8cf6bd35b4e335cd7e682617c0cc39af18ed8f238064eebce2bd7f7d39e5f6f8 (Accessed May 15, 2015).

Cases: Schools in Austria, the United Kingdom and Spain, schoolchildren in California, kindergartens in England.

All Austrian schools were advised by the government that sex education must be oriented toward the "plurality of values, respect for same-sex forms of partnership." Instructional personnel and informational material with differing points of view were no longer allowed. This also applied to Christian schools.[30]

All schools in Great Britain, including Christian schools, are prohibited by Sexual Orientation Regulations (SOR) to teach sexual morality "as if it was objectively true." Should they not obey SOR, they will lose public funding.

All Spanish schools under the Zapatero regime had to introduce a compulsory subject called Educación para la Ciudadanía (EpC), a type of civics class with a curriculum in sharp conflict with Christian ethics. 55,000 parents protested against it on the basis of conscience. 2,300 sued in court.[31]

In Germany school education for children from 6 to 14 years is compulsory. Homeschooling is forbidden. On this legal ground parents are forced to send their children to sexual education classes. If they withdraw children from sex-education classes they are heavily fined. There have been around twenty cases where parents refused to pay the fine. Some of them were put into coercive detention, their children into state custody. Since 2014, new federal laws extend sexual education to all age groups and all subjects in order to achieve acceptance of non-heterosexual lifestyles.[32]

All of these cases show that things are becoming tough for Christians and for any citizen who wants to stay true to his conscience. Looking at

30. http://www.intoleranceagainstchristians.eu/case/christian-sexual-education-jeopardized-by-government.html. Keyword: *Austria sexual education.*

31. http://www.intoleranceagainstchristians.eu/case/new-educational-program-spreads-secularist-ideas-55-000-parents-opt-out.html (accessed October 7, 2015).

32. "2007 German Horror Tale," *Washington Times*, February 27, 2007, http://www.washingtontimes.com/news/2007/feb/27/20070227-084730-5162r/; "More problems for homeschoolers in Germany," *Washington Times*, June 15, 2008; http://www.washingtontimes.com/news/2008/jun/15/more-problems-for-home-schoolers-in-germany/; "Wunderliches re-gain freedom to leave but vow to stay and fight," Home School Legal Defense Association, http://www.hslda.org/hs/international/Germany/201408280.asp.

"The Perils of Political Propaganda," Randall Smith writes: "The state recognizes that it depends heavily on the personal moral consciences of its citizenry, and that to force them to *violate* that conscience is to pollute the very wellspring of the common moral life of the state: namely, the *personal* moral conscience of each individual within the state."[33]

The fate of Christians in Nigeria, Sudan, Pakistan, Indonesia, Iraq, Syria, Turkey and North Korea shows the bloody abyss of persecution of Christians in our time. In Europe, Christians do not yet fear for life and limb, but ideological consequences can quickly lead to physical ones. Cardinal Francis George made the famous statement: "I expect to die in bed, my successor will die in prison and his successor will die a martyr in the public square." And he added: "His successor will pick up the shards of a ruined society and slowly help rebuild civilization, as the Church has done so often in human history." (He died in bed on April 17, 2015.) The transformation from a democratic society, founded on Christian faith, to a hedonistic totalitarian one does not happen in just one step. There are no signs that this trend will stop, unless people rise to defend their values and democratic rights.

33. Randall Smith, "The Perils of Political Propaganda: Mass Hysteria over Indiana," *Public Discourse*, April 2, 2015. http://www.thepublicdiscourse.com/category/conscience-protection/ (accessed October 7, 2015).

15

Resistance

The only thing necessary for evil to triumph is for good men to do nothing.

Edmund Burke

IT WOULD SEEM there is no stopping the global sexual revolution. The political power and huge financial resources of the UN, the EU, the governments of the United States and other countries, and the billions controlled by foundations, global corporations, and NGOs, have been thrown behind the effort to deconstruct the binary gender order, deregulate sexual norms, dissolve the family, and reduce the world population.

But there is resistance, and there is successful resistance. Around the world, Christian churches, NGOs, individuals and institutions are working for a culture that respects the dignity of the human person and fights for life, marriage and family. A report of the Friedrich Ebert Stiftung, the intellectual activist center of the German Social Democratic Party (SPD), shows that the gender activists are becoming alarmed over the growing resistance to "gender politics" seen at the grass-roots level (e.g., *La Manif pour tous* movement in France and *Demo für alle* in Germany) and expressed in referendums held in several countries across Europe.[1]

The Eastern-European countries who had to endure Communist oppression were spared from the sexual revolution in the West—an irony of history, since it was Communism that wanted to destroy the family through "liberated" sexuality.

---

1. Gabriele Kuby, "Gender Activists Alarmed: New Report on the 'Anti-Gender Mobilizations in Europe' by Left-Wing Think Tank," July 31, 2015, http://europeandignitywatch.org/day-to-day/detail/article/gender-activists-alarmed-new-report-on-the-anti-gender-mobilizations-in-europe-by-left-wing-think.html (accessed October 7, 2015).

Let us first look at two countries in more detail. First, Spain, a country that had a radical gender-revolutionist for prime minister who did what he could to destroy the old Christian culture of his country; then, Hungary, a country which had suffered greatly under Communist dictatorship, and the left-wing government after 1989, and returned to a Christian constitution on January 1, 2012, through landslide elections.

Spain

From 2004 to 2011, Spain was governed by socialist José Luis Rodríguez Zapatero, a radical gender ideologue who knew what he wanted: "Today Spain is on the cutting edge of a radical international project that will deeply affect the family . . . a far-reaching project to change the cultural values that will determine Spain's social and historical identity for a long time."[2] This "radical international project" marched behind a concept of freedom that had been "emancipated" from reality. In Zapatero's words, "It is freedom that makes us true. Not the truth that makes us free."

During his time in office, Zapatero used "legislation as the decisive key to cultural change." The following laws were passed under his regime:

- A law against gender violence.
- A quickie divorce law (divorces jumped from 51,000 in 2004 to almost 122,000 in 2008).
- Legalization of abortion-on-demand (abortions increased from 49,500 in 1997 to 112,000 in 2007). [3]
- Free distribution of the "morning after pill" without a prescription.
- Legalization of artificial methods of reproduction.
- Free choice of gender identity.
- Legalization of homosexual "marriage."
- Legalization of therapeutic cloning.
- Introduction of obligatory sex education in favor of "diversity" and against "homophobia."
- Equal treatment and anti-discrimination laws.
- Introduction of obligatory education in gender ideology.
- Reform of the law on religious freedom.

2. "Demographic Deficit. Family rights and human capital in Europe. Experiments on families—Member States experiences and consequences: SPAIN," ECR Group, Brussels (Instituto de Politica Familiar, November 17, 2010).

3. Ibid.

As Zapatero said, "We stand before a global project of social transformation with the goal of destroying the old order and building a new order. We have never passed so many laws in such a short time that change the lives of the individual."[4]

A strong opposition movement formed against this policy. It fights for the right to life, for marriage and family, parents' rights, freedom of religion, and against the new gender indoctrination in schools (under the label of Educación para la Ciudadanía, or EpC). In June 2005, more than 2 million Spaniards protested in favor of the family and against homosexual "marriage." The movement received strong support from Pope Benedict XVI, who visited this once-Catholic country three times (in June 2006 for the World Meeting of Families in Valencia, in November 2010 at Santiago de Compostela and Barcelona for the consecration of the Church of the Holy Family, and in August 2011 in Madrid for World Youth Day).

The Zapatero regime came to an abrupt end. Both destruction of the culture and extreme financial mismanagement led to the government's ousting in 2011. The new prime minister was Mariano Rajoy of the conservative Partida Popular. On January 31, 2012, the new minister of education struck the subject Educación para la Ciudadanía from the school curriculum. For the family movement, this was a great success after a five-year struggle.

Zapatero's dream was over for now, but the legally mandated cultural revolution during his seven-year regime has left behind a deeply torn society. The fight for life, for the family, and for the inviolable dignity of the person has not been won. The European Union is pursuing very similar anti-life goals for the 500 million residents of its member states.

Hungary

The Hungarians are a patriotic, freedom-loving, pro-European people. They paid for this with blood during the 1956 uprising against their Soviet occupiers and had to endure a brutal Communist dictatorship for more than 30 years afterward. It was the Hungarians who opened the Iron Curtain, thereby triggering the final collapse of Soviet Communism. Then the process of westward integration began with entry into NATO in 1999, and membership in the European Union on May 1, 2004.

After a left-wing, self-serving, five-year government, and parliamentary elections, the conservative *Fidesz* party won by a landslide in April 2010. The two-thirds majority they achieved gave them the ability,

4. Ibid.

under Prime Minister Orbán, to change the constitution. After the overthrow of Communist dictatorship in 1989, the constitution had merely been patched up, but did not provide Hungary with a new foundation. Now Hungary would dare to overthrow the old Communist structures that had permeated all aspects of society, and begin anew, based on values to which Catholic Hungary had been committed for ten centuries. This caused an international uproar, led by members of the European Parliament.

The new constitution came into force on January 1, 2012. Since then, the media have given the impression that Hungary is on the verge of fascist dictatorship, that basic democratic rights are being nullified, judicial independence abolished, freedom of the press compromised and human rights violated. But here are the real bones of contention:

• Recognition of God: the first sentence of the constitution says, "God bless Hungary."
• Recognition of the nation and its traditions: the Constitution makes reference to the "Holy Crown" of King Stephen in the 10th century.
• Recognition of the family: the Constitution sees the family as "the foundation of society's strength and of the honor of each person." It says that "Marriage is a life partnership between a man and a woman."
• Recognition of the right to life of the unborn child: "The life of the fetus is entitled to protection from the time of conception."
• Recognition of man as a creation of God: the government bans cloning humans and using body parts for profit.

The new law on the family defines the family as "an autonomous communion of a man and a woman whose task is fulfilled in the rearing of children." It must be respected by the state for reasons of national survival. The law designates parents as the primary authority in raising children.

For the good of all, Hungary wishes to reestablish fundamental Christian values in order to bring down a culture of death and develop a culture of life. It acknowledges God, nationhood, the family and the sanctity of life from conception until death—evidently a reason for the European Union to unleash a crusade against Hungary. The volume has been turned down somewhat since the reelection of Viktor Orbán with a supermajority of two-thirds in April 2014.

But neither marriage and family nor the protection of life nor the passage of a constitution comes under EU authority. Viviane Reding, the EU justice commissioner, has no qualms about encroaching on the

country's national sovereignty and demanding "real changes or abandonment of the new legislation."[5]

Prime Minister Orbán attended the January 18, 2012 discussion at the
European Parliament. Guy Verhofstadt, a former prime minister of Belgium, lost his composure and, in a burst of rage, screamed about what
was really bothering the EU. The problem was not "this or that article,
but the whole philosophy behind the operation of what is happening at
the moment."[6] There may be questionable individual provisions in the
constitution, but they are far from "violations of human rights," of
which the new government was loudly accused.

In January 2012, Dr. Eva Maria Barki, an attorney of Hungarian origin, initiated a petition called *Hungaria semper libera. Una et eadem lib-
ertas.* It says:

> We know that this fight is harder than battling against tanks. Our
> weapons are only words, law and European values. It is difficult
> because it is not we, but the European Union, that suffers from a lack
> of democracy. We are at its mercy, because to this day, the European
> Union has not met the obligation it has assumed and is still not
> signed on to the European Convention for Human Rights; its bodies
> can therefore not be prosecuted before the European Court of
> Human Rights. It is not we who have abandoned European values,
> but the center of power in Brussels. It is not we who are betraying
> democracy but the European institutions that lack democratic legiti-
> macy.
>   Europe is in an economic and political crisis, and in moral decline.
> This is not what we imagined the new Europe to be! We must build a
> new Europe. A Europe that is not centrally structured, but is multi-
> centered, a Europe that will return to its Christian roots and values, a
> Europe in which the people and the nation are sovereign, not the
> financial oligarchy. A Europe in which the democratic will of the peo-
> ple is respected.[7]

France

The mass movement La Manif Pour Tous sprang up at the beginning of
2013 to oppose the new gender agenda. Socialist president François Hol-

5. http://www.europeandignitywatch.org/day-to-day/detail/article/hungary-eu-fun
ded-pro-life-poster-banned-by-the-commission.html (accessed October 7, 2015).

6. Cf. J. C. von Krempach, https://c-fam.org/turtle_bay/god-save-the-hungarians-iii-
the-eus-crusade-against-hungary-likely-to-end-in-defeat-and-ridicule / (accessed October 7, 2015).

7. http://www.petitionen24.com/selbstbestimmung_und_souveranitat_ungarns.

lande's plan to legalize homosexual "marriage" with the slogan *Marriage pour tous* ("Marriage for All") brought millions of protesters onto the streets of Paris and other French cities. The law was passed anyway, but the movement was able to stop a new family law intended to change the definition of family. La Manif Pour Tous is actively spreading to other European countries.

Germany

La Manif pour tous moved to Germany, where it built up resistance to the state's forced sexualization of children in the schools—*a demonstration for all*, as the movement's name says in French and in German: *Demo für alle*.[8] In no time, 200,000 citizens signed a petition against an instructional curriculum in Baden-Württemberg that intended to teach children to accept all types of non-heterosexual lifestyles (LGBTTIQ). Since then, demonstrations are regularly held in Stuttgart: "Marriage and family to the fore! Stop gender ideology and sexualization of our children!"

Switzerland

Even Switzerland puts the pedal to the metal when it comes to sexualizing children from kindergarten on. But revelations in the tabloid press about the "Basel sex box" disturbed the Swiss populace.[9] This box contained plastic reproductions of male and female genitalia to be used for "enlightening" kindergarten children. In June 2011, a citizens' initiative formed against it, drew up petitions against early sexualization, and in three months collected more than 90,000 signatures. Now there is an initiative to hold a referendum. Under pressure from the citizenry, the "Competence Center for Sexual Pedagogy" at the University of Teacher Education Lucerne (PH Luzern) was closed.

Slovakia

Slovakia has not legalized civil partnerships or same-sex marriage. In the Constitution (2014) marriage is defined as the union between one man and one woman. Three initiatives in parliament to legalize same-sex partnerships were unsuccessful. In spring 2015 a referendum was held to prohibit same-sex adoption in the Constitution and allow parents to withdraw children from sex education in school, in order to

8. https://demofueralle.wordpress.com
9. Philipp Gut, "Porno für Kindergärtler," *Die Weltwoche* (Zürich: n.p., October 6, 2011).

ward off the interventions of the EU. The referendum was not valid because only 20% of the people took part in it.

Poland

Under the government of Jarosaw Kaczynski (July 2006 to September 2007), Poland dug in its heels against the EU reform treaty. Education minister Roman Giertych spoke out against legalization of abortion and same-sex "marriage." Despite campaigns for legalized abortion and same-sex partnerships, they were still prohibited in 2014. There is no sex education in schools, but "family life education." But even in Poland, Christian values are in the midst of an overthrow. Elections in October 2011 brought the new party led by Janusz Palikot onto the scene, and it won 10 percent of the votes in the first run-off. This multimillionaire is fighting for legalization of abortion, homosexual rights, soft drugs, in vitro fertilization, and free contraception for all.

Croatia

In 2013, a civic movement forced the leftist government to hold a referendum for the purpose of constitutionally defining marriage as a union between a man and a woman. Despite relentless, unified resistance by the government and the media, the referendum passed, and the Constitution had to be changed to reflect it. After this victory by the conservative opposition, the government hurried to legalize same-sex legal partnership.

Norway

In Norway, a trailblazer country for gender mainstreaming, unexpected resistance arose from a popular comedian, Harald Eia, who subjected the Norwegian creed of gender equality to a reality check. It had struck him that in his country—which had promoted and supported gender equality for decades—still only 10 percent of engineers were women and only 10 percent of nursing staff were men, just like everywhere else in the world. Despite massive gender equality programs, these numbers have stood fast in Norway since the 1980s. Eia took the "gender paradox" by the horns and produced seven highly informative half-hour videos titled *The Gender Equality Paradox*[10] on the hot topics of gender, homosexuality, violence, sex and race that were broadcast on Norwegian television. His films triggered a national debate and contributed to the Norwegian government's reduction of funding for gender research.

10. https://www.youtube.com/watch?v=tiJVJ5QRRUE&index=2&list=PLPPa8aTP2j 2MPyEzYwqmCOMHLi1bmu95e (accessed October 7, 2015).

The European Union

Resistance to the LGBT anti-family agenda is newly emerging in the European Parliament. Resolutions promoting this agenda used to skate right through into law. Now this is changing. One breakthrough was rejection of the "Estrela Report" on sexual and reproductive rights. (Edit Estrela is a Socialist member of the European Parliament from Portugal.) This report demanded early sex education for children, a "right" to abortion, and curbs on doctors' and nurses' freedom of conscience. New cooperation between pro-family NGOs throughout Europe led to acceptance of an alternative report from the more conservative faction of the European Parliament (the European People's Party [EPP]).

The civic initiative One of Us, carried out in all European member states, aimed at banning financing for embryo-destructive research throughout the EU. It was the most successful citizens' initiative ever, gaining more than 1.7 million signatures. Nonetheless, the EU commission vetoed the initiative the last day before adjourning for 2014, demonstrating its contempt for participatory democracy.[11]

The United States

Resistance to the anti-life, anti-family, pro-LGBT agenda in the United States is beyond the scope of this book.[12] The country is split on the issues of abortion, LGBT privileges, homosexual "marriage" and sex education. However, both Gallup and Rasmussen polls indicate that record numbers of Americans identify themselves as pro-life, outnumbering those who say they are "pro-choice." In fact, the majority of Americans now say they oppose all or most abortions. Moreover, abortion has dropped to its lowest level since the *Roe v. Wade* decision legalized it in 1973. A 13-percent decline from 2008 to 2011 can be seen as a great success for the pro-life movement, which brings hundreds of thousands of people to Washington every year. Despite the major media all but ignoring the event, attendance has grown from 250,000 in 2009 to 650,000 in 2013.

One battle with the radical pro-LGBT, anti-family, anti-life agenda of the Obama administration is covered here:

Through the Health and Human Services (HHS) mandate, the health care reforms pushed through by President Obama force all employers to offer insured workers prescription contraceptives, the "morning-after

---

11. http://europeandignitywatch.org/day-to-day/read-excerpts/browse/2.html (accessed October 7, 2015).

12. Excellent information is provided at www.lifesitenews.com.

pill," and sterilization free of charge. Even religious organizations such as churches, universities, hospitals, and charitable organizations are to be forced to do so.

This stirred up a storm of resistance that the Obama administration may not have expected. The administration has been deluged with lawsuits, letters of protest, and signature petitions. All Catholic bishops, 65 Orthodox bishops, 2,500 pastors, leaders of Evangelical churches, university presidents, and many others have let President Obama know that they will not bend to the law. Rick Warren, who delivered the sermon at Obama's inauguration, said, "I'd go to jail rather than cave in to a government mandate that violates what God commands us to do [Acts 5:29]. Would you?"

The attorneys general of 13 US states announced legal action against the Department of Health and Human Services. In an open letter to HHS secretary Kathleen Sebelius and other cabinet members, they declared: "[The HHS mandate] conflicts with the most basic elements of the freedoms of religion, speech, and association, as provided under the First Amendment. . . . We believe [the HHS mandate] represents an impermissible violation of the Constitution's First Amendment virtually unparalleled in American history."[13]

It appears that the mandate has struck a nerve in freedom-minded Americans. It remains to be seen how this battle will end.

The Catholic Church

The world's leading voice in resisting this moral disorientation is the Catholic Church. It is therefore under constant attack from the media and the powers promoting deregulation of sexual norms.[14]

Since late 2013, several bishops' conferences have issued uncompromising declarations against the ideology of genderism, affirming the biblical assertion that human beings are created as man and woman.

In several South American countries, such as Peru,[15] Venezuela[16] and

---

13. http://www.ncregister.com/DAILY-NEWS/bishops-conference-attorneys-submit-comment-to-hhs-on-contraceptive-mandate (accessed October 7, 2015).

14. This reached a new pinnacle in the United Nations. On February 5, 2014, the UN Committee on the Rights of the Child pressured the Holy See to abandon its stand on abortion, contraception, same-sex "marriage" and youth sex.

15. http://www.esposiblelaesperanza.com/index.php?option=com_content&view=article&id=338:la-ideologia-de-genero-sus-peligros-y-alcances-conferencia-episcopal-peruana&catid=348:magisterio-conferencias-episcopales&Itemid=24 (accessed October 7, 2015).

16. http://www.esposiblelaesperanza.com/index.php?option=com_content&view=article&id=1252:ante-el-proyecto-de-ley-organica-para-la-equidad-e-igualdad-de-gener

Panama,[17] bishops' conferences have spoken out against genderism and the sexualization of children.

The first was the lone warrior among Swiss bishops, Dr. Vitus Huonder, with his declaration *Gender: Die tiefe Unwahrheit einer Theorie* (Gender: The Deep Falsehood of a Theory)[18] on December 10, 2013, which earned him a demonstration from the Catholic Women's Organization. Since 2013, bishops' conferences have followed with very clear, uncompromising pastoral declarations, such as those of Slovakia,[19] Poland[20] and Croatia.[21]

A year earlier, on December 21, 2012, Pope Benedict XVI had used his Christmas address to the Curia and the College of Cardinals to remind them that "[the Church] must propose with all clarity the values she recognizes as fundamental and non-negotiable." In his speech he clarified the depth of what he called an "anthropological revolution":

> While up to now we regarded a false understanding of the nature of human freedom as one cause of the crisis of the family, it is now becoming clear that the very notion of being—of what being human really means—is being called into question. He [the Great Rabbi of France, Gilles Bernheim] quotes the famous saying of Simone de Beauvoir: "one is not born a woman, one becomes so" (*on ne naît pas femme, on le devient*). These words lay the foundation for what is put forward today under the term "gender" as a new philosophy of sexuality. According to this philosophy, sex is no longer a given element of nature, that man has to accept and personally make sense of: it is a social role that we choose for ourselves, while in the past it was chosen for us by society. The profound falsehood of this theory and of the anthropological revolution contained within it is obvious. People dispute the idea that they have a nature, given by their bodily identity, that serves as a defining element of the human being. They deny their

o-conf-episcopal-venezolana&catid=348:magisterio-conferencias-episcopales &Itemid= 24 (accessed October 7, 2015).

17. http://www.esposiblelaesperanza.com /index.php?option =com_content&view= article&id=434:obispos-de-panama-ante-ley-de-sexualidad&catid=348:magisterio-con-ferencias-episcopales&Itemid=24 (accessed October 7, 2015).

18. http://www.bistum-chur.ch/wp-content/uploads/2013/12/Wort_des_Bischofs_ VIII_2013.pdf (accessed October 7, 2015).

19. http://www.familiam.org/pls/pcpf/v3_s2ew_consultazione.mostra_pagina?id_pa gina=5708 (accessed October 7, 2015).

20. http://torontocatholicwitness.blogspot.ca /2014/01/the-polish-bishops-conferenc e-denounces.html.

21. http://torontocatholicwitness.blogspot.de/ 2014/11/croatian-bishops-conference-denounces.html.

nature and decide that it is not something previously given to them, but that they make it for themselves. According to the biblical creation account, being created by God as male and female pertains to the essence of the human creature. This duality is an essential aspect of what being human is all about, as ordained by God. This very duality as something previously given is what is now disputed. The words of the creation account—"male and female he created them" (Gen 1:27)—no longer apply. No, what applies now is this: it was not God who created them male and female—hitherto society did this, now we decide for ourselves. Man and woman as created realities, as the nature of the human being, no longer exist. Man calls his nature into question. From now on he is merely spirit and will. The manipulation of nature, which we deplore today where our environment is concerned, now becomes man's fundamental choice where he himself is concerned. From now on there is only the abstract human being, who chooses for himself what his nature is to be. Man and woman in their created state as complementary versions of what it means to be human are disputed. But if there is no pre-ordained duality of man and woman in creation, then neither is the family any longer a reality established by creation. Likewise, the child has lost the place he had occupied hitherto and the dignity pertaining to him. Bernheim shows that now, perforce, from being a subject of rights, the child has become an object to which people have a right and which they have a right to obtain. When the freedom to be creative becomes the freedom to create oneself, then necessarily the Maker himself is denied and ultimately man too is stripped of his dignity as a creature of God, as the image of God at the core of his being. The defense of the family is about man himself. And it becomes clear that when God is denied, human dignity also disappears. Whoever defends God is defending man.[22]

22. http://www.vatican.va/holy_father/benedict_xvi/speeches/2012/december/documents/hf_ben-xvi_spe_20121221_auguri-curia_en.html.

16

The Slippery Slope
to a New Totalitarianism

We think we're not free or truly ourselves until we follow only our own will. God seems to be in the way of our freedom. We need to get free of Him, or so we think: Only then will we be free. This is the fundamental rebellion that runs throughout history, and the fundamental lie that distorts our lives. When man stands against God, he stands against His truth, and is therefore not free, but alienated. We are not free in our truth until we are one with God.

Pope Benedict XVI[1]

The Dialectics of Freedom

LET US REPEAT the question posed at the beginning of this book: *Is it right to view current social developments in the context of totalitarianism?* When you look at the incomprehensible horror committed by the Communist and National Socialist dictatorships and the leaden terror that oppressed their people, this seems wrongheaded and disrespectful to the hundreds of millions of victims whose lives were crushed in an infernal machine wrought by man. After all, we live well! We're free!

Yes, we do live well. We see no misery on the streets, but the lines at the soup kitchens keep getting longer. The state social network has a large enough buffer to keep unemployed millions fed. Admittedly, neighborhoods have burned in Paris, London, and Ferguson; but the fires were put out quickly. The financial crisis has been rocking Europe, but in the heart of Europe the crisis doesn't seem to affect people much—prices are still stable, and consumer sentiment is unbroken.

The only strange thing is that more and more people are anxious and depressed, and mental illness and suicide rates keep climbing. Accord-

---

1. Pope Benedict XVI, Maundy Thursday sermon (April 5, 2012).

ing to the Robert Koch Institute, more than a quarter of children and teenagers have mental disorders and behavioral problems.[2] In three out of four households, there are no children, and half of the rest have only *one* child. Starting in 2020, there will be massive demographic upheavals. But who cares? The pill and the over-the-counter morning-after pill, abortion on demand (paid for by medical insurance)—that is the government's demographic policy.

We're seeing what happens when greed becomes the driver of the economy. Deregulation of the restrictive standards in financial markets has allowed an out-of-control financial oligarchy to throw entire nations into economic ruin. Deregulation of the restrictive standards of sexuality is the precondition for an out-of-control sex drive to throw people, families and the whole society into mental and social chaos. Poverty and demoralization are a dangerous mix that can give rise to totalitarian forms of power.

The great promise of our time is freedom and limitless sexual satisfaction as the way to happiness. Do whatever you want to increase your fun, your pleasure, your happiness, and your well-being. You are independent, autonomous, and no one should put rules in your way—least of all the Church. God is dead, and so is the devil. You construct your own world, decide whether you want to be a man or a woman, whether your nose should be crooked or straight, your breasts small or large, and whether to satisfy your sexual needs with men or women or both. You decide whether your child should live or die, whether it should have blue or brown eyes. You decide whether and when you should get a lethal injection once you've had enough of life. Whatever stands in the way of your freedom is deconstructed: gender identity as man or woman, morality, the family, the Church, the sanctity of life.

But there is nothing to show that unbridled freedom fulfills the promise of happiness. An ideology that promises the limitless freedom to redesign oneself and achieve self-gratification plunges the person into the no-man's-land of egotism, hands him over to the tyranny of his untamed urges, and makes him "who conceals the largest, most powerful tyrant in his own soul"[3] into a tyrant over his own people. This dialectic of absolute freedom was already described by Plato two and a half millennia ago.

Inner freedom is a great good that can be achieved only by learning virtue, specifically the unwavering will to do what is good. People are born selfish. Virtue must be cultivated in them. This requires the expe-

---

2. www.rki.de/kiggs.
3. Plato, *The Republic*, Book IX.

rience of loving acceptance, role models and guidance, knowledge and self-knowledge. Each person must learn wisdom, justice, bravery, and restraint throughout his entire life. If that doesn't happen, he will use his abilities to strive toward money, sex, and power. These three work as a team and open the door to one another. The Bible calls them idols—false gods who have nothing good in store for people. Those who serve them will exploit and harm others to come out on top. When there is no binding standard imparted through tradition, example, authority, and religious upbringing protected by the legal system, then whoever is strongest wins. Those who are more intelligent, more ruthless, and more brutal succeed in reaching positions of power, and enslave the weak, just as they themselves are enslaved by their own urges.

The 21st century's looming totalitarianism wears a different costume from that of the 20th—no mustache, no jackboots. It goes unrecognized because people today ease their consciences by pointing to the crimes of their forefathers, never seeing that in every era evil emerges in a different form. The new totalitarianism is flexible and can adapt to the values that are popular today. It even wears the cloak of freedom, while step-by-step destroying the conditions necessary for freedom. It is adept at controlling new communication and monitoring technologies, and uses their potential for total control. It mixes, blends, and distorts every truth with lies and every lie with a grain of truth, so that people can no longer distinguish truth from falsehood, until truth itself becomes suspect and our freedoms may be pruned. A torrent of public opinion ensues and becomes so powerful that people no longer trust their own perceptions and are willing to replace them with ideologies—even those that their own eyes and experience show them are lies, such as the denial of the binary structure of human existence.

The realm of intellectual freedom and the search for truth becomes poisoned by ideology. Reality is forced into an ideological framework in the service of power politics that hide behind seemingly good intentions. The end justifies every means—every lie, every fraud, every manipulation. What starts out as intentional falsification leads to violence against people. Karl Marx never killed anyone as he wrote *Das Kapital* at his desk. But within a century, hundreds of millions of people were exterminated for the sake of a utopia that was nothing other than a pretext for criminal gangs taking total power.

Marxism promised to relieve the real problems of the working class, and the women's movement arose to give women equal rights. Both movements' objectives were based on the plight of the masses. In contrast, the current Cultural Revolution is a top-down revolution. It does not aim to improve the situation of a large, oppressed segment of the population, but to transform the entire society into a new image of man according to the will of a small minority. The ideological fraud that noble objectives are being pursued, that the interest of the majority is being served, must hold out until irreversible changes have been achieved and cement the minority's domination through totalitarian power structures.

Today there seems to be no unified ideology with a stranglehold on interpretation of reality such as Marxism had. Now the individual seems to be given complete freedom to interpret his own existence, his gender, and his moral values—a freedom that denies what is necessary for humanity to exist and that, like any ideology, finally turns against people.

Abuse of Sexuality and Abuse of Power

Let's focus a little more sharply on sexuality to see how freedom divorced from truth and responsibility leads down the slippery slope to a totalitarian society. If the sex act is reduced to pursuit of pleasure, it is no longer integrated into the dynamic of conceiving and giving life. Man loses his place in the continuum of past and future, remains imprisoned in his little self, and becomes his own end. His heart is turned in on itself—"*cor in se incurvatus*," in the words of St. Augustine.

Celibacy for the sake of the kingdom of God is no contradiction to this. It is meant to be a freely chosen way of life for spiritual fertility that gives true fulfillment and makes one free to serve one's neighbor. For this reason, priests are called "Father" and senior women religious are called "Mother."

Trivializing sexuality as a tool for pleasure turns the sexual partner into an object. By *using* the other for sexual gratification, the other is robbed of personal dignity, even if he or she doesn't feel that way at first. The concept of inviolable dignity that is the basis of human rights and the constitutions of democratic countries is derived from Christian anthropology. According to biblical revelation, man is created in the image of God as man and woman *for his own sake*. He consists of mortal flesh and an immortal soul, having a spirit that enables him to know himself and God. Each person is unique, existing only once in the entire cosmos. Only the sexual act consummated in personal love and openness to life does justice to the dignity and uniqueness of the human person.[4] One *knows* the other as the unique person that he or she is and transcends the self in unity with the other. The two become co-creators

---

4. Today, Natural Family Planning (NFP) is a reliable method for a couple to plan their family size without artificially blocking the woman's fertility.

of a new person who embodies the unity of this man and woman forever. In the Bible, this deepest knowledge of the other person is so thoroughly deemed to be the essence of the sex act that the act has traditionally been described with the verb *to know*.

The dignity of the human being is not to be violated, because his life is holy—received from the hand of God—and he is endowed with an immortal soul. To be exploited by anyone for any reason is always an attack on his dignity.[5] Even those who do not share this faith dimension can see from the feelings of disappointment, emptiness, humiliation, and disgust produced by sexual (mutual) exploitation that their dignity has been damaged and that the yearning for a deep bond of love has not been met. With time, these acutely painful feelings become dulled if the person has separated his heart from his body's experience of pleasure. These experiences of pleasure do not lead to the fulfillment of the actual yearning for the unity of personal love, but drive the person to ever more sexual stimulation with a sequence of new partners, often to the point of sexual addiction and crime.

If someone can exploit another within the deepest realm of his being, what is to keep him from exploiting people to satisfy his egotistical interests in other aspects of life? As for the person who *allows* himself to be exploited in his innermost being, where is he to muster the power to defend his personal dignity against omnipresent incursions by those more powerful? In all realms of society, it is hard enough for any person not to lose himself to his drives. However, when a society's moral compass has been broken, when good is called evil and evil called good, when citizens and voters in a democratic society have no solid, day-to-day orientation or renewal of moral substance, when those who govern have no obligation toward the common good, then society is on the slippery slope to a new totalitarianism.

The uprooted person mistakes seducers for prophets, can no longer distinguish between truth and lies, and can be limitlessly manipulated with today's limitless manipulation techniques. Long before the popularization of television and the invention of the internet, Aldous Huxley posed the question of whether a regime that succeeds in redefining perversion as normality and normality as perversion "will get clever enough to redefine the techniques of servitude to become so pleasurable that no one notices the horror anymore or has the will to object."[6]

---

5. Cf. Karol Wojtyla, *Love and Responsibility* (San Francisco: Ignatius Press, 1960), Chapter One: The Person and the Sexual Urge.

6. Quoted in E. Michael Jones, *Libido Dominandi*, loc. cit., 16, note 2.

The Böckenförde Dictum

In Germany, former constitutional judge Ernst-Wolfgang Böckenförde has stated the fundamental problem of the secular state. The first sentence of his analysis has become known as the Böckenförde dictum:

> The liberal secular state lives by assumptions that it cannot itself guarantee. It is the great venture that it has entered for the sake of freedom. On the one hand, as a liberal state, it can only survive if the freedom it grants its citizens is regulated from the inside through the moral substance of the individual and the homogeneousness of the society. On the other hand, it cannot guarantee these forces of regulation from within itself—that is, try to guarantee it using legal coercion and authoritarian decree—without giving up its liberalism and on the secular level sliding back into the totalitarian demands it freed itself from in religious civil wars.[7]

If the state cannot itself create the conditions for a free society, then the liberal constitution has to depend on non-state institutions to achieve this. The "moral substance" from which European high culture flowered is Christianity. Through the beauty of churches, monasteries, urban development, painting, and music, it has unfolded over centuries in every country in its own way. Through the Church, and in the churches, everyone came into contact with the highest achievements of the culture: the language of the Bible, painting, music, and architecture; everyone could experience the true, the good, and the beautiful and was marked by them. Now the flood of images from the media is neither true, nor beautiful, nor good, and even engulfs small children.

From the basic anthropological concept that every man is made in God's image came a legal system in which everyone is equal before the law, in which state power is limited and committed to the common good. Society needs a substructure that constantly renews moral substance. This is what the Church and the family achieved. Over many centuries, the Church prodded believers toward the good, and every religious service was a wake-up call to the conscience, an activation of moral substance. In principle, the Ten Commandments applied to the leaders as much as to the followers. The Church created a social realm of true equality, specifically the equality of the sinner before God, whether king or beggar.

The "Church Militant," the Church of the earthly pilgrims, is made up

---

7. Ernst-Wolfgang Böckenförde, *Staat, Gesellschaft, Freiheit* (Frankfurt: Suhrkamp Verlag, 1976), 60.

not of saints, but of people who are guilty of sin, fall, and get back up. They are most attacked by those who have no interest in holiness, but have great interest in sins not being called sins. Despite all the clouds that have hung over its sacred mandate, the Church has survived for 2,000 years. That is the greatest miracle of all. There is always an undercurrent of grace. Though parts of the Church were corrupted under totalitarian regimes, it cannot be concluded that a society without religious moorings can withstand new forms of totalitarianism any better.

The spiritual bulwark against the West's cultural identity is the monastic idea of poverty, chastity, and obedience. Monasticism worked like the source of an irrigation system that traversed many levels into the cells of the culture.

What makes a person strong enough to contribute positively to society and keep freedom alive? How does he obtain the spiritual and material independence to resist the mainstream and, when necessary, oppose the state's claim to dictatorial power? He needs a stable, positive identity. This is nourished by many factors: affirmation of one's own existence; solid roots in one's own family; respect for one's parents and ancestors; tradition handed down from one generation to the next; love of home, country and one's own culture; the feeling of true self-esteem that arises when one uses one's own gifts and capabilities for the good of society; joy from seeing one's own children thrive; and—first and foremost—the experience of being loved by God. A religious person's roots reach beyond life on earth into eternity and provide an identity that is not shaken by earthly challenges. Millions of martyrs have witnessed to this with their blood.

But today everything that makes people strong has become weak.

The Conscience

Back to Böckenförde. A liberal state can only survive "if the freedom it grants its citizens is regulated from the inside through the moral substance of the individual." A person's moral monitor is the conscience. It is like a seismograph calibrated to good and evil that communicates its signal through self-esteem—biting, burning guilt feelings when wrong is done; and joy, serenity and calm sleep after good deeds. Because the conscience is the highest authority by which a person must judge himself, our legal system protects freedom of conscience in the constitution.

But what is the standard? Is there any objective, absolute standard, or in the age of relativism is everyone entitled to his own subjective conscience? Must a society fall apart if it no longer has any binding moral values—because such values are rejected as illegitimate limits on individual freedom?

The seismograph of the conscience depends on the moral level at which a person lives. The more a person ignores his conscience, the more he becomes comfortable with what is bad or even evil, the less he *desires* the good. The more the conscience is formed and cultivated by choosing the good over the comfortable even in small matters, the more the person recognizes and *desires* the good.

In his essay "Conscience and Truth," Joseph Ratzinger (Pope Benedict XVI) clarifies the paradox that conscience is recognized as the highest authority by law, yet it can err:

> Is conscience the protective mantle of subjectivity in which man can shelter and hide himself from reality? Or is conscience the window that gives man a clear view of the common truth that grounds and supports us all? Firm subjective conviction and the resulting lack of doubt or scruples provide the person no justification. . . . The guilt feelings that break through a falsely tranquil conscience, which can be called the conscience's request to speak against my self-satisfied existence, is as necessary to a person as physical pain signaling that normal life functions are being disturbed. . . . An acquired blindness to guilt, the numbing of the conscience . . . is a more dangerous illness of the soul, as guilt is still recognized as guilt.[8]

Even if a person momentarily *must* follow what he takes for the voice of his conscience, this does not mean that he has actually chosen what is good. Ratzinger continues:

> A person who equates conscience with subjective conviction identifies with a pseudo-rational certainty woven from self-righteousness, conformity and inertia. The conscience is degraded to an excusal mechanism, when it really represents the person's transparency to the divine and the true dignity and greatness of man. . . . A man of conscience is one who never buys tolerance, well-being, success, public image and the approval of prevailing opinion at the price of the truth.

In fact, the concept of conscience is only meaningful if there is such a thing as objective truth that is written on the person's heart. Once the existence of God is no longer acknowledged, the person recognizes no authority over himself to which he owes his life and that will someday hold him to account, the concept of conscience loses its substance—but the conscience itself does not lose its capacity to disturb. Even if the inner seismograph no longer registers in the conscience, one cannot tear it completely out of one's soul.

8. Joseph Ratzinger, "Gewissen und Wahrheit," in Rehder and Wolff, *Der Wahrheit verpflichtet* (Würzburg: Johann Naumann, 1998).

What does one do with the guilt feelings, the oppressive burden of knowing that you have not given what you should have or have taken what is not yours? People of all eras and cultures have been confronted with this question and have developed sacrificial rites to return to the deity what they believed they owed, and thus reconciled could live anew. Is it an angry, punitive, vengeful god who must be appeased with hearts cut from the bodies of virgins—as the Aztecs believed—or is it, as Christians believe, a merciful God who gave himself as a sacrifice and forgives every sinner who repents and accepts His sacrifice?

What does a culture do when it no longer has a way of cleansing guilt because it has made men their own gods? It must silence the conscience, in the vain hope that then inner peace will be found. There are various strategies for this:

- Create ideologies that make sin appear good.
- Drag everyone into the sin.
- Defame, shun, and persecute everyone who gives voice to his conscience.

If we look at the global sexual revolution, we can see that this is exactly what is happening.

If there is a God, then he has written his law on the hearts of the people he has created. "*I will place my law within them, and write it upon their hearts; I will be their God, and they shall be my people*" (Jeremiah 31:33). Man cannot drive away guilt even if he turns the whole world on its head to do it. Because this strategy cannot bring inner peace, there is never a limit for the sexual revolutionaries.

Admittedly, we can decide not to believe that God exists. But if there is a God—a rumor that stubbornly persists—not believing in Him won't erase His existence.

At an ecumenical religious service on September 23, 2011, at the Augustinian monastery in Erfurt, Germany, Pope Benedict XVI asked:

Does man need God, or do things go fine without Him? In the first phase of God's absence, if His light continues to glow and the rules of human existence hold together, it looks like things go well even without God. But the farther the world gets away from God, the clearer it becomes that in the hubris of power, in the emptiness of the heart, and in the longing for fulfillment and happiness, man loses his life.

A New World Order?

The cultural revolution described in this book is taking place behind people's backs—top-down. It emanates from the power elites and is propelled by minorities who define themselves by sexual orientation and seek to topple the world order. Indeed, a change in values can only lead to a change in the world order. Because the changes are global, it is to be expected that the development aims at a new global order.

Rootless, dependent, malleable masses may be ready to celebrate a new—global—savior. The cultural revolution of our time increasingly limits individual freedom and broadens the power of the state over the individual and of international organizations over the states—in the service of the financial oligarchy and for toppling the moral order. With this baggage, we are skidding into great crises that are appearing on the horizon, one of which is dead certain—monumental demographic change. Within 100 years, from 1950 to 2050, the median age in most industrialized nations is expected to shift from 36 to over 50, and half of the population will then be over 50—a situation unique in the history of the world. There will be a lack of children; a shortage of workers, technical employees and scientists; and not enough soldiers to defend our countries. The shrinking younger generation will not be able to care for their own offspring or for the elderly. There will be distribution conflicts between the generations and euthanasia will be accepted as a solution. South of the Mediterranean, however, there is a "youth bulge," a surplus of young people who have barely any future in their own countries and increasingly migrate to the West, as do millions of refugees from Islamic terror.[9] Every politician knows the demographic scenario, but no party and no leading politicians are developing a vision for turning the situation around—toward a culture of life.

What carries people through in a crisis? Families are the social safety net, because they stick together and are willing to share. Faith is the spiritual safety net that gives people refuge in their misfortune and an unshakable hope. We don't know what phase of human history we are in, but Christians know that the story will come out well.

---

9. Cf. Richard Jackson, *The Graying of the Great Powers: Demography and Geopolitics in the 21st Century* (*CSIS*, 2008). http://csis.org/publication/graying-great-powers-0.

Afterword

Dear Readers,

My warmest thanks for taking the time to read this book. If you now feel you understand our times more clearly and ask yourself, "What can I do?," then it has been worth the effort—both yours and mine. If the question is pressing enough, you will find an answer.

It is always the individual who gets things moving—for better or for worse, however small or large the scale. They have a goal, commit themselves to it, inspire others, and create new opportunities—each person in his own walk of life. A bishop, a politician, an investor, a managing editor, a media celebrity, a philanthropist—each has special responsibilities and possibilities of influence; but everyone can make his own distinctive contribution to the good cause. At the advanced stage of sexual deregulation we are in now, we will all need courage to do that. As Lao Tzu said, a journey of a thousand miles begins with a single step. No one can stop you from starting by putting your own house in order, if need be. This can give you knowledge, courage, persuasiveness, vigor, and—last but not least—joy of life.

If the destruction of our social foundations is to stop, and a change is to be initiated, certain goals are absolutely essential:

- Family mainstreaming instead of gender mainstreaming.
- Marriage only between one man and one woman.
- Legal enforcement of the right of the child to their biological mother and father.
- Legal enforcement of the right of parents to raise their children according to their values.
- No sexualization of children and teenagers through mandatory Comprehensive Sex Education in schools.
- No inclusion of "sexual identity" or "sexual orientation" in anti-discrimination laws.
- International and nationwide campaigns against pornography.
- Protection of the right to life from conception to natural death.

Since 2013, resistance has been growing throughout society. We can change things! There are thousands of initiatives working on behalf of human dignity. It is worthwhile to work toward a spiritual and moral renewal of Europe, which has its unique culture largely thanks to Christianity—the true source of individual and political freedom. The crisis ensuing from the uncontrolled mass immigration to Europe since autumn of 2015, mainly of young muslim men and primarily to Germany, will reveal the gender agenda to be the delusion of a decadent society and put us back on the solid ground of human reality—man and woman, father, mother, and children. It is the family that sustains human life, especially in a crisis. The victory of evil only sets the stage for the triumph of good. Certain of this, I wish you hope, confidence, and courage.

GABRIELE KUBY

Index

GABRIELE KUBY was a student at the Free University of Berlin in 1967, a pivotal year of upheaval and rebellion among students. She completed her Masters degree under the direction of Ralph Dahrendorf at the University of Konstanz, following which she worked as a translator and interpreter for twenty years. After her conversion to the Catholic faith in 1997, she became a successful author of books on spiritual and political issues and an international speaker. "As a sociologist, I observe the developments of our society; as a mother I am committed to the future of the next generation; as a Catholic, I try to live what I believe." www.gabriele-kuby.de

Printed in Great Britain
by Amazon